ATLANTA, GEORGIA — THE COMMERCIAL CENTER — *Drawn by Horace Bradley,* in the February 12, 1887 issue of HARPER'S WEEKLY.

THE JUNIOR ASSOCIATES
OF
THE ATLANTA MUSIC CLUB
PRESENT

ATLANTA COOKS for COMPANY

1968

Conger Printing Company
Atlanta, Georgia

First printing   October, 1968   5,000
Second printing   December, 1968   10,000

The proceeds from the sale of this book are to be used for charitable purposes.

COPYRIGHT © 1968

THE ATLANTA MUSIC CLUB, INC.

All rights reserved including the right to reproduce this book or parts thereof in any form. Library of Congress Catalog Card Number: A 28898

TO
JANETTE LANE BRADBURY

who, with selfless devotion,
has inspired our aims and
challenged our energies
to follow her dynamic leadership.

HISTORY
OF
THE JUNIOR ASSOCIATES OF THE ATLANTA MUSIC CLUB

The history of the Junior Associates of the Atlanta Music Club would not be complete without first relating some of the history of the Atlanta Music Club which fostered the Junior Associates.

The Atlanta Music Club was created in 1915 by a group of ladies who realized that the musical muse in Atlanta was being neglected. The Club began its first season with a concert by the famed pianist, Leo Ornstein. Because the first concert was such a success, the Atlanta Music Club sponsored a variety of concerts: the All-Star Concert Series, the Membership Series and the Salon Concert Series. Through these concerts Atlantans have enjoyed such greats as Paderewski, Galli-Curri, Pons, Rubinstein, London, Sutherland and Moffo.

Besides bringing artists to Atlanta, the Music Club has encouraged many musical ventures within the city. In 1940, the Atlanta Music Club formed the Choral Guild; and in 1945, the Club founded the Atlanta Symphony which has grown to be a very important part of Atlanta's musical life. Realizing the need of Atlanta's amateur instrumentalists to perform in a challenging ensemble group, the Music Club created the Atlanta Community Orchestra in 1958. A professional opera workshop was begun in 1963 when Opera-Atlanta was organized.

The Atlanta Music Club launched a new group in 1963, the Junior Associates of the Atlanta Music Club, to give younger members of the Atlanta Music Club an opportunity to excel in projects related to the Club. Consequently, the Junior Associates support all the concerts and activities of the Music Club, while initiating programs that are uniquely their own.

Operettas have been produced by the Junior Associates and performed for children in hospitals and orphanages, as well as for the general public. The proceeds from the public performance have gone to the Atlanta Music Club Scholarship Fund.

The Junior Associates have also designed a pre-school musical program featuring types of musical experiences which encourage creative musical expression at an early age.

EDITOR
Mrs. McNeill Stokes

GRAPHICS DIRECTOR	Mrs. Harry G. Haisten, Jr.
EDITORIAL DIRECTOR	Mrs. Thomas I. Sangster
HISTORICAL DIRECTOR	Mrs. Harry G. Haisten, Jr.
WINE DIRECTOR	Mrs. Dan M. Hodges
MARKETING DIRECTOR	Mrs. Robert Minnear
PROMOTIONAL DIRECTOR	Mrs. Solon P. Patterson
PUBLICITY DIRECTORS	Mrs. Andrew N. Foster Mrs. Thomas I. Sangster
DISTRIBUTION DIRECTORS	Mrs. Robert B. Ansley, Jr. Mrs. Clifford Baum

STAFF

Mrs. John R. Barnett, Mrs. Albert W. Boam, Mrs. William Bugg, Jr., Miss Marjorie Chisholm, Mrs. Tyrone S. Clifford, Mrs. J. Robert Douglas, Jr., Mrs. Bernard Haight, Miss Martha Haines, Mrs. Paul L. Hanes, Mrs. Kevin Heeney, Mrs. John C. Hopkins, Jr., Miss Jean Hunter, Mrs. Wendell Kitchens, Mrs. Ernest Lewis, Miss Diane Love, Mrs. Rausey Mason, Mrs. William Matthews, Mrs. H. Perry Michael, Mrs. C. M. Moye, Miss Mary Norris, Mrs. Adolphus B. Orthwein, Jr., Miss Mary Ann Rogers, Mrs. Charles Scharitz, Mrs. DeFoor Vaughan, Mrs. Jack R. Worrill.

We sincerely appreciate each and every recipe of the hundreds submitted by Southern hostesses. Regretably we were unable to incorporate all of the recipes due to a lack of space.

ATLANTA COOKS FOR COMPANY

ATLANTA COOKS FOR COMPANY will support the Atlanta Music Club Scholarship Fund, the Junior Associates' pre-school musical guidelines program and individual programs of music education.

The Atlanta Music Club Scholarship Fund has a significant history of providing education and training for outstanding young musicians. The recipients of the Scholarship Fund are chosen by audition, based on talent and need, and receive grants or loans from the Atlanta Music Club. Some of the nation's most widely acclaimed musicians have received support from this Fund at the beginning of their careers. The Junior Associates of the Atlanta Music Club believe that the proceeds from ATLANTA COOKS FOR COMPANY will be a worthy contribution to the work of the Scholarship Fund.

The Junior Associates recognize the child's need for music while his responses are spontaneous and strong. Therefore, the emphasis of this group's pre-school musical program is on types of musical experiences which allow the child to express himself creatively: singing, rhythm and movement, dramatization, and listening and appreciation.

The guide recommends children's records and songbooks and where they may be purchased, musical game instructions, easy-to-make rhythm instruments, and musical outings.

In addition, the Junior Associates of the Atlanta Music Club offer workshops to demonstrate how the musical activities may be developed by teachers, Mothers in play groups, or by parent and child.

With each of these programs—the Scholarship Fund, Musical Guidelines, and individual programs of music education—the Junior Associates sincerely hope that ATLANTA COOKS FOR COMPANY will aid in furthering their development.

HISTORY OF ATLANTA

Hospitality is Atlanta!

Since the first Western and Atlantic trains came chugging into town, everyone has turned out to meet and entertain cousins and friends at brunches, luncheons and teas, with dinners, "at home" gatherings and holiday festivities. Pride in this Southern hospitality sparked the writing of these menus. Also included is a collection of ideas for entertaining and a hostess' guide to wines. These sections await the reader who seeks Atlanta's approach to entertaining, which has been greatly influenced by its history and traditions.

Indian Territory

There were a few scattered folks in these parts even before the railroad boom. It all started back in 1814 when George Rockingham Gilmer was ordered to build a fort in Indian territory on the Chattahoochee at the Standing Peachtree. Pioneer Walsh Collier said he remembers as a child the beautiful peach tree growing on top of the Indian mound. After James Montgomery began operating a ferry at the trading post, the Standing Peachtree site was referred to as Montgomery's Ferry. We can follow the original Indian trail to Standing Peachtree by starting at Stone Mountain, passing Sears on Ponce de Leon, turning right at Peachtree going on to Buckhead and down West Paces Ferry to the river. An Indian path—later a wagon road—led to a trading post which was then flanked by railroad tracks and now finally emerges into the busy, honking thoroughfare of world-famous Peachtree Street, which still partly follows the original Indian path. Peachtree Street could not have had a more interesting evolution.

The Settlers of the 1820's and 1830's

Visualize the 1820's, the earliest of the by-gone days of what is now Atlanta, then only a small segment of DeKalb County. You probably picture the large land holdings and plantation life similar to middle and east Georgia. However, ante-bellum life did not exist in the early days of our city. The original settlers were plain people, usually from Virginia, North Carolina, South Carolina and the Northeastern counties of Georgia. Instead of plantation life, the virgin timber country was dotted with simple log cabins built on a couple of hundred acres of land each. If still standing, the cabin of Atlanta's first settler and large-scale landowner, Hardy Ivy, would be on Courtland and Ellis in the middle of downtown Atlanta!

At the junction of the Peachtree and Sandtown trails, a community known as Whitehall began to bustle. The chief business section of West End at Lee and Gordon Streets is its lineal descendant. Whitehall in its heyday was a tavern stage, coach stop, post office, and election precinct. The big social event was "Muster day" held at the tavern. The prize for marksmanship was a yearling cow. The winner did not have a chance to walk away with the prize as the cow was immediately slaughtered, cooked and served.

Heading out today's Peachtree to Brookhaven, yesterday's traveler would find himself at the home of Soloman Goodwin, which was built in 1831 and is still standing. In earlier times, the kitchen and dining room were located fifty feet from the main house. Because of the intense heat, most kitchens were detached from the main house until the wood burning stove was introduced.

THE RAILROADS OF THE 1840'S

The birth of Atlanta truly began with the building of the Western and Atlantic Railroad in 1838. John Thrasher was engaged to grade a terminal site near the present Atlanta Terminal. Thrasher's workers built their shacks in the general vicinity of the present Federal Reserve Bank. This transient village, known as Terminus, was abandoned by 1840.

Associated with Terminus is the story of Mrs. Mulligan, who some consider Atlanta's very first hostess. Mrs. Mulligan's husband was the best railroad foreman in the area, but he would not accept the job of building the railroad unless his spouse joined him. With her arrival, Mrs. Mulligan had her heart set on a lodging place with wooden floors. "Cousin" John Thrasher had to fetch the lumber from Collier's sawmill and plank Mrs. Mulligan's shack. Right away she gave a party, one of Atlanta's first "balls." Mr. Thrasher was not even daunted when he caught his heel in the floor; he just hippity-hopped through the evening.

With railroads from Chattanooga, Augusta, Macon, and Savannah, the settlement grew rapidly. In 1842, plans were underway for incorporating under Marthasville; but by 1845, the name was changed to Atlanta. The name, most likely, was formed from WESTERN AND ATLANTIC, not from ATTALANTA, the name of a Greek goddess. Some of the names of Atlanta's earlier suburban areas were Lick Skillet, Rough and Ready, Tight Squeeze, Bull Sluice, Sandtown, Slabtown, Snake Nation, Hambug Square, and Beaver Slide.

In the mid 1840's, the village extended one mile in all directions from the railroad terminal. The social situation is described thusly in an arriver's journal: "The people here bow and shake hands with everybody they meet, as there are so many coming in all the time that they cannot remember with whom they are acquainted."

THE BOOM TOWN OF THE 1850'S

By the 1850's Atlanta was considered a boom town. The muddy streets and free livestock did not deter the enormous amount of activity. As the price of land was still low, Nathan Carroll bought forty acres at Peachtree and Cain for one five-dollar pony in 1851. Many citizens, such as Ephraim G. Ponder, began building substantial homes. Located on Marietta Road and Ponder Avenue, N.W., the Ponder home was constructed of stone covered with white plaster. The kitchen was still a separate building but located only a few feet from the main house. Other Atlantans began building residences on Peachtree. One of the first Peachtree residences built was that of

Dr. Crawford W. Long.

The Athenaeum, Atlanta's first theater, was built in 1855. James E. Williams, who needed more room for his produce business, built a large brick building on Decatur Street between Peachtree and Pryor. The second story was designed as a theater while the first floor was used for grain and produce. Mr. and Mrs. W. A. Crisp presented the first performance amid the pungent odor of nearby corn and hay.

During the same year, fifty ornamental gas lampposts were erected throughout the city. The lamplighter became one of Atlanta's familiar sights.

The War and the 1860's

In the years before the burning of the city, the town's most fashionable residents were constructing imposing homes in the Washington Street area, East of Whitehall. In 1860, Marcus Aurelius Bell built his picturesque, antebellum home at Wheat and Collins, now Auburn and Courtland. For more than forty years, this massive, sturdy homestead whose walls were built of stone from Patrick Lynn's rock quarry, was known as the Calico House. The subcontractor, who had worked for a book-binder, displayed his skill by "marbleizing" the interior walls of the house. Co-incidentally, during the same year, a dress manufacturer came out with the same "Calico" pattern. During the war, the house was used for making and storing supplies for the army. The rooms were occupied every day by groups of women knitting, sewing and "pulling lint." The long ell of the house was converted into a temporary hospital for the wounded. Since it was one of the few homes left standing in Atlanta after the War, it became a meeting place and entertainment center. There were shows and plays and regular Friday night band concerts. The Calico House was purchased in 1904 by Asa G. Candler for the first home of Wesley Memorial, now Emory University Hospital. In 1924, the Calico House was torn down to make way for progress.

Atlanta's prosperity was stymied by the outbreak of the Civil War in 1861. During this period there were many domestic hardships in the menempty homes. Since ice was not available, a great deal of food was wasted even though salt was used as a preservative. Food prices were extremely high. Eggs cost as much as three dollars a dozen! Due to high prices, it became necessary to find substitutes for food favorites. Sugar cane, called long sweetening, was used in parched corn coffee. Long sweetening was also used on biscuits and corn dodgers.

During the War, the men's thoughts were home-centered. One soldier's letter plaintively shows this yearning-for-home spirit when he describes the evening scene as the men would wearily retire from a day of fighting. As the men rested, the buglers from both sides would join together and play the refrains from "Home Sweet Home."

Atlanta was a strategic point for both sides. On September 2, 1864, Mayor James M. Calhoun surrendered the city to avoid further destruction. On

September 4th, General Sherman issued the order that the city was needed for military purposes, and all persons except those officially detained should leave the city. In 1864, the year the city was destroyed by fire, it consisted of several thousand dwellings. The property value of business totaled millions of dollars and the city was soon burned to the ground. Only one business and a number of dwellings, including a few handsome residences, remained.

After the men returned from the War, there was an interim that could be described as a breathing spell. In 1868, Laurent de Give purchased the unfinished Masonic Temple on the corner of Marietta and Forsyth. The DeGive Opera House opened with E. Rosse Dalton's presentation of RICHELIEU. About ten years later, when Edwin Booth was the leading attraction, it was impossible even to obtain standing room.

The Recovery Period of the 1870's

With a zeal that has always characterized Atlanta, the city was making a speedy recovery after its tragic destruction in 1864. H. I. Kimball, an imaginative entrepreneur, built the finest hotel South of New York on the old Atlanta Hotel site, bounded by Decatur, Pryor, Wall and Whitehall. To local citizens, the Kimball House was an indication that Atlanta was headed toward metropolitan importance. It was also one of the pivoting spots of social activity for many years. In 1883, the Kimball House was destroyed by fire and two years later an elaborate formal re-opening was staged. By 1960, the Kimball House had outlived its usefulness and was torn down.

With Atlanta's growth in the state's population, the city was named the state capitol in 1868. On October 27, 1870, the State acquired—for $100,000 —the James' home at Peachtree and Cain for use as an Executive Mansion. At the time of construction, it was the costliest residence built in Atlanta. It became the scene of official hospitality for more than fifteen Georgia governors. This landmark was demolished in 1923 to make way for the Henry Grady Hotel.

Who were the people rebuilding Atlanta after the War? According to Dr. Wilson's book, published in 1871, they were business people who came to Atlanta to work. He presents a man's point of view about the ladies: "As to our women (bless them) they, as a general rule, find ample occupation in the domestic duties they so gracefully assume, as in works of charity and benevolence, leaving them but little time for fashionable calls, balls, parties, theatres, etc."

The Expositions and Clubs of the 1880's

At this point, Atlanta blinked her eyes and began to take note of the world around her. The International Cotton Exposition was held in Atlanta in 1881. An actual model cotton factory was built in an attempt to bring together the cotton grower and the manufacturer. October 27 was officially designated as Governor's Day. An elaborate social program was planned for the visitors, which included a special reception at the Executive Mansion.

Afterwards, Atlanta's leading citizens opened their homes to entertain the out-of-town guests.

The fashionable Kimball House was the scene of many fun and stimulating ideas. In 1883, one group of Kimball House regulars formed Atlanta's first permanent social club, the Capital City Club. They first leased the elegant residence of Dr. H. V. M. Miller on the corner of Walton and Fairlie Streets. In 1884, the Capital City Club moved to Peachtree and Ellis, the present site of Davison's. It was not until the next century, 1911, that the present home at Peachtree and Harris was purchased. Early guests included President and Mrs. Grover Cleveland, Presidents McKinley and Taft, and the beloved President of the Confederacy, Jefferson Davis.

Since the International Cotton Exposition was so successful, another similar event was planned in 1887, The Piedmont Exposition. In Washington, Senator Alfred H. Colquitt personally presented President Cleveland his elaborate invitation to the Piedmont Exposition. The invitation, inspired by Henry W. Grady, was engraved on sheets of Dahlonega gold and enclosed in a case of native hardwoods and precious stones. Opening day was exciting for the Piedmont Exposition with choruses, bands, horse races, exhibits, a bicycle parade, an art gallery, and a balloon ascension. At one luncheon for the ladies, given by Mrs. James Porter at her elegant Peachtree home, there were twelve courses lasting for more than three hours.

In the planning of the Exposition, there was a stormy session concerning the purchase of property for the exposition and whether the riding facilities of a driving club should be combined with the annual exhibits of a fair. The next week a more harmonious meeting took place and the Walker property was bought. The Atlanta Constitution announced that a handsome park and club house were in view with plans for annual fairs. The Piedmont Exposition Company and the Gentlemen's Driving Club were chartered. The men kept the Walker home for the club house and leased the remaining land to the Exposition Company. Later, the City of Atlanta bought the land used by the Piedmont Exposition and created Piedmont Park.

The survey of the 80's would not be complete without a glimpse of the early life of Coca-Cola. In 1886, a wholesale druggist and chemist, Dr. J. S. Pemberton, developed a headache remedy, Coca-Cola, which local druggists began dispensing with soda water. One young druggist, Asa Griggs Candler, set about to gain controlling interest in Coca-Cola. Later, two Tennessee attorneys gained permission to bottle this popular beverage. Its growth exceeded the most optimistic expectations.

THE SOCIAL HEYDAY OF THE 1890'S

By the 1890's, Atlanta had begun to make her way in the financial world; consequently, the ladies began to have more leisure time. A marvelous idea from New York was introduced. Each lady of standing had her own "At Home" day when she received her friends and served tea. Social activity assumed an unusual importance. Frequent balls, debut parties, and wedding "collations" served as appropriate backgrounds.

Another popular form of entertainment was the trolley system's *Nine Mile Circle*. For only five cents one could circle through the wooded northeastern section of the city. On Sunday afternoons, the cars on the Circle were so crowded that the seats had to be turned back for the ladies to be seated. Meanwhile, the men jammed the steps that ran the length of the car. From these excursions, hostesses began issuing invitations for trolley parties. These picnickers would charter a car, spread lunch in the woods, and return to the city at dusk. Typical of the day, utmost politeness and decorum were executed in issuing and accepting invitations to such a party.

Beginning during this period—and continuing for nearly twenty-five years—was the Bell House establishment, first cousin to a select private club. The widow, Mrs. Bell, bought the famed Leyden house. This Peachtree home had been used as a Confederate lookout and as headquarters for General John B. Hood. In order to be a resident or a "Bell House Boy," an applicant had to be recommended by three members in good standing, then approved by an executive committee. High standards were enforced. Even the meals were served in a formal manner. Mrs. Bell's talent for encouraging young businessmen became legendary as many residents became prominent social and civic leaders.

On January 8, 1898, society was set astir by an article in the LOOKING GLASS, a homegrown publication. Even though scandalous at the time, some astute observations were made. "In the strictest sense of the word, Atlanta is not a Southern city as far as manner and customs are concerned, and its society is by no means characteristic of the old regime. On the contrary, it is essentially a new town and its wealth is for the most part in the hands of individuals who have accumulated fortunes since the War." A list of Atlanta's new society followed the article. Immediately, there was a group who refuted the original article with a new list of their own. The argument grew, but people acknowledged that Atlanta recognized everyone who had made a contribution to the city's progress.

The 1900's Onward
CONCLUSION

The twentieth century began a new era. Times have changed since the 1800's, but Atlanta is still dispensing hospitality with warmth and zeal. Congeniality entwined with a unique history lends Atlanta her own approach to entertaining.

We are grateful to the Atlanta Historical Society for information from both printed and manuscript materials in its Margaret Mitchell Memorial Library.

TABLE OF CONTENTS

PROLOGUE   2-16
    HISTORY   9-14

BRUNCHES   17-56

LUNCHEONS   57-120

TEAS   121-168

AT HOME   169-200

DINNERS   201-272

HOLIDAYS   273-291

WINES   292-299

INDEX   300-303

    Any menu item which not been further detailed by a recipe may be found in more basic cookbooks. This book has been designed as a guide to entertainment through hospitality.

BRUNCHES

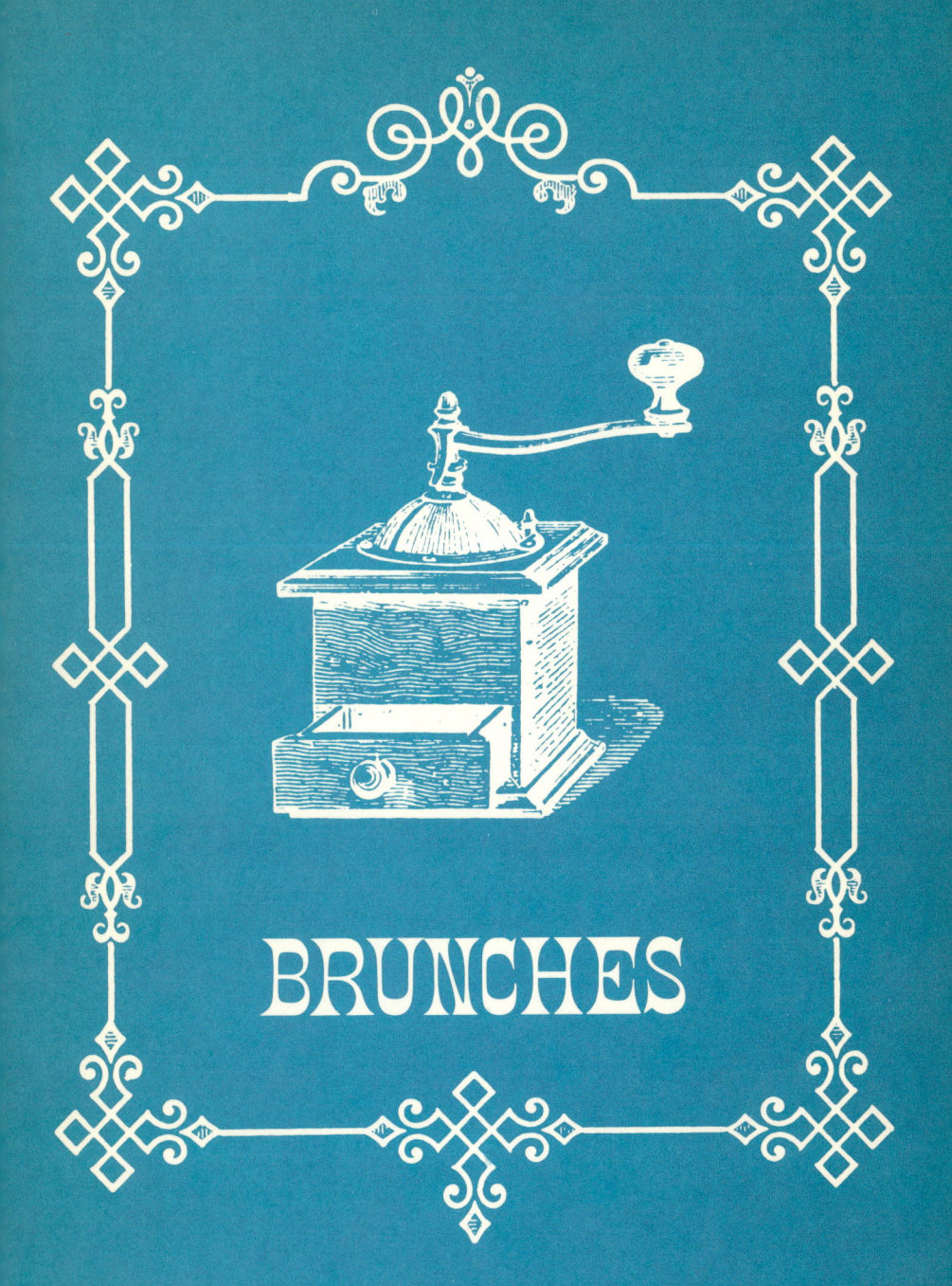

BRUNCHES

Picture, please, the radiant beauty of Atlanta. In the springtime, the dogwoods, azaleas, and peach blossoms are in full bloom. In autumn, the trees are ablaze with the warmth that is so symbolic of Atlanta. Picture, please, Atlanta in any season.

With such a setting, who could resist a party! Because of the hour, brunch is a party favorite as everyone seems to be in a particularly relaxed and gay mood. Invite guests to come between ten-thirty and three. Be sure to have plenty of freshly brewed coffee in evidence for any sign of early-morning grumpiness. The men-folk relish the idea of a morning party, especially when heralded with a tasty bracer.

Seating and Service

If you are having a small familiar group, guests may be seated in the dining room. For a larger party, buffet service is appropriate.

Buffet Service

Spread the buffet serving table with a pretty cloth or leave it uncovered. If card tables are used, cover with party cloths or attractive place mats.

Organize the service so that plates, silver and napkins are arranged at a logical starting place at one end of the table. Place platters of food at intervals along the table with service forks and spoons alongside each platter. The food should be bountiful so that second helpings are available. Place water and coffee on a side table or tea cart where guests may serve themselves. Dessert may also be offered from a side table or tea cart.

Buffet Seating

At a large brunch, guests may find their places in the living room or at card tables placed throughout the entertaining area. Eight to twelve guests can serve themselves from a sideboard or service buffet and may be seated at a graciously appointed table.

Whether buffet or seated, feature gay, cool colors when brunch is served in the garden or on the patio. Set tables with light-colored pottery, porcelain dinnerware and silver flatware. A blend of china and colored glasses provides an unusual setting.

For four people or forty, a brunch is an ideal party to precede another event. For example, it's fun to get together before the Tech, Georgia or Atlanta Falcons' games. Invitations may be printed on brown paper in the shape of footballs, and as the center of attraction, a football helmet could be filled with autumn flowers or leaves, accented with miniature school pennants. A big red or gold bow tied to the mailbox says, "Welcome," the minute guests arrive.

Nearly any event can foster a brunch. At the turn of the century, there was a poker group of prominent Atlanta businessmen called the Ice Picks.

BRUNCHES

These gentlemen played cards every Saturday night with a ten-cent limit on all bets. The game ended promptly at midnight with breakfast served afterward. Their breakfast menus sounded like ideal brunches. After enjoying champagne cocktails, they had either Smithfield ham, birds from around Albany, or kidney and mushroom stew.

Centerpieces

Whatever the occasion, the centerpiece should mirror the event. You may prefer emphasizing the casual mood of the party with a china cow standing in a field of daisies or greenery nestled in an old-fashioned coffee mill. For a garden brunch, paper butterflies on a basket of ivy would be an ideal touch.

For a refreshing summertime idea, use a scalloped melon shell, (See page 285 Dinner Section) or a scooped out pineapple boat as a container for flowers. After removing the fruit, drain the shell and brush with melted paraffin. Pansies give a special note of cheer with their velvety faces peeping over the scalloped edge of a watermelon shell. Marigolds have an affinity for cantaloupe halves. Arrange them individually on small tables and in clusters of three for larger areas. Snapdragons are pretty in a pineapple boat. A split zucchini makes an unusual receptacle for blue verbena, ageratum or blue asters in dwarf form, accented with a splash of coral, pink or yellow flowers. While such arrangements add immeasurably to a brunch, they will enhance any party setting.

Elegant effects can be achieved with a garland of fruit either in a wreath or extending the length of the table or an arrangement of gilded fruit. To gild fruit, spray a fresh pineapple and a variety of fruits, such as apples, pears, bananas, lots of grapes and nuts, gold. Protect the pineapple leaves by wrapping them in aluminum foil, then spray the pineapple and other fruits and nuts. After drying, remove foil from the pineapple leaves. Spread green leaves in the center of the table, and place a compote or block of wood on the greens. Set the pineapple on the stand, and cluster the fruits and nuts around it, building them up from the table to the pineapple. Arrange the heavy fruits on the table and lighter ones, such as grapes, at the base of the pineapple.

Atlanta hostesses favor either a branch of dogwood, peach blossoms or azaleas in a low bowl.

Wicker cornucopias filled with sweet rolls in various shapes, sizes and colors spilling onto a party cloth offer an attractive, edible centerpiece.

Watering cans are delightful containers for flowers and are adorable "pitchers" for serving cold beverages.

For an eggs-quisite centerpiece, try ovals of white that go back into the refrigerator when the party's over. Build a pyramid on a chicken-wire cone covered with floral clay which holds the eggs firmly in place. Tuck in berries or cherries, wheat and fern.

Brunches preceded some of our city's earliest social events. In the 1900's,

BRUNCHES

during the Metropolitan Opera's first appearance in Atlanta, the members of the company were entertained at a brunch. One of their favorite Southern dishes was Georgia grits. Ummm, especially those golden cheese grits. Rush on to the menus and have a brunch—Atlanta style!

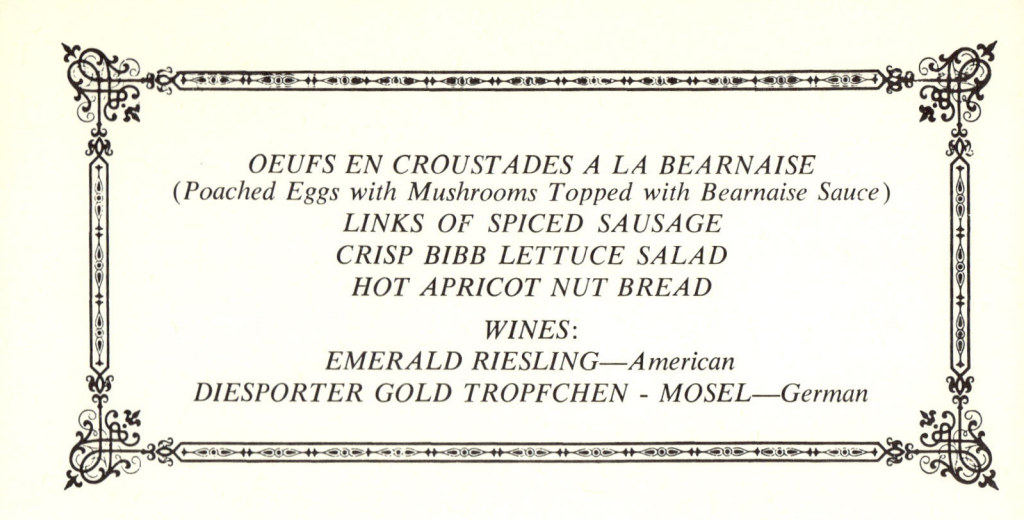

OEUFS EN CROUSTADES A LA BEARNAISE
(Poached Eggs with Mushrooms Topped with Bearnaise Sauce)
LINKS OF SPICED SAUSAGE
CRISP BIBB LETTUCE SALAD
HOT APRICOT NUT BREAD

WINES:
EMERALD RIESLING—American
DIESPORTER GOLD TROPFCHEN - MOSEL—German

OEUFS EN CROUSTADES A LA BEARNAISE
(Poached Eggs with Mushrooms Topped with Bearnaise Sauce)

Yield: 8 Servings

1 Pound Fresh Mushrooms, Minced
3 Tablespoons Green Onions, Minced
3 Tablespoons Butter
1½ Tablespoons Flour
¼ Cup Port
½ Cup Heavy Cream
½ teaspoon Salt
Dash Pepper
8 Patty Shells
8 Poached Eggs
2 Cups Bearnaise Sauce

1. Twist mushrooms in towel to eliminate excess moisture.
2. Saute mushrooms and onions in butter for 8 minutes.
3. Add flour and stir over moderate heat for 3 minutes.
4. Stir in wine and simmer 1 minute. Stir in ⅔ of the cream and add seasonings.
5. Simmer 3 minutes, adding more cream by spoonfuls if mixture becomes too thick.
6. Just before serving, reheat mushrooms, patty shells and eggs. Place 3 Tablespoons of mushroom mixture into each patty shell. Place poached egg over mixture and coat with Bearnaise Sauce.

Bearnaise Sauce

Yield: 2 Cups

1 Cup Butter
4 Egg Yolks, Slightly Beaten
4 teaspoons Tarragon Vinegar
2 Tablespoons Parsley, Chopped
½ teaspoon Pepper, Freshly Ground
2 teaspoons Chives, Chopped

1. Place ½ cup of the butter in top of double boiler with egg yolks and Tarragon vinegar, stirring constantly until butter is melted. Add rest of butter and stir until thick.
2. Remove from heat and add freshly ground pepper. Add parsley and chives.

— Miss Peggy Reeves

APRICOT NUT BREAD

Yield: 1 Loaf

½ Cup Dried Apricots, Diced
1 Cup Water
1 Egg, Well-Beaten
1 Cup Sugar, Granulated
2 Tablespoons Butter, Melted
2 Cups Flour, Sifted
1 Tablespoon Baking Powder
¼ teaspoon Soda
¾ teaspoon Salt
½ Cup Orange Juice, Strained
¼ Cup Water
1 Cup Brazil Nuts or Almonds, Sliced

1. Preheat oven to 350 degrees. Grease loaf pan.
2. Soak apricots in water for 30 minutes. Drain and dice.
3. Beat egg until light; add sugar and blend well.
4. Add butter. Sift flour with baking powder, soda and salt. Add alternately with orange juice and water.
5. Add nuts and apricots and blend well.
6. Bake in greased loaf pan for 1½ hours at 350 degrees.

— Miss Martha Haines

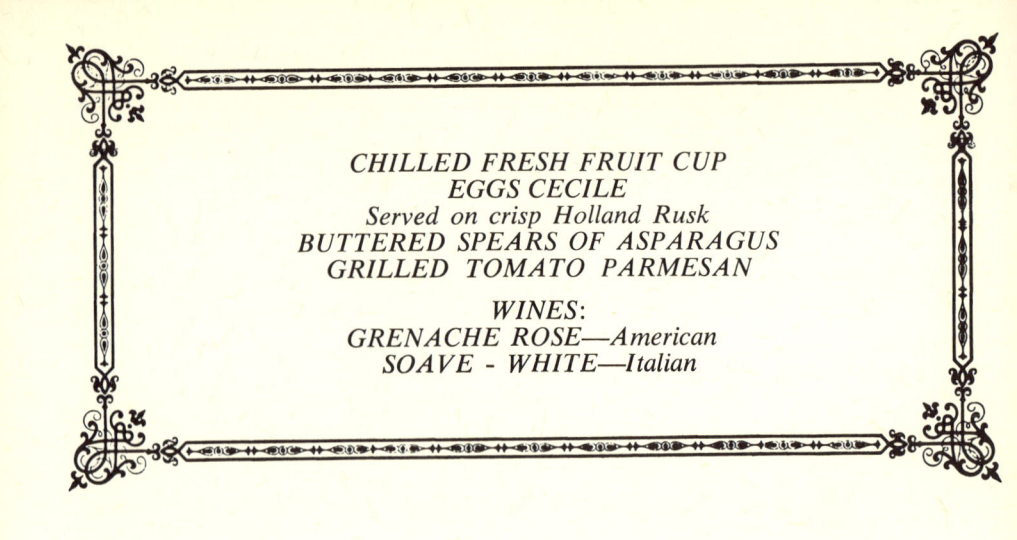

CHILLED FRESH FRUIT CUP
EGGS CECILE
Served on crisp Holland Rusk
BUTTERED SPEARS OF ASPARAGUS
GRILLED TOMATO PARMESAN

WINES:
GRENACHE ROSE—*American*
SOAVE - WHITE—*Italian*

EGGS CECILE

Yield: 4 Servings

6 Pieces Ham, Grilled
1 Cup Cecile de Vin Sauce
6 Poached Eggs
¾ Cup Hollandaise Sauce
6 Buttered Holland Rusk
Sprigs of Parsley

1. Place ham on top of buttered holland rusk and top with Cecile de Vin Sauce.
2. Place poached eggs next on the combination and top with Hollandaise Sauce.
3. Garnish with sprig of parsley.

Cecile de Vin Sauce

Yield: 1 Cup

2 Tablespoons Butter, Melted
2 Tablespoons Flour
¾ Cup Heavy Cream
¼ Cup Chicken Broth
¼ Cup Swiss or Gruyere Cheese, Grated
2 Tablespoons Sherry
Salt

BRUNCHES

1. Melt butter and add flour, cooking until bubbly. Add cream and broth slowly and cook until thickened.
2. Add cheese and blend thoroughly. Add sherry and season to taste.

Blender Hollandaise Sauce

Yield: ¾ Cup

3 Egg Yolks
2 Tablespoons Lemon Juice
¼ teaspoon Salt
Dash Pepper
½ Cup Butter, Melted

1. Place egg yolks, lemon juice and seasonings in blender jar and blend briefly.
2. Pour melted butter very slowly into egg yolk mixture while blending at top speed. (DO NOT POUR IN SALT RESIDUE OF BUTTER.)
3. This may be stored in the refrigerator and re-heated at a later date.

— Mrs. Louie Lathem

GRILLED TOMATO PARMESAN

Yield: 4 Servings

4 Firm Medium Tomatoes
Salt and Pepper
Butter
Grated Parmesan Cheese

1. Preheat oven to 350 degrees. Slice off the tops of the tomatoes. Season and dot with butter.
2. Bake at 350 degrees for 10 minutes, until thoroughly heated.
3. Sprinkle Parmesan cheese on top of the baked tomato and serve piping hot.

— Miss Janet Barnes

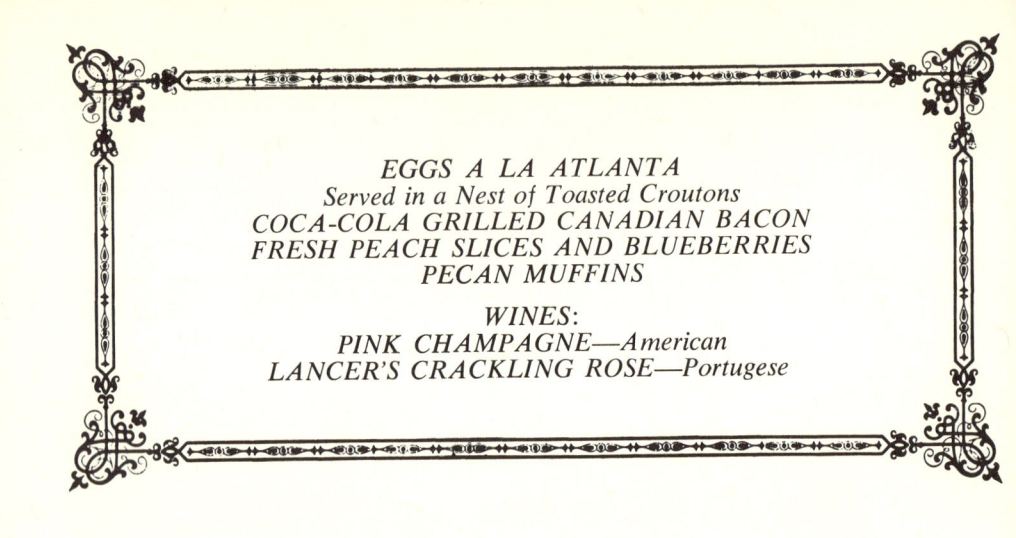

EGGS A LA ATLANTA
Served in a Nest of Toasted Croutons
COCA-COLA GRILLED CANADIAN BACON
FRESH PEACH SLICES AND BLUEBERRIES
PECAN MUFFINS

WINES:
PINK CHAMPAGNE—American
LANCER'S CRACKLING ROSE—Portugese

EGGS A LA ATLANTA

Yield: 4 Servings

4 Poached Eggs
2 Cups Buttered Toasted Croutons
1 Cup Cheddar Cheese, Grated
1 Cup Brandied Cream Sauce

1. Poach eggs and place in a nest of toasted croutons. Top with grated cheddar cheese and brandied cream sauce.
2. Garnish with a sprinkle of paprika and a sprig of parsley.

Brandied Cream Sauce

Yield: 1 Cup

2 Tablespoons Butter, Melted
2 Tablespoons Flour
¾ Cup Evaporated Milk, Heated
¼ Cup Chicken Broth, Heated
2 Tablespoons Brandy
Salt

BRUNCHES

1. Melt butter and stir in flour, cooking until bubbly.
2. Gradually add heated evaporated milk and chicken broth, stirring constantly until sauce thickens.
3. Add brandy and season to taste.

— Mrs. McNeill Stokes

COCA-COLA GRILLED CANADIAN BACON

Yield: 4 Servings

8 Slices Canadian Bacon
½ Cup Coca-Cola

1. Add coca-cola to Canadian bacon in skillet and cook until done.
2. If desired, serve with coca-cola syrup developed through cooking.

— Mrs. Harry G. Haisten, Jr.

PECAN MUFFINS

Yield: 12 Medium Muffins

2 Cups Flour, Sifted
4 teaspoons Baking Powder
½ teaspoon Salt
2 Tablespoons Sugar, Granulated
2 Eggs, Well-Beaten
1 Cup Milk
¼ Cup Butter, Melted
½ Cup Pecans, Chopped

1. Preheat oven to 425 degrees. Grease muffin tins.
2. Mix and sift dry ingredients together.
3. Mix egg and milk together. Add to dry ingredients.
4. Stir in melted butter and chopped pecans.
5. Fill muffin tins three fourths full and bake at 425 degrees for 20 to 25 minutes until golden brown.

— Mrs. Charles C. Ford

HEARTY EGG DELIGHT
BUTTERED SPEARS OF BROCCOLI
Topped with Mushroom Crowns
RED SPICED CRABAPPLE
HOT CORNBREAD SHORTCAKE
Served with Marmalade

WINES:
DRY SAUTERNE—*American*
WEHLENER SONNENUHR - MOSEL—*German*

HEARTY EGG DELIGHT

Yield: 6 Servings

This is a real favorite with us men!

1 Pound Bacon, Uncooked and Diced
3 Medium Potatoes, Diced
12 Eggs
½ Cup Milk

1. Fry bacon until almost done.
2. Add diced potatoes. Cook until golden brown and tender (about 15 to 20 minutes).
3. Blend eggs and milk together. Scramble egg mixture over medium heat and serve with cornbread shortcake.

— Reverend Charles B. Weesser

CORNBREAD SHORTCAKE

Yield: 9 Servings

¾ Cup Flour, Sifted
4 teaspoons Baking Powder
2 Tablespoons Sugar, Granulated
1 teaspoon Salt
1½ Cups Cornmeal
1¼ Cups Milk
1 Egg, Well-Beaten
4 Tablespoons Shortening, Melted

1. Preheat oven to 425 degrees. Grease an 8 inch square pan.
2. Sift together flour, baking powder, sugar, and salt. Add cornmeal and blend well.
3. Add milk, well-beaten egg and melted shortening.
4. Pour into greased 8 inch square pan. Bake at 425 degrees for 25 minutes.
5. Split while hot (first cutting into 9 pieces).

— Miss Wanda White

MOCK EGGS BENEDICT
Served on Toasted English Muffins
HOT CINNAMON FRUIT COCKTAIL
CHILLED TOMATO QUARTERS
Garnished with a Sprig of Parsley

WINES:
CHAMPAGNE, EXTRA DRY—American
SCHLOSS VOLLRAD - RHEIN—Germany

MOCK EGGS BENEDICT

Yield: 4 Servings

4 English Muffins, Toasted
4 or 8 Pieces Canadian Bacon, Grilled
6 Eggs
Hollandaise Sauce
Chopped Chives

1. Using a fork, split English muffins in half. Toast and butter each half.
2. Top each half with slice of grilled canadian bacon.
3. Pile high with soft-scrambled eggs. Top with Hollandaise Sauce and a sprinkling of chopped chives.

— Mrs. Adolphus B. Orthwein, Jr.

Never Fail Hollandaise Sauce

Yield: 4 Servings

2 Egg Yolks
¼ teaspoon Salt
Dash Cayenne Pepper
½ Cup Butter, Melted
1 Tablespoon Lemon Juice

1. Beat egg yolks until thick and lemon-colored. Add salt and pepper.
2. Add 3 Tablespoons of the melted butter, a little at a time, beating constantly.
3. Slowly blend in rest of butter, adding alternately with lemon juice.

— Mrs. Everett P. Bean

CINNAMON FRUIT COCKTAIL

Yield: 4 Servings

1 No. 303 Can Fruit Cocktail
1 Tablespoon Cinnamon
½ teaspoon Nutmeg
1 teaspoon Allspice
¼ Cup Butter

1. In a saucepan blend all ingredients together and heat until bubbly.
2. Serve in baking cups, custard dishes, or scalloped orange shells.

— Mrs. McNeill Stokes

EGGS SARDOU
Served on Hearts of Palm
GOLDEN CHEESE GRITS
CHILLED MELON A LA GALAX
CINNAMON MUFFINS

WINES:
PINOT CHARDONNAY—American
LACRIMA CHRISTI—Italian

EGGS SARDOU

Yield: 6 Servings

6 Poached Eggs
1 10-Ounce Package Chopped Frozen Spinach
12 Slices Hearts of Palm
¾ Cup Hollandaise Sauce (See Page 27)

1. Poach eggs. Cook frozen spinach according to package directions.
2. Slice hearts of palm ¾ of an inch thick and place 2 slices per serving on heated platter.
3. Place poached egg on top of sliced hearts of palm.
4. Top with buttered spinach and Hollandaise Sauce.
5. Garnish with a sprinkle of paprika and serve.

— Mrs. Frank Briggs

GOLDEN CHEESE GRITS

Yield: 8 Servings

This makes the best company or family treat brunch ever! It's a great way to introduce Yankees to grits!

1¼ Cups Grits, Uncooked
3½ Cups Boiling Water
1 Roll Garlic Cheese or Bacon-Flavored Cheese
½ Cup Butter
2 Eggs
1 Cup Milk
⅓ - ½ Cup Cheddar Cheese, Grated

1. Preheat oven to 350 degrees. Grease 2 quart casserole.
2. Cook grits in boiling water. Crumble cheese and butter into cooked grits.
3. Blend eggs and milk together. Mix egg-milk mixture with grits.
4. Pour into greased casserole and bake at 350 degrees for 45 minutes uncovered.
5. Sprinkle with grated cheddar cheese and bake uncovered 15 minutes more until cheese is melted.

— Mrs. Neil Williams

CHILLED MELON A LA GALAX

Yield: 6 Servings

12 - 18 Galax Leaves (from Florist)
6 Slices Cantaloupe
Fresh Strawberries, Honeydew Melon Balls
Cantaloupe Balls, Blueberries
Confectioner's Sugar
Sprigs of Mint

1. Place 2 - 3 Galax leaves or 1 large green maple leaf on serving plate.
2. Peel cantaloupe and slice in half. Cut 3 - 4 rings from each half and place on leaves.
3. Spill fresh, chilled fruit over the circle of melon.
4. If desired, sprinkle Confectioner's sugar over fruit and top with sprig of mint.

— Mrs. McNeill Stokes

CINNAMON MUFFINS

Yield: 12 Medium Muffins

2 Cups Flour, Sifted
4 teaspoons Baking Powder
½ teaspoon Salt
2 Tablespoons Sugar, Granulated
2 Eggs, Well-Beaten
1 Cup Milk
¼ Cup Butter, Melted
Cinnamon Sugar

1. Preheat oven to 425 degrees. Grease muffin tins.
2. Mix and sift dry ingredients together.
3. Blend egg and milk together. Add to dry ingredients and stir in melted butter.
4. Fill muffin tins three fourths full and top with cinnamon sugar. Bake at 425 degrees for 20 to 25 minutes until golden brown.

— Mrs. Solon P. Patterson

POACHED EGGS EMILE
Served on Patty Shells and Topped with Hollandaise
BUTTERED GREEN BEANS
Sprinkled with Whole Kernels of Corn
HOT RASPBERRY PEAR

WINES:
RIESLING—*American*
MATEUS ROSE—*Portugese*

POACHED EGGS EMILE

Yield: 4 Servings

This is a real taste treat!

3 Firm Medium Tomatoes, Chopped
4 Shallots, Chopped
½ Cup Butter
¼ Cup Parsley, Chopped
4 Patty Shells
4 Poached Eggs
1 Cup Hollandaise Sauce (See Page 27)

1. Saute chopped tomatoes and shallots in butter until tender. Add parsley and remove from heat.
2. Fill patty shell with tomato mixture and top with poached egg, covered with Hollandaise Sauce.
3. Sprinkle with paprika and add a sprig of parsley for color.

— Mrs. Terrell Burnley

HOT RASPBERRY PEAR

Yield: 4 Servings

4 Pear Halves
¼ Cup Raspberry Preserves
4 teaspoons Butter

1. Preheat oven to 350 degrees. Place 1 teaspoon butter in the hollow of each pear half.
2. Top with 1 Tablespoon raspberry preserves.
3. Bake at 350 degrees for 10 minutes until preserves are melted and pear is thoroughly heated.

— Mrs. McNeill Stokes

EGGS ROYALE
Served on Brandied Liver Pate
BUTTERED SESAME SPINACH
RED SPICED KIEFFER PEAR
PARKERHOUSE ROLLS

WINES:
GEWURTZTRAMINER—American
CHABLIS—French

EGGS ROYALE
Yield: 4 Servings
Brandied Liver Pate
4 Poached Eggs
1 Cup Hollandaise Sauce (See Page 27)
1. Place patty of brandied liver pate on heated plate.
2. Top with poached egg and Hollandaise Sauce.
3. Garnish with a sprinkle of paprika and a sprig of parsley.

Brandied Liver Pate
Yield: 4 Servngs

1 Pound Chicken Livers
2 Medium Onions, Coarsely Chopped
½ Cup Butter
½ Cup Cognac, Heated
2 Eggs
2 teaspoons Salt
¼ teaspoon Pepper
Pinch of Allspice
½ teaspoon Thyme
1 Clove Garlic, Pressed
1 Hard-Cooked Egg

1. Saute chicken livers and onion in butter. Remove from butter and put in blender.
2. Heat cognac in butter to remove raw alcohol taste. After heating, pour butter and cognac into blender.
3. Place remaining ingredients in blender and blend until it reaches desired consistency.
4. You may wish to add a little more melted butter if pate seems a bit dry. Form into patty and serve.
— Mrs. Harry G. Haisten, Jr.

BUTTERED SESAME SPINACH
Yield: 4 Servings

1 10-Ounce Package Frozen Spinach
Butter
Salt and Pepper
¼ Cup Sesame Seeds

1. Cook frozen spinach according to package directions.
2. Add butter and seasonings to taste. Remove spinach from any remaining liquid and gently stir in sesame seeds.

TOMATO BOUILLON
OMELETTES AUX CHAMPIGNONS
BUTTERED HERB BREAD
CHILLED ROMAINE SALAD
Sprinkled with Toasted Croutons

WINES:
SYLVANER—American
CHABLIS—French

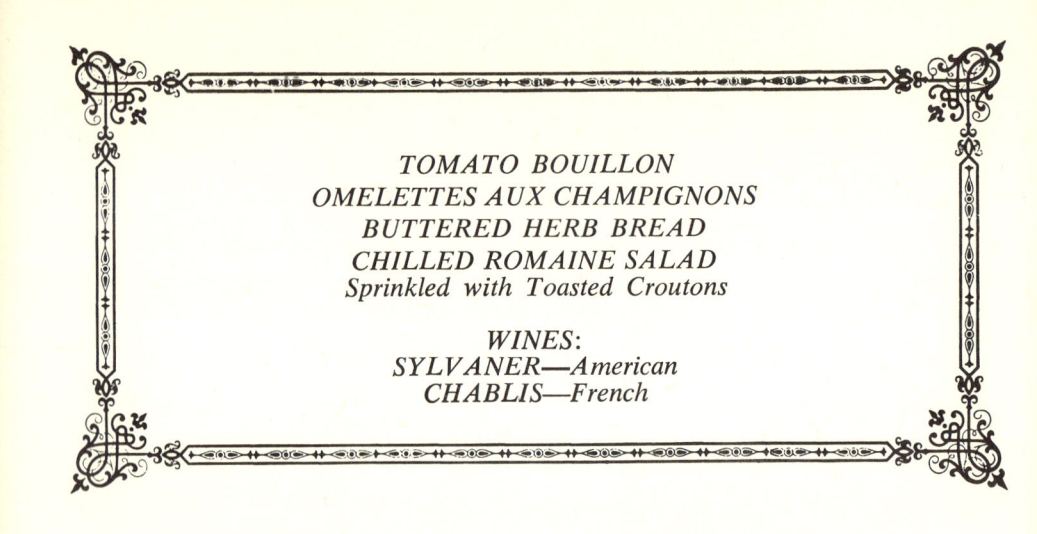

OMELETTES AUX CHAMPIGNONS

Yield: 3-4 Servings

6 Eggs
1 Tablespoon Cold Water
¼ teaspoon Salt
Pinch Pepper, Freshly Ground
1 Tablespoon Butter
1 3-Ounce Can Sliced Mushrooms

1. Add water and seasonings to eggs.

2. Beat vigorously with fork or wire whip (not a mechanical beater) for 30 seconds.

3. Heat omelette pan until butter sizzles when placed in the pan.

4. Pour in eggs. Stir once or twice with a fork, lifting the edges as the omelette cooks, letting the liquid part run under. Shake the pan back and forth to keep the omelette free.

5. Preheat broiling unit of range; and, after omelette has cooked sufficiently on the bottom, place pan under broiler to cook liquid on top of omelette.

6. After liquid has solidified on top, turn the left side of the omelette to the center, sliding the omelette well to the right edge of the pan, and turn out in three folds on the platter.
7. Garnish with Mushroom Sauce (see page 47) and whole mushroom cap.

— Mrs. Tom Slaughter

HERB BREAD

Yield: 1 Loaf

1 Package Active Dry Yeast
1¼ Cups Warm Water
3 Cups Flour, Sifted
2 Tablespoons Butter, Softened
2 Tablespoons Sugar, Granulated
2 teaspoons Salt
1 Tablespoon Caraway Seed
1 teaspoon Nutmeg
1 teaspoon Sage
1 teaspoon Basil

1. Preheat oven to 350 degrees.
2. In mixing bowl, dissolve yeast in 1¼ cups warm water.
3. Add butter, sugar, salt, all herbs and half the flour.
4. Beat 2 minutes at medium speed with electric mixer. Scrape sides of bowl frequently.
5. Add rest of flour and stir until smooth. Scrape batter from sides of bowl.
6. Cover with damp tea towel and let rise in warm place until doubled (approximately 30 minutes).
7. Stir batter about 25 strokes. Spread evenly in greased pan, 9 x 5 x 3 inches.
8. Lightly flour top of loaf of dough.
9. Let rise a second time until batter is 1 inch from top of pan, (approximately 40 minutes).
10. Bake bread 45-50 minutes at 350 degrees until golden brown.
11. Immediately remove bread from pan and place on cooling rack.
12. Brush top of bread with melted butter. Cool before cutting.

— Mrs. Adolphus B. Orthwein, Jr.

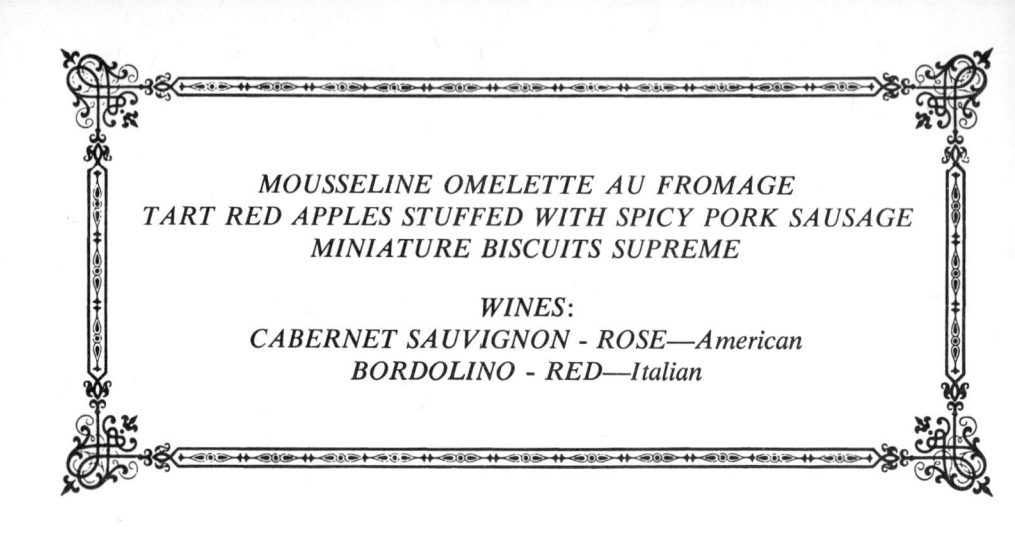

MOUSSELINE OMELETTE AU FROMAGE
TART RED APPLES STUFFED WITH SPICY PORK SAUSAGE
MINIATURE BISCUITS SUPREME

WINES:
CABERNET SAUVIGNON - ROSE—*American*
BORDOLINO - RED—*Italian*

MOUSSELINE OMELETTE AU FROMAGE

Yield: 3-4 Servings

This is an exceptionally creamy, delicate and delicious way of preparing an omelette. It is quite special!

3 Egg Yolks, Well-Beaten
Salt and Pepper
1 Tablespoon Heavy Cream
4 Egg Whites, Stiffly Beaten
2½ Tablespoons Butter, Melted
½ Cup Flaked Crabmeat
⅓ Cup New York Sharp Cheese, Grated

1. Beat yolks until pale and thick with salt, pepper, and cream.

2. Beat the whites until stiff, not dry. Gently fold egg whites into egg yolk mixture.

3. Melt butter in omelette pan and when sizzling, pour in eggs, stirring with a spoon and bringing the outer edges in toward the center until they begin to take on a certain consistency.

4. Cook slowly and shake pan periodically to keep omelette from sticking. (More butter may be added if necessary.)

BRUNCHES

5. Place flaked crabmeat and cheese in center of omelette and fold out double on a platter.
6. This is especially good when topped with a Brandied Cream Sauce. (See page 24.)

— Mrs. Steve J. Dixon

APPLES STUFFED WITH SAUSAGE

Yield: 4 Servings

4 Apples, Baking
½ Pound Pork Sausage
Salt and Pepper

1. Preheat oven to 325 degrees.
2. Core apples but do not go all the way through.
3. Season inside of cored apples and stuff sausage into hole.
4. Bake at 350 degrees in oven for 15-20 minutes.

— Mrs. Harry G. Haisten, Jr.

MINIATURE BISCUITS SUPREME

Yield: 8-10 Tiny Biscuits

1 Cup Flour, Sifted
2 teaspoons Baking Powder
¼ teaspoon Salt
1 Tablespoon Sugar, Granulated
¼ Cup Shortening, Chilled
⅓ Cup Evaporated Milk

1. Preheat oven to 425 degrees.
2. Sift dry ingredients together. Cut in shortening until mixture resembles coarse crumbs.
3. Add milk all at once and stir until dough follows fork around bowl.
4. Place dough on lightly floured surface, gently patting out dough to ¾ inch thick.
5. Use either small biscuit cutter or a knife which works quite well in getting the desired size and a unique shape. They can be cut into miniature diamonds or any shape desired.
6. Bake at 425 degrees for 10-12 minutes on an ungreased cooky sheet.

— Mrs. McNeill Stokes

CHARMING CHEESE SOUFFLE
or
PARSLIED CHEESE SOUFFLE
LEMON BUTTERED ASPARAGUS
CHILLED CINNAMON APPLE SALAD
HOT CRESENT ROLLS

WINES:
JOHANNISBERGER—American
MOSELBLUEMCHEN—German

CHARMING CHEESE SOUFFLE

Yield: 6 Servings

½ Cup Butter, Melted
2 Tablespoons Flour
1 Cup Milk (Room Temperature)
¼ teaspoon Cayenne Pepper
½ teaspoon Salt
16 Ounces Cracker Barrel Cheese, Cubed
7 Egg Yolks, Well-Beaten
7 Egg Whites, Stiffly Beaten

1. Preheat oven to 325 degrees for 45 minutes. Grease souffle dish.

2. Melt butter in top of double boiler. Add flour and milk and stir.

3. Add Cayenne pepper and salt and blend. Add cubes of Cracker Barrel cheese and stir until smooth. Remove from heat and allow mixture to cool.

4. Beat room temperature egg yolks until thick and lemon-colored. Add Souffle mixture to egg yolks and allow mixture to cool further for 30 minutes.

5. Beat egg whites until stiff. Fold in stiffly beaten egg whites into souffle mixture gently and pour into souffle dish.

6. Bake at 325 degrees for 45 minutes.

— Mrs. Adolphus B. Orthwein, Jr.

PARSLIED CHEESE SOUFFLE

Yield: 6 Servings

1½ Cups Milk
5 Tablespoons Flour, Sifted
5 Tablespoons Butter
¾ teaspoon Salt
Dash Pepper
1½ Cups Sharp Cheddar Cheese, Grated
5 Egg Yolks, Well-Beaten
5 Egg Whites, Stiffly Beaten
Sprigs of Parsley

1. Prepare a cream sauce of flour, butter, and milk. Season and add grated cheese.
2. When cheese is thoroughly blended, remove from heat and cool.
3. When mixture is lukewarm, add beaten egg yolks and fold in stiffly beaten egg whites. Pour into greased souffle dish.
4. Bake at 350 degrees for 45 minutes to 1 hour or until knife comes out clean.
5. Heat may be increased to 375 degrees during the last 15 minutes.
6. Top with sprigs of parsley and served immediately.

— Mrs. Everett P. Bean

CHILLED CINNAMON APPLE SALAD

Yield: 6 Servings

6 Tart Apples
1 Cup Red Cinnamon Candies
2 Cups Water
½ Cup Miracle Whip
1 Cup Miniature Marshmallows
½ Cup Celery, Diced
1 Cup Dark Seedless Raisins
⅓ Cup Pecans, Chopped

1. Pare and core apples.
2. Cook candies in water, add apples and simmer until tender, turning frequently.
3. While apples are cooking, blend Miracle Whip with other ingredients.
4. After apples have cooked until tender, drain and fill centers with Miracle Whip mixture.

— Mrs. Jack Pipkin

GOLDEN CHEESE SOUFFLE
Surrounded by Shrimp and Chicken Liver Kabobs
BUTTERED SPEARS OF ASPARAGUS
Topped with Strip of Pimiento
FROSTED BOWL OF FRESH FRUIT
PIPING HOT QUICK YEAST ROLLS
CHOCOLATE MERINGUE PIE
WINES:
JOHANNISBERGER RIESLING—American
PUILLY FUISSE—French

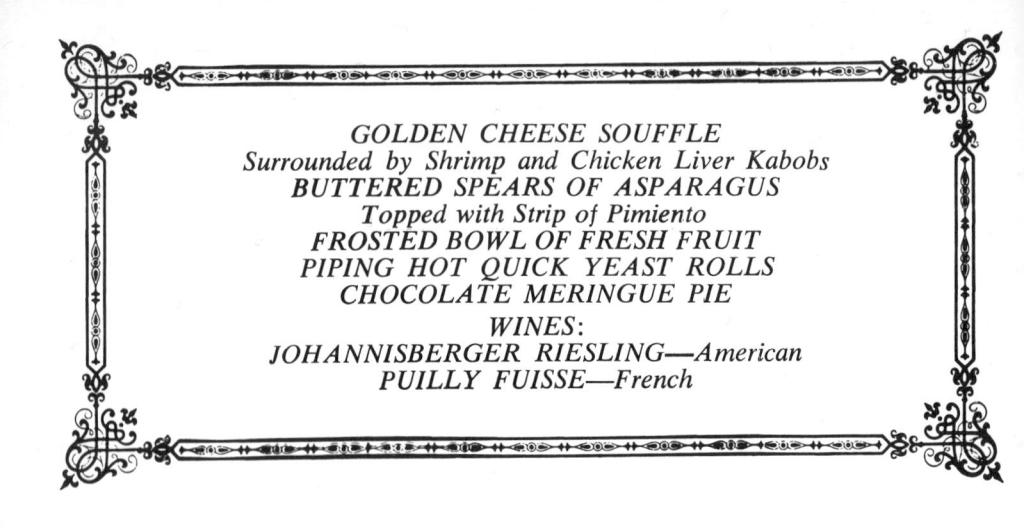

GOLDEN CHEESE SOUFFLE

Yield: 6 Servings

This makes an ulta-easy brunch as it can be made the day before.

4 Eggs
2 Cups Milk
1 teaspoon Dry Mustard
1 teaspoon Salt
½ Pound Cheese, Grated
5 Slices Bread, Cubed

1. Preheat oven to 350 degrees. Grease casserole.
2. Blend together first five ingredients. Pour over bread cubes in greased casserole and refrigerate at least one hour or overnight.
3. Place casserole in shallow pan of water.
4. Bake at 350 degrees for one hour.
5. Place cooked shrimp and sauteed chicken livers on small skewers to serve with souffle.

— Mrs. Thomas L. Johns, Jr.

QUICK YEAST ROLLS

Yield: 12 Each

These rolls are best prepared 2 hours before baking.

1 Cake Compressed Yeast
½ Cup Milk, Scalded
½ Cup Water
2 Tablespoons Vegetable Oil
1 teaspoon Salt
2 Tablespoons Sugar, Granulated
Flour

1. Preheat oven to 375 degrees. Grease shallow pan.
2. Scald ½ cup milk, pour into ½ cup water and slowly pour over cake of compressed yeast, being careful the liquid is not too hot.
3. Add vegetable oil, salt, sugar and enough flour to make soft dough.
4. Roll out and cut with biscuit cutter. Fold once, brush on melted butter and place in well-greased pan. Bake at 375 degrees for 15 to 20 minutes until golden brown.

— Mrs. J. P. Ashmore, Sr.

CHOCOLATE PIE

Yield: 8 Servings

This is a marvelous "splurge" dessert!

5 Egg Yolks, Well-Beaten
2 Cups Sugar, Granulated
½ Cup Butter
1 Tablespoon Flour
2 1-Ounce Squares Semi-Sweet Chocolate
1 Cup Milk
1 teaspoon Vanilla Extract
1 9-Inch Unbaked Pastry Shell

1. Preheat oven to 400 degrees.
2. Beat egg yolks; add sugar, butter, flour, melted chocolate and thoroughly blend together. Add milk and vanilla extract. Blend well.
3. Pour into unbaked pastry shell and bake 10 minutes at 400 degrees. Reduce heat to 350 degrees and bake until crusty on top (20 minutes) Cool and top with meringue.

Pastry Shell

Yield: 1 9-Inch Single Crust Pastry Shell

¾ Cup Flour, Sifted
½ teaspoon Salt
½ Cup Shortening
4-5 Tablespoons Cold Water

1. Sift flour and salt together.
2. Cut in shortening with pastry blender until mixture is the size of large peas.
3. Sprinkle cold water, a Tablespoon at a time, and mix thoroughly.
4. Using your hands as little as possible, form dough into ball, flatten and roll out to fit pie pan.

— Mrs. Jordan Stokes, III

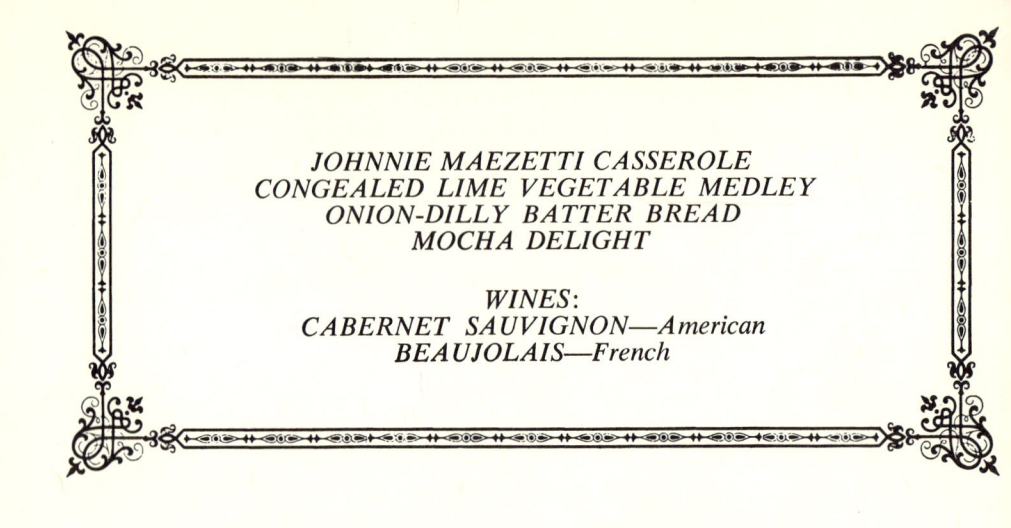

JOHNNIE MAEZETTI CASSEROLE
CONGEALED LIME VEGETABLE MEDLEY
ONION-DILLY BATTER BREAD
MOCHA DELIGHT

WINES:
CABERNET SAUVIGNON—American
BEAUJOLAIS—French

JOHNNIE MAEZETTI CASSEROLE

Yield: 6 Servings

3 Tablespoons Butter
2 Pounds Ground Beef
¼ Pound Ground Pork
1 Large Onion, Diced
1 3-Ounce Can Sliced Mushrooms
1 Can Tomato Sauce
1 teaspoon Celery Salt
1 teaspoon Salt
Dash of Lowry's Salt
1 Box Spaghetti
½ Pound Cheddar Cheese, Grated

1. Preheat oven to 350 degrees. Grease casserole.
2. Saute meat and onions in butter. Add mushrooms.
3. Add tomato sauce, celery salt, salt, and Lowry's Salt.
4. Cook spaghetti according to package directions.
5. Add cheese to the meat mixture and combine with the cooked spaghetti in greased casserole.
6. Bake at 350 degrees for one hour.

— Mrs. Charles P. Netherton

BRUNCHES

CONGEALED LIME VEGETABLE MEDLEY

Yield: 4-6 Servings

1 3-Ounce Package Lime Gelatin
¾ Cup Boiling Water
1 Cup Evaporated Milk
¼ Cup Vinegar
1 teaspoon Salt
1 teaspoon Onion, Grated
1 Cup Unpeeled Cucumber, Grated
¼ Cup Radishes, Grated
2 Tablespoons Bell Pepper, Chopped

1. Oil salad mould(s).
2. Add boiling water to gelatin, stirring until dissolved. Cool.
3. Stir in milk and vinegar (mixture will look curdled).
4. Chill until partially set, stirring occasionally to keep smooth.
5. Fold in remaining ingredients and ladle into individual moulds or one quart mould. Chill until set.

— Mrs. Robert B. Ansley, Jr.

ONION-DILLY BATTER BREAD

Yield: 1 Loaf

1 Package Active Dry Yeast
¼ Cup Warm Water
1 Cup Creamed Cottage Cheese, Heated to Lukewarm
2 Tablespoons Sugar, Granulated
1 Tablespoon Instant Minced Onion
1 Tablespoon Butter
2 teaspoons Dill Seed
1 teaspoon Salt
¼ teaspoon Soda
1 Egg
2¼ - 2½ Cups Flour, Sifted

BRUNCHES

1. Preheat oven to 350 degrees. Grease an 8 inch diameter casserole.
2. Soften yeast in warm water.
3. Combine in mixing bowl: cottage cheese, sugar, onion, butter, dill seed, soda, egg, and softened yeast.
4. Add flour to form a stiff batter, beating well after each addition. Cover.
5. Let rise in a warm place, 85 to 90 degrees, until light and doubled in size (approximately 1 hour).
6. Punch down dough. Turn into well-greased casserole. Let rise in warm place until doubled again (approximately 30 to 40 minutes).
7. Bake at 350 degrees for 45 minutes until golden brown.
8. Brush with softened butter and sprinkle with salt.

— Miss Harriet Lichti

MOCHA DELIGHT

Yield: 6-8 Servings

This is a real "fun" dessert for guests, particularly when it is served in a large frosted glass compote.

2 Packages Coconut Macaroons, Crushed
¼ Cup Rum (Add as Desired)
1 Quart Mocha Ice Cream
1 Cup Heavy Cream
½ teaspoon Instant Coffee
Semi-sweet Chocolate Shavings

1. Crush coconut macaroons. Add rum until it reaches a thick, dry, pasty consistency.
2. Press macaroon mixture to sides of compote or individual sherbet dishes.
3. Fill containers with mocha ice cream and round off top with back of spoon.
4. Cover with aluminum foil (to prevent ice crystals) and freeze.
5. Whip cream and add instant coffee while whipping. (This eliminates the flat taste of whipped cream.)
6. Top the dessert with whipped cream and shaved chocolate.

— Mrs. McNeill Stokes

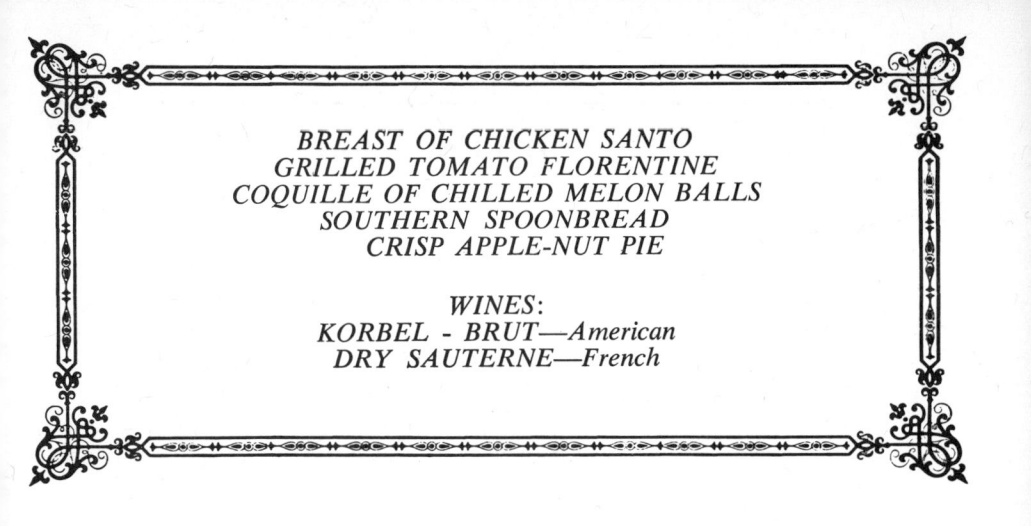

BREAST OF CHICKEN SANTO
GRILLED TOMATO FLORENTINE
COQUILLE OF CHILLED MELON BALLS
SOUTHERN SPOONBREAD
CRISP APPLE-NUT PIE

WINES:
KORBEL - BRUT—*American*
DRY SAUTERNE—*French*

BREAST OF CHICKEN SANTO

Yield: 8 Servings

8 Half Breasts of Chicken
(6 Ounces per Half Breast)
2 Cups Rice (Soaked in Water Overnight)
2 Cans Onion Soup
1 Soup-Can Water
2 Cans Cream of Mushroom Soup
1 Soup-Can Water
3 Cups White Santo Wine

1. Preheat oven to 250 degrees.

2. Soak rice overnight. Pour cans of onion soup and water over rice.

3. Pour cans of mushroom soup and water over chicken.

4. Place rice at one end of casserole and chicken breasts at the other end so soup can be poured as directed.

5. Pour wine over all of ingredients in casserole and cover with foil.

6. Bake at 250 degrees for two hours. Remove foil during last half hour.

— Mrs. C. Y. Bumgarner

BRUNCHES

COQUILLE OF CHILLED MELON BALLS

Yield: 8 Servings

1. Slice a honeydew melon in half. Then slice one half into 6 pieces, using part of the other half for the remaining 2 pieces.
2. Using a French ball cutter or a Tablespoon measure, ball the fruit from watermelon, cantaloupe, the remaining part of the honeydew melon and any other melon in season that you desire.
3. Spill these melon balls and other fresh fruits (blueberries, Thompson seedless grapes or strawberries) over the boat of honeydew.
4. Top with a fresh sprig of mint.

— Mrs. McNeill Stokes

GRILLED TOMATO FLORENTINE

Yield: 8 Servings

8 Firm Medium Tomatoes
Salt and Pepper
Butter
1 10-Ounce Package Frozen Spinach

1. Preheat oven to 350 degrees. Cook spinach according to directions on package.
2. Cut top off tomatoes, season with salt and pepper and dot with butter. Bake at 350 degrees for 10 minutes or until heated through.
3. Puree spinach in blender and place on top of tomatoes.

— Mrs. McNeill Stokes

SOUTHERN SPOONBREAD

Yield: 8 Servings

1 1/3 teaspoon Sugar, Granulated
1 1/2 teaspoon Salt
1 Cup Cornmeal

1⅓ Cup Boiling Water
3 Eggs, Well-Beaten
1 Tablespoon Baking Powder
1⅓ Cup Milk

1. Preheat oven to 350 degrees. Grease 2 quart casserole.
2. Mix sugar and salt with cornmeal. Blend well.
3. Pour boiling water over cornmeal, stirring constantly. Cool.
4. Beat eggs until foamy. Add beaten eggs and baking powder to mixture. Add milk.
5. Pour mixture into greased 2 quart casserole and dot with butter. Place casserole in shallow pan of hot water in a 350 degree oven for 35 minutes.

— Mrs. J. Lee Edwards

APPLE-NUT PIE

(A Do-It-Itself Crust)

Yield: 8 Servings

2 Eggs
1 Cup Sugar, Granulated
½ Cup Flour, Sifted
2 teaspoons Baking Powder
¼ teaspoon Salt
1 Apple, Diced
¾ Cup Pecans, Chopped
¼ teaspoon Vanilla Extract

1. Preheat oven to 350 degrees. Grease 9 inch pie pan.
2. Beat eggs, add sugar, mixing well. Sift flour, baking powder and salt together.
3. Add to egg mixture, stir just enough to mix (don't beat).
4. Add apples, pecans, vanilla extract and mix (do not overmix).
5. Pour into pan and bake 25 to 30 minutes at 350 degrees.

— Mrs. Charles N. Morris

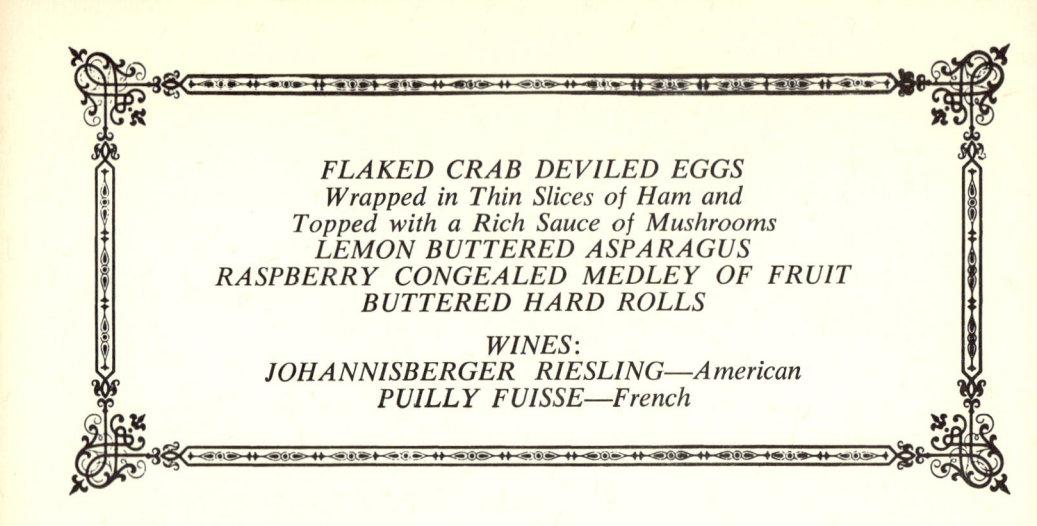

FLAKED CRAB DEVILED EGGS
Wrapped in Thin Slices of Ham and
Topped with a Rich Sauce of Mushrooms
LEMON BUTTERED ASPARAGUS
RASPBERRY CONGEALED MEDLEY OF FRUIT
BUTTERED HARD ROLLS

WINES:
JOHANNISBERGER RIESLING—American
PUILLY FUISSE—French

FLAKED CRAB DEVILED EGGS
Wrapped in Thin Slices of Ham
and Topped with a Rich Sauce of Mushrooms

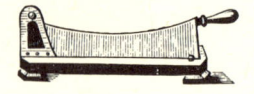

Yield: 6 Servings

- 6 Flaked Crab Deviled Eggs
- 6 Medium Thick Slices of Ham
- 2 Cups Mushroom Sauce (See Page 47)
- 1 3-Ounce Can Mushroom Crowns

1. Preheat oven to 300 degrees. Grease shallow pan.

2. Place 2 halves of the Flaked Crab Deviled Eggs together to make one whole egg again.

3. Wrap ham slices around each egg and secure with pick. Place in greased shallow pan.

4. Pour mushroom sauce over ham, leaving some in reserve for serving.

5. Bake at 300 degrees for 45 minutes until done.

6. Pour remaining sauce over each individual serving. Top with mushroom crown and paprika, garnishing with parsley.

Flaked Crab Deviled Eggs

Yield: 6 Servings

6 Hard-Cooked Eggs
2 Tablespoons Mayonnaise
1 teaspoon Vinegar
½ teaspoon Salt
Dash Pepper
¼ teaspoon Paprika
1 teaspoon Prepared Mustard
⅓ Cup Flaked Crabmeat

1. Halve hard-cooked eggs lengthwise. Remove yolks and mash.
2. Add remaining ingredients to mashed egg yolks and refill whites.
3. Add crabmeat last.

Mushroom Sauce

Yield: 2 Cups

¼ Cup Butter
¼ Cup Flour
1 Cup Cream of Mushroom Soup, Undiluted
1 Cup Evaporated Milk, Heated
Salt and Pepper
1 6-Ounce Can Sliced Mushrooms

1. Melt butter, stir in flour and cook until bubbly.
2. Gradually add mushroom soup and evaporated milk that has been heated together. Add seasonings to taste.
3. Stir until sauce is thick and add sliced mushrooms.

— Mrs. McNeill Stokes

RASPBERRY CONGEALED MEDLEY OF FRUIT

Yield: 6-8 Servings

1 6-Ounce Package Raspberry Gelatin
1 Cup Boiling Water
1 Cup Fruit Juice
1 No. 303 Can Grapefruit Sections
1 No. 303 Can Mandarin Oranges
1 Cup Blanched Almonds

1. Oil salad mould(s).
2. Add boiling water to gelatin and stir until dissolved.
3. Add fruit juice from cans to gelatin mixture.
4. Place in mould(s) and chill for 30 minutes or until partially set. Add fruit and chill until firm.

— Mrs. Robert B. Malone

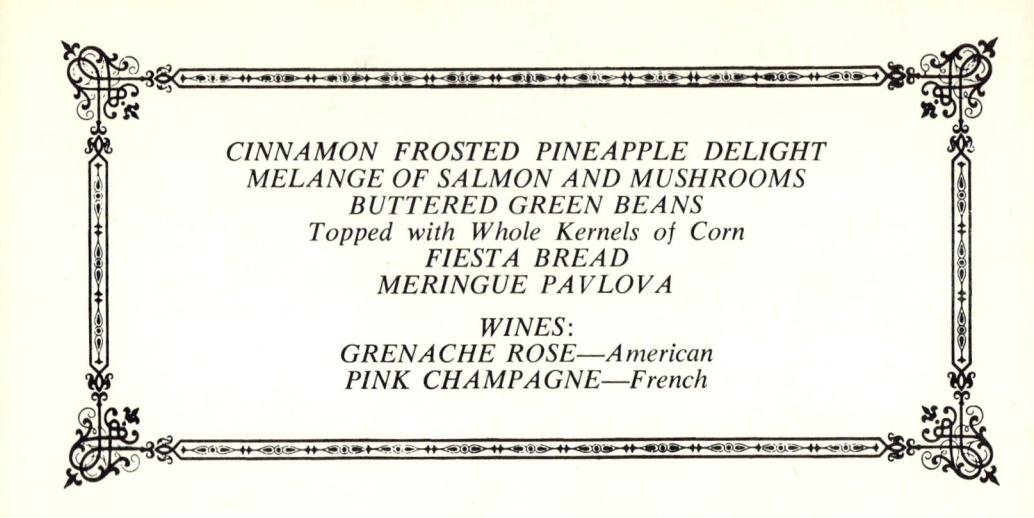

CINNAMON FROSTED PINEAPPLE DELIGHT
MELANGE OF SALMON AND MUSHROOMS
BUTTERED GREEN BEANS
Topped with Whole Kernels of Corn
FIESTA BREAD
MERINGUE PAVLOVA

WINES:
GRENACHE ROSE—*American*
PINK CHAMPAGNE—*French*

CINNAMON FROSTED PINEAPPLE DELIGHT

Egg White
Cinnamon Sugar Mixture
Pineapple Juice, Chilled
Fresh Pineapple Rings
Maraschino Cherries
Sprigs of Mint

1. Dip rim of juice glass in egg white.
2. Dip rim of juice glass in cinnamon sugar mixture and freeze.
3. Fill glass with chilled pineapple juice.
4. As a garnish for something extra pretty, add a ring of fresh pineapple, Maraschino cherry, and sprig of mint.

— Mrs. McNeill Stokes

MELANGE OF SALMON AND MUSHROOMS

Yield: 4 Servings

This is a tasty way to serve fish extra quick and extra easy.

1 Large Can Salmon
1 Large Bermuda Onion, Sliced
1 Can Cream of Mushroom Soup (Cream of Celery or Cream of Chicken Soup may be substituted)

BRUNCHES

1. Preheat oven to 400 degrees. Grease casserole.
2. Arrange rings of Bermuda onion on bottom of casserole.
3. Add salmon and onion in alternate layers, ending with salmon.
4. Top with soup and bake in 400 degree oven for 30 minutes or until browned and bubbly.

— Mrs. John C. Hopkins, Jr.

FIESTA BREAD

Yield: 6-8 Servings

¼ Cup Butter, Softened
1 Cup Cheddar Cheese, Grated
½ Cup Catsup
⅓ Cup Ripe Olives, Pitted and Chopped
⅓ Cup Bell Pepper, Chopped
⅓ Cup Onion, Chopped
1 Large or 2 Small Loaves French Bread

1. Split bread lengthwise in half.
2. Mix all ingredients but the bread together.
3. Spread each half of bread with butter mixture.
4. Wrap each half in foil and heat in oven or on grill, or place halves together and wrap in foil before heating.

— Mrs. Paul Hanes

MERINGUE PAVLOVA

Yield: 4 Servings

4 Meringue Shells
1 Pint Heavy Cream
½ Pint Strawberries
2 Bananas, Sliced

1. Fill a large meringue shell with a small thin layer of sweetened whipped cream.
2. Cover this with a layer of strawberries or bananas.
3. Top with big puffs of whipped cream. (This may be made with any fruit.)

— Mrs. John C. Hopkins, Jr.

CAJUN SHRIMP CREOLE
Served on White Rice
CHILLED BIBB LETTUCE SALAD
CHEESE DROP BISCUITS
LEMON FLUFF PIE

WINES:
SAUVIGNON BLANC—American
WHITE RHONE—French

CAJUN SHRIMP CREOLE

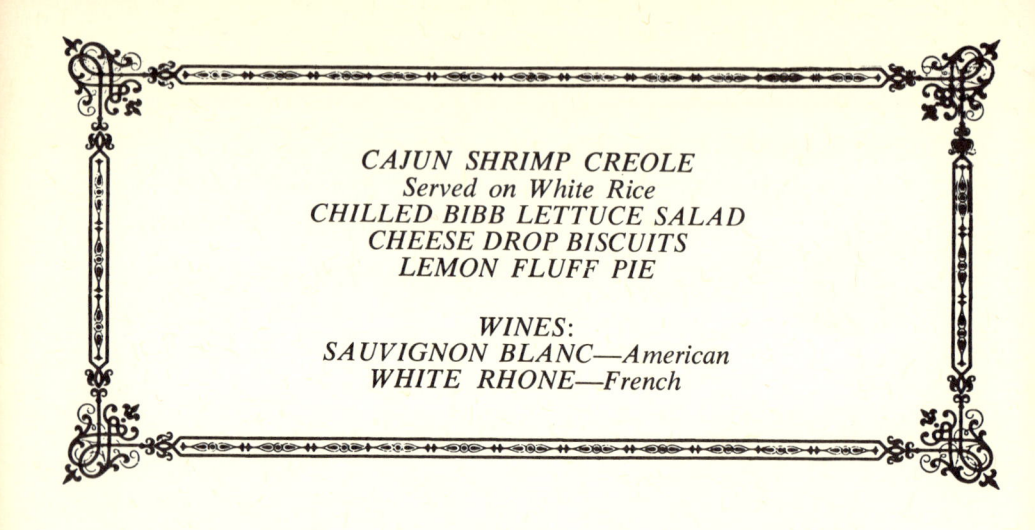

Yield: 6-8 Servings

¼ Cup Vegetable Oil
2 Medium Onions, Sliced
1 Large Bell Pepper, Cut in Strips
¼ Pound Fresh Mushrooms, Sliced
¼ Cup Flour
1 teaspoon Salt
¼ teaspoon Pepper
1 teaspoon Oregano
2 Cans Solid Pack Tomatoes
2 Pounds Shelled and Deveined Shrimp

1. In a saucepan, heat oil; add onions, Bell pepper and mushrooms.
2. Cook until ingredients are tender, stirring occasionally.
3. Add flour and seasonings. Mix well.
4. Add tomatoes. Cook, stirring constantly, until thickened.
5. Cover and cook over low heat 10 minutes.
6. Add shrimp and cook 5 minutes more.

— Mrs. Paul Hanes

CHEESE DROP BISCUITS

Yield: 2½ Dozen

2 Cups Sharp Cheese, Grated
¼ Cup Shortening
2 Eggs, Well-Beaten
2 Cups Flour, Sifted
3 Tablespoons Baking Powder
1 teaspoon Salt
¼ teaspoon Cayenne Pepper
½ Cup Water

1. Preheat oven to 425 degrees; grease cooky sheet.
2. Mix first three ingredients together.
3. Add remaining ingredients, blending thoroughly.
4. Drop onto greased cooky sheet. Biscuits should be the size of small walnuts.
5. Bake at 425 degrees for about 15 minutes or until golden brown.

— Mrs. Edna De Foor

LEMON FLUFF PIE

Yield: 8 Servings

3 Egg Yolks, Well-Beaten
¾ Cup Sugar, Granulated
1 Tablespoon Butter
Grated Rind and Juice of 1 Lemon
3 Tablespoons Cold Water
¼ Cup Sugar, Granulated
1 9-Inch Baked Pastry Shell (See page 39)

1. Mix first 5 ingredients in top of double boiler.
2. Cook in double boiler until thick and add ¼ cup sugar.
3. Pour mixture into baked 9 inch pastry shell and brown quickly under the broiler unit of the range.

— Mrs. Chester E. Martin

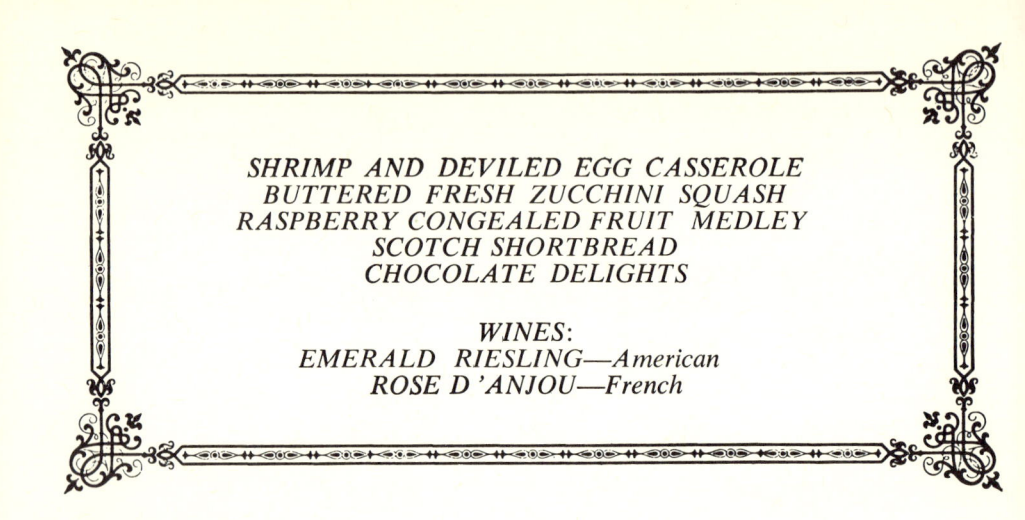

SHRIMP AND DEVILED EGG CASSEROLE
BUTTERED FRESH ZUCCHINI SQUASH
RASPBERRY CONGEALED FRUIT MEDLEY
SCOTCH SHORTBREAD
CHOCOLATE DELIGHTS

WINES:
EMERALD RIESLING—American
ROSE D'ANJOU—French

SHRIMP AND DEVILED EGG CASSEROLE

Yield: 8 Servings

2 Pounds Shrimp, Uncooked
4 Cups Light Cream Sauce
8 Hard-Cooked Eggs
½ Cup Sharp Cheddar Cheese, Grated
2 Cups Soft Bread Crumbs, Well-Buttered
½ teaspoon Dry Mustard
¼ Cup Mayonnaise
1½ teaspoons Light Cream
½ teaspoon Lemon Juice
Dash Pepper
Dash Tabasco Sauce
Finely Chopped Sweet Pickle (Optional)

1. Preheat oven to 350 degrees. Grease casserole.
2. Cook shrimp in seasonings as usual.
3. Prepare four cups light cream sauce, add ½ cup sharp cheddar cheese.
4. Mash egg yolks. Devil eggs with salt, dry mustard, mayonnaise, light cream, lemon juice, pepper and Tabasco Sauce.
5. Place cooked shrimp in bottom of greased casserole. Pour sauce over this.
6. Place deviled eggs on top and sprinkle with soft bread crumbs.
7. Bake at 350 degrees for 30 minutes or until heated through and topping is golden brown.

Light Cream Sauce:

Yield: 4 Cups

    3 Tablespoons Butter
    2 Tablespoons Flour
    4 Cups Milk, Heated
    ¾ teaspoon Salt

1. Melt butter. Add flour and salt. Cook until bubbly.
2. Add heated milk gradually until sauce is slightly thickened.

— Mrs. George W. Rowbotham

RASPBERRY CONGEALED FRUIT MEDLEY

Yield: 8 Servings

1 Envelope Plain Gelatin
½ Cup Cold Water
1 3-Ounce Package Raspberry Gelatin
1 Jar Maraschino Cherries
1 Jar Spiced Peaches, Diced
1 Large Can Crushed Pineapple, Drained
1 Cup Pecans, Chopped

1. Oil mould(s) with salad oil. Dissolve plain gelatin in ½ cup cold water.
2. Heat juice from fruit and add enough water to make 2 cups. Pour hot juice over raspberry gelatin. Add softened plain gelatin to hot mixture.
3. Combine all other ingredients and add to liquid mixture.
4. Pour into oiled mould(s) and chill until set (about 2 - 3 hours).

— Mrs. Thorne Winter

SCOTCH SHORTBREAD

Yield: 8 Servings

It's crisp, delicious and easy!

½ Cup Butter
½ Cup Margarine
⅔ Cup Sugar, Granulated
2¼ Cups Flour, Sifted

1. Preheat oven to 275 degrees. Cream together butter, margarine and sugar.

2. Add flour and knead for 10 minutes.

3. Separate dough into halves and pat each into round circle on 2 cooky sheets. Make each circle about ⅛ inch thick. Prick circles of dough with fork.

4. Bake at 275 degrees for 30 to 40 minutes or until slightly browned.

5. Cut into pie-shaped wedges and cool on wire rack.

— Mrs. J. Robert Douglas, Jr.

CHOCOLATE DELIGHTS

Yield: 2 Dozen

½ Cup Milk
½ Cup Cocoa
½ Cup Butter
2 Cups Sugar, Granulated
½ Cup Coconut, Shredded
3 Cups Quick Oats

1. In a saucepan, combine milk, cocoa, butter and sugar. Cook 2 minutes.

2. Add coconut and oats. Mix well. Drop onto waxed paper or pan with teaspoon or cooky dropper to make drop cookies. Chill and serve.

— Mrs. Walker Nelson

HOSTESS' NOTES

LUNCHEONS

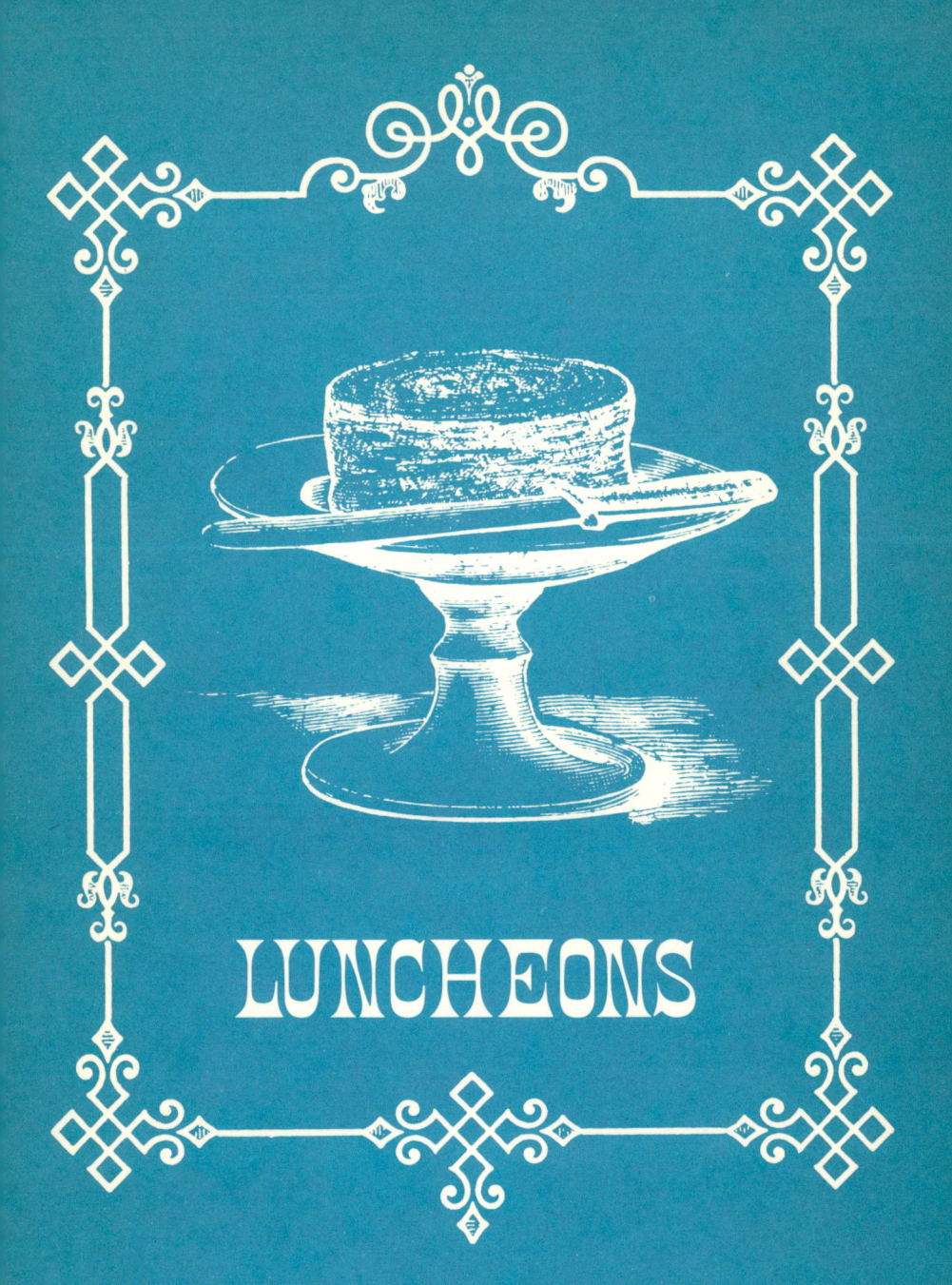

LUNCHEONS

A golden wheelbarrow ladened with lilies, geraniums and roses graced the dining table; handsome Dresden china candelabras in which burned ten golden candles flanked the sides. Small doll ladies dressed in silk net and colored sashes lingered at the door of a vine-clad candy cottage on one end of the table. Suspended from the chandelier to the four corners of the table were pink ribbons from which swung a myriad of little Chinese lanterns. This most imaginative and elegant luncheon took place in an Atlanta home in the late 1800's, with many a belle and beau present. Not everyone, of course, can entertain on such a grand scale. But there are no limitations on the use of imagination and originality, by which you can achieve the same effect in more modest surroundings.

Because luncheons are more personal, they are one of the most popular habits of entertaining among women. Invitations are the same as for a coffee or tea. Telephone a few friends and write individual notes to a larger group. Six to twelve make a pleasant group and can be handled without additional help.

A nice gesture is to focus the attention on an honoree. When President and Mrs. Theodore Roosevelt visited Atlanta, they were honored at a luncheon after the President's speech at Piedmont Park. They also visited Bullock Hall in nearby Roswell, the childhood home of President Roosevelt's mother, the former Martha Bullock.

About that same time, an article appeared in the Atlanta Constitution stating that buffet luncheons were the most fashionable mode of entertainment in New York and Chicago as they did not conflict with afternoon engagements of cards, tea, or calling. Another amusing description of a long-ago luncheon read, "Twenty-eight young ladies partook of a tempting feast, and never did sweeter lips than theirs sip of champagne when responding to the numerous toasts. Thirteen courses were daintily served with claret and champagne."

Seating

Seat your guests at the dining table when serving a small group. For a larger number, card tables can be set in the living room or adjoining rooms. There is available an extension top which fits over a card table and increases the seating capacity to six. If the weatherman's predictions are favorable, lunch may be served on the patio or on a flowering garden path.

Do take time for those little extras that make ladies' luncheons so memorable. Set the table with a pretty, delicate cloth. Place attractive napkins in the center of the luncheon plate or to its left. Place cards located directly above the plate give a personal air to any setting. In 1909, when cars were an innovation, one Atlanta hostess cleverly used car cut-outs for her place cards. You will want to use your own ingenuity in selecting place cards.

LUNCHEONS

Party Ideas

Welcome spring with a lunch party for your neighbors. Decorate lavishly with pots of blooming spring plants that can be planted in your garden later. Geraniums, hyacinths, tulips and daffodils are quite appropriate for spring. Set a miniature berry basket of blooming flowers lined with colored tissue paper at each guest's place, or use tiny potted flowering plants. These can be table decorations and favors combined. Purchase, from your florist, wooden identification sticks on which guests' names may be written and attach to arrangements for place cards. Packets of seeds tied to place cards with ribbon also make excellent seasonal favors.

For your next bridge-party luncheon, use a flower theme. Place small arrangements of different kinds of flowers on card tables. Distribute tallies that correspond with the table decorations. For a three-table bridge luncheon, there might be four daffodil tallies, four rose tallies, and four tulip tallies. By matching the tally flowers to the table flowers, guests can find their places. Dessert might be served in tiny clay flower pots, with a flower springing from the center, (see page 284).

Centerpieces

In the fall a hollowed-out pumpkin, coated with melted wax and filled with rust-colored chrysanthemums and bittersweet reflects the coolness of the season. You may prefer a wreath of autumn leaves beneath a wooden bowl overflowing with green pears, green grapes and assorted nuts or colorful gourds and dried flowers.

As a wintertime centerpiece, or whenever flowers are scarce, you will be amazed at the effectiveness of highly polished red apples in a silver bowl. A basket of evergreens or a bird cage filled with trailing ivy also provide gay; flowerless arrangements. For sheer simplicity, feature a Lazy Susan or small bowl of pink carnations or geraniums. For a casual setting, select vegetables that are the ripest in color and shape and combine them with freshly cut ivy. Vegetables are especially becoming in a rustic container such as a wooden or pewter bowl, an antique washbowl or a basket.

Highlight your springtime luncheon table with azaleas or camellias in a silver or crystal dish. Try a table decoration of yellow tulips, daffodils and variegated ivy in an olive green bowl. Red roses on a pink cloth achieve a beauty classic. Violets nestled in a pretty white basket add a delicate touch.

Geraniums arranged in a rather low wicker basket or blackberries heaped in demitasse cups set in a circle are favorite summertime standbys. A pretty tea cup is just the right size and color for flowers on a small table.

If you do not have enough stem holders to take care of your summer crop of sweetpeas, you can make your own with a potato or apple. Slice the apple and punch holes in the rounded part to hold the stems. Be careful not to make the hole too large.

As you prepare your luncheon, make the most of the little flourishes so dear to the female heart. Rose the radishes, curl the carrots, and mould the butter.

Be a little adventurous; sprinkle a few candied violets on the dessert. A recipe that appeared in an Atlanta Constitution paper in 1890 read: "The dainty and expensive sweets, preserved violets, are easy and simple to prepare. Boil one pound of loaf sugar in as much water as it will absorb until when dropped into cold water it becomes hard and brittle. Throw the violets, the large double variety, and with no stems, into syrup a few at a time and keep them in until sugar boils again. Stir the sugar around the edge of the pan until it is white and grains, then gently stir flowers about until sugar leaves them. Drain them on fine white cloth, set on sieve to dry in slightly warm oven. Turn carefully two or three times and watch them lest they cool before they dry."

You might be overwhelmed at the thought of so much work; however, candied violets are available in specialty shops for your convenience. Save your vigor for preparing the Shrimp Aux Champignons luncheon dish listed in the menu section and your vitality for your special guests.

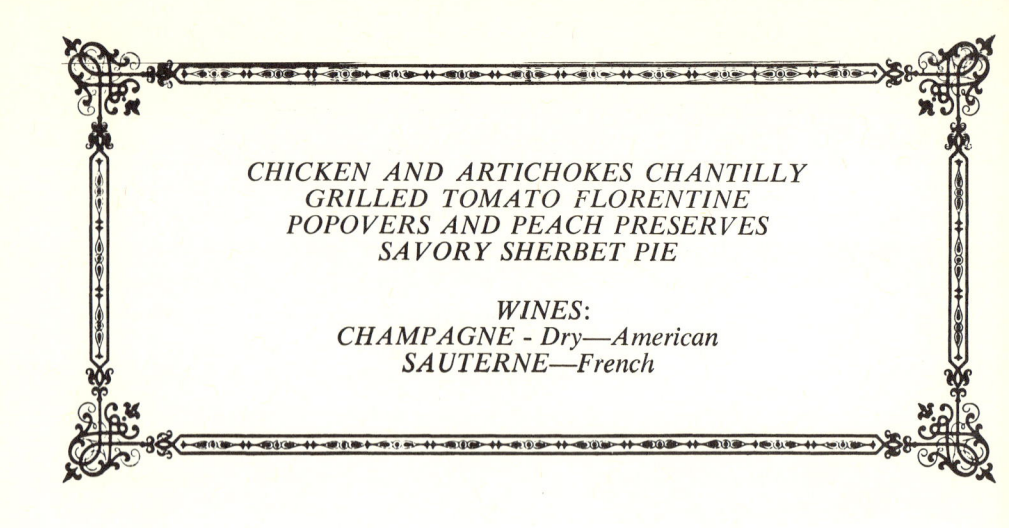

CHICKEN AND ARTICHOKES CHANTILLY
GRILLED TOMATO FLORENTINE
POPOVERS AND PEACH PRESERVES
SAVORY SHERBET PIE

WINES:
CHAMPAGNE - Dry—American
SAUTERNE—French

CHICKEN AND ARTICHOKES CHANTILLY

Yield: 6 Servings

6 Half Breasts of Chicken
    (6 Ounces per Half Breast)
¼ Cup Vegetable Oil
¾ Cup Chicken Broth
¾ Cup Sauterne
1 10-Ounce Package Frozen Artichoke Hearts
Wedges of Tomato, Onion, Bell Pepper
Salt and Pepper
2 Cups Rice, Cooked

1. Season, flour and brown chicken breasts at 360 degrees in electric skillet. Add chicken broth and Sauterne. Cover.

2. Bake for 45 minutes at 300 degrees in covered pan.

3. Add package of artichoke hearts and wedges of tomato, onion and Bell pepper.

4. Bake about 15 minutes more at 300 degrees. Serve over fluffy, white rice or toasted croutons.

— Mrs. Neil Williams

GRILLED TOMATO FLORENTINE

(See Page 44)

POPOVERS AND PEACH PRESERVES

Yield: 8 - 10 Each

3 Eggs
1 Cup Milk
¾ Cup Flour, Sifted
1 teaspoon Salt

1. Blend all ingredients together well. Pour into greased muffin tins, filling each well about ⅓ full.

2. Place in a cold oven for 45 minutes at 450 degrees. (Do NOT preheat your oven).

— Mrs. Everett P. Bean

SAVORY SHERBET PIE

Yield: 8 Servings

1 Cup Flour, Sifted
¼ Cup Sugar, Granulated
½ Cup Butter
½ Cup Pecans or Walnuts, Chopped
2 Pints Orange Sherbet

1. Preheat oven to 350 degrees. Blend together well flour, sugar, butter and nuts. Place on cooky sheet and roll to desired thickness.

2. Bake at 350 degrees for 15 minutes. While still warm from baking, break the baked mixture into small pieces. Line a 9 inch pie pan with broken pieces, reserving ¾ cup of the broken pieces.

3. Add 2 pints sherbet and top with remaining ¾ cup broken pieces.

— Mrs. A. E. Greene

POULET AUX FROMAGES
MARINATED TOMATO SLICES
BUTTERED GREEN BEANS AND WATER CHESTNUTS
PRESTIGE PRUNE CAKE

WINES:
JOHANNISBERGER—American
SOAVE—Italian

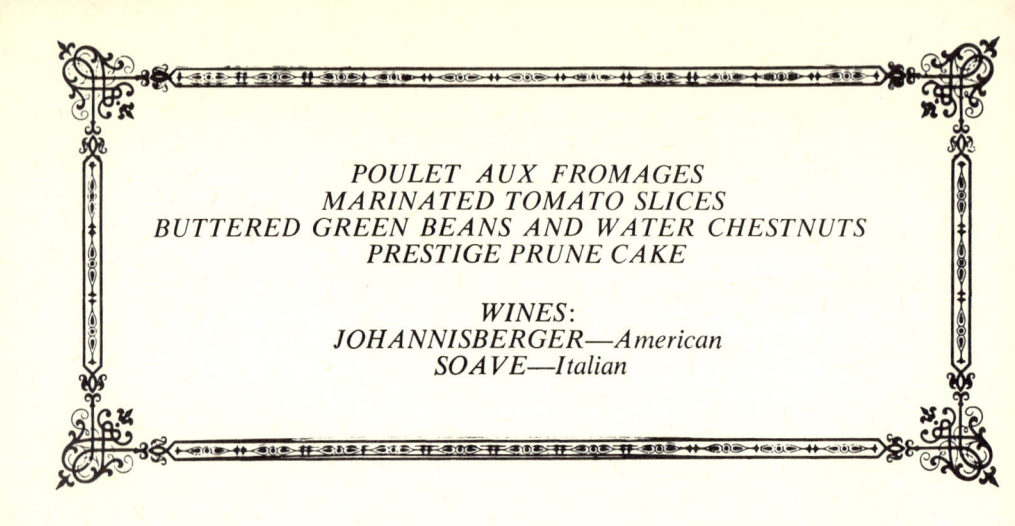

POULET AUX FROMAGES

Yield: 8-10 Servings

8 Ounces Wide Noodles, Uncooked
2½ Cups Mushroom Sauce
3 Cups Chicken, Diced
1½ Cups Cream-Style Cottage Cheese
2 Cups American Cheese, Grated
½ Cup Parmesan Cheese, Grated

1. Preheat oven to 350 degrees. Grease 9 x 12 inch casserole.
2. Prepare noodles according to package directions.
3. In greased casserole, alternate layers of cooked noodles, mushroom sauce, chicken and cheese.
4. Bake at 350 degrees for 45 minutes.

Mushroom Sauce

½ Cup Onion, Chopped
½ Cup Bell Pepper, Chopped
3 Tablespoons Butter
1 Can Cream of Chicken Soup
⅓ Cup Milk
1 6-Ounce Can Sliced Mushrooms
¼ Cup Pimiento, Diced
½ teaspoon Basil

1. Saute onion and Bell pepper in butter. Blend in rest of ingredients.

— Mrs. Carroll Schoen

PRESTIGE PRUNE CAKE

Yield: 12 Servings

1½ Cups Sugar, Granulated
1 Cup Vegetable Oil
3 Eggs
2 Cups Flour, Sifted
1 teaspoon Soda
1 teaspoon Nutmeg
1 teaspoon Allspice
1 teaspoon Cinnamon
1 teaspoon Salt
1 Cup Buttermilk
1 teaspoon Vanilla Extract
1 7½-Ounce Jar Junior Baby Food Prunes
1 Cup Pecans, Chopped Finely

1. Preheat oven to 350 degrees. Grease and flour 9 x 13 inch pan.
2. Blend together thoroughly sugar and vegetable oil.
3. Add eggs, one at a time, to sugar mixture and blend after each addition.
4. Sift together flour, soda, nutmeg, allspice, cinnamon, and salt.
5. Add dry ingredients to sugar-egg mixture alternately with mixture of buttermilk and vanilla extract.
6. Fold in prune pulp and pecans. Pour into greased pan.
7. Bake at 350 degrees for 35-45 minutes.

Glaze

1 Cup Sugar, Granulated
½ Cup Buttermilk
½ teaspoon Soda
1 teaspoon Light Corn Syrup
¼ to ½ Cup Butter
½ teaspoon Vanilla Extract

1. Blend all ingredients together and cook to soft ball stage (234 to 238 degrees).
2. Remove from heat and beat briefly until bubbles disappear.
3. Dribble over cake and serve!

Mrs. Walker Nelson

CRUNCHY CHICKEN
PARSLIED RICE WITH MUSHROOMS
CHILLED TOMATO QUARTERS
GEORGIA PEACH JUBILEEE
SOUTHERN SPOON BREAD
SWIRLED LEMON SHERBET AND
CREME DE MENTHE PARFAIT
WINES:
CABERNET SAUVIGNON—American
BORDOLINO—Italian

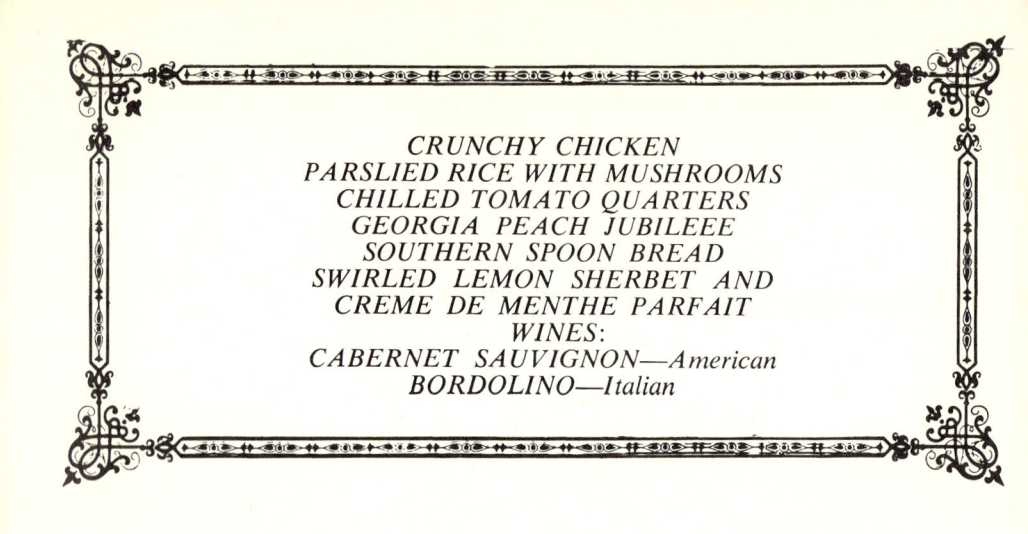

CRUNCHY CHICKEN

Yield: 8 Servings

2 Fryers, Cut in Parts
2 Cups Ritz Cracker Crumbs
¾ Cup Parmesan Cheese
¼ Cup Parsley, Chopped
1 Clove Garlic, Pressed
2 teaspoons Salt
⅛ teaspoon Pepper
1 Cup Butter, Melted

1. Preheat oven to 350 degrees.
2. Blend together Ritz cracker crumbs, Parmesan cheese, parsley, garlic, salt, and pepper.
3. Dip each piece of chicken in melted butter and then in Ritz cracker crumb mixture.
4. Arrange in open shallow pan or casserole.
5. Pour remaining butter over chicken and bake one hour at 350 degrees. Do NOT turn chicken.

— Miss Martha Haines

PARSLIED RICE WITH MUSHROOMS

Yield: 8 Servings

This makes an especially good buffet item, and it's pretty too!

1 Bell Pepper, Chopped
1 Onion, Chopped
3 Tablespoons Butter
1½ Cups Rice, Uncooked
1 Cup Parsley, Chopped
1 3-Ounce Can Sliced Mushrooms
2 Eggs, Well-Beaten
2 Cups Sharp Cheese, Grated
1½ teaspoons Salt
Dash Pepper

1. Preheat oven to 325 degrees.
2. Saute bell pepper and onion in butter.
3. Prepare rice according to package directions. Add parsley, mushrooms, bell pepper, and onion to the cooked rice.
4. Add milk, eggs, cheese, salt and pepper.
5. Blend together and bake at 325 degrees for 1 hour.

— Mrs. James H. Dolvin, Jr.

GEORGIA PEACH JUBILEE

Yield: 6 Servings

1 3-Ounce Package Cream Cheese
2 Tablespoons Mayonnaise
6 Maraschino Cherries, Chopped
2 No. 303 Cans Peach Halves

1. Blend together cream cheese, mayonnaise and Maraschino cherries.
2. Put about a Tablespoon of this mixture in center of one or two peach halves on a bed of lettuce.

— Mrs. James Jarrell

SOUTHERN SPOON BREAD

Yield: 4 or 5 Servings

2¼ Cups Milk, Scalded
2 Tablespoons Butter
1 teaspoon Salt
⅔ Cup Yellow Cornmeal
3 Egg Yolks, Slightly beaten
3 Egg Whites, Stiffly Beaten

1. Preheat oven to 375 degrees. Grease a 1½ quart casserole.
2. Scald milk. Add butter and salt.
3. Stir in corn meal and cook 1 minute, stirring constantly.
4. Remove from heat and cool slightly.
5. Stir in egg yolks and fold in stiffly beaten egg whites.
6. Pour into greased casserole and bake 35 to 40 minutes at 375 degrees.
7. Serve with lots of butter.

— Mrs. Carrol Schoen

SOUTH AMERICAN CHICKEN
WHITE ASPARAGUS SPRINKLED WITH LE SEUR PEAS
CHILLED MELON A LA GALAX
PIPING HOT PRUNE BREAD
LUSCIOUS LEMON SQUARES

WINES:
GRENACHE ROSE—American
SCHLOSS VOLLRAD—German

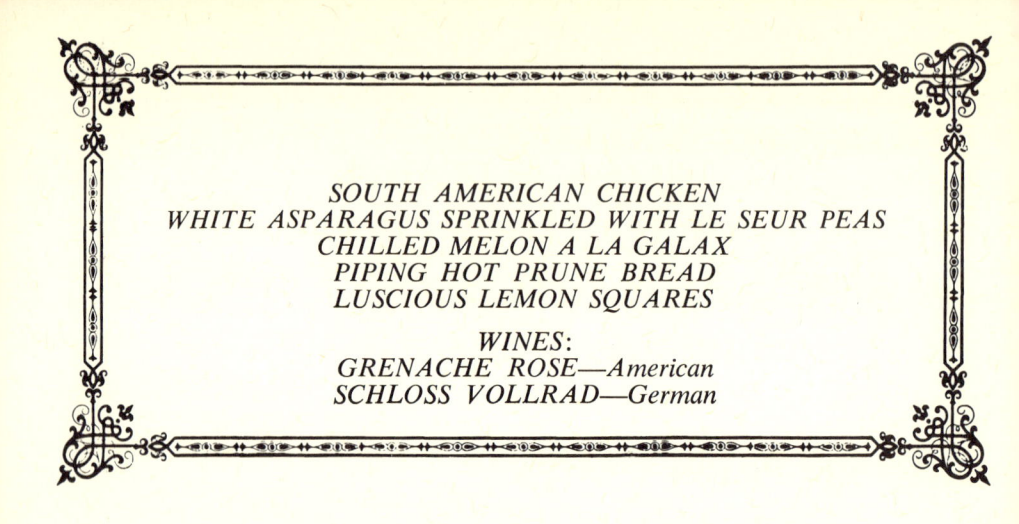

SOUTH AMERICAN CHICKEN

Yield: 8 Servings

¼ Cup Vegetable Oil
¼ teaspoon Pepper
¼ Cup Onion, Minced
1 Clove Garlic, Minced
1 Cup Rice, Uncooked
2 Cups Chicken Stock
2 teaspoons Salt
1 teaspoon Paprika
1 Cooked Hen, Diced
1 Cup Cooked Ham, Slivered
½ Cup Stuffed Olives, Sliced

1. In large skillet, heat vegetable oil and pepper. Simmer until golden in color. Add onion, garlic and rice.

2. Add chicken stock, salt and paprika. Cover and simmer until rice is cooked.

3. Add diced chicken, ham and olives. Heat thoroughly and place in center of large platter.

4. Surround with cooked white asparagus tips and green peas.

5. Garnish with strips of pimiento.

— Mrs. William L. Holland

LUNCHEONS

CHILLED MELON A LA GALAX

(See Page 29)

PIPING HOT PRUNE BREAD

Yield: 1 Loaf

2 Tablespoons Shortening
1 Cup Sugar, Granulated
1 Egg
½ Cup Prune Juice
1 Cup Sour Milk or Buttermilk
1 Cup Flour (Graham or Whole Wheat)
1½ Cups Flour, Sifted
1½ teaspoons Baking Powder
½ teaspoon Soda
1 Cup Cooked Prunes, Chopped Coarsely
1 Cup Pecans or Walnuts, Chopped

1. Preheat oven to 350 degrees. Grease loaf pan. Cream together shortening and sugar, add eggs and blend well.

2. Blend in prune juice and sour milk. Combine dry ingredients and add to egg-milk mixture.

3. Dust nut meats with a little flour and add them with the prunes, last. Pour into greased loaf pan.

4. Bake for 1 hour at 350 degrees.

— Miss Martha Haines

LUNCHEONS

LUSCIOUS LEMON SQUARES

Yield: 3 Dozen Small Squares

½ Cup Butter
1 Cup Flour, Sifted
¼ Cup Confectioner's Sugar

1. Preheat oven to 350 degrees. Mix butter with flour and add Confectioner's sugar. Press mixture into bottom of 9 inch square pan.
2. Bake at 350 degrees until done and cool for 15 minutes.

Filling:

2 Tablespoons Lemon Juice
1 Lemon Rind, Grated
2 Eggs, Well-Beaten
1 Cup Sugar, Granulated
2 Tablespoons Flour
½ teaspoon Baking Powder

1. Blend ingredients together well. Place on baked layer of Confectioner's sugar mixture.
2. Bake at 350 degrees for 25 minutes.

Frosting:

¾ Cup Confectioner's Sugar
1 teaspoon Vanilla Extract
1 Tablespoon Butter
1 Tablespoon Milk
1 Cup Coconut, Shredded

1. Blend all ingredients together well. Spread over filling.
2. Cut into small squares to serve.

— Mrs. William L. Holland

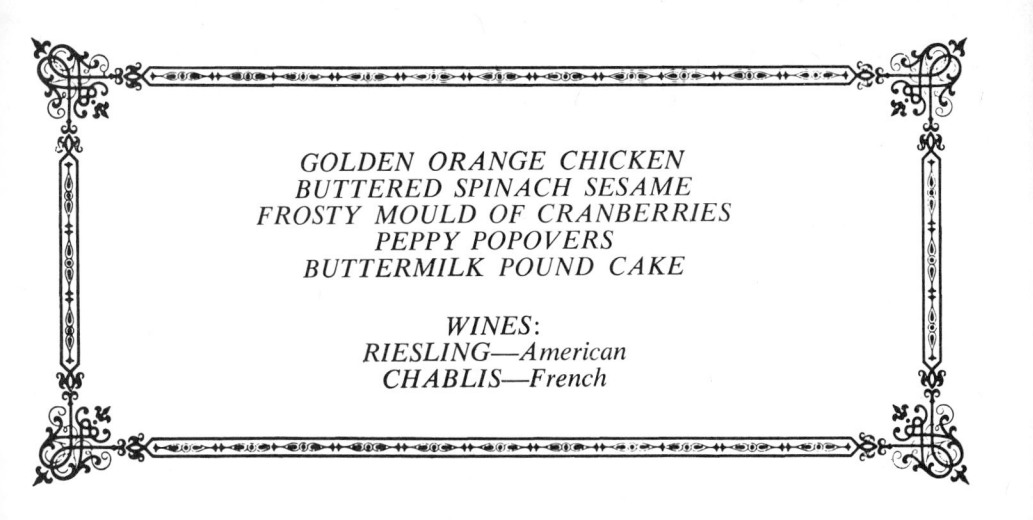

GOLDEN ORANGE CHICKEN
BUTTERED SPINACH SESAME
FROSTY MOULD OF CRANBERRIES
PEPPY POPOVERS
BUTTERMILK POUND CAKE

WINES:
RIESLING—American
CHABLIS—French

GOLDEN ORANGE CHICKEN

Yield: 12 Servings

This is particularly pretty when served as a buffet entree.

12 Slices of White Bread
2 teaspoons Salt
2 teaspoons Orange Rind, Grated
4 Eggs, Well-Beaten
2/3 Cup Orange Juice
8 Pounds Chicken Parts
3/4 Cup Butter, Melted

1. Dry bread slices at 200 degrees for about an hour. Place 6 slices in 3 clear plastic bags. With a rolling pin, crush finely.
2. In a shallow dish, combine the bread crumbs wth salt and orange peel.
3. In a second shallow dish, beat eggs with a fork until blended. Stir in orange juice.
4. Using kitchen tongs, dip chicken parts first into orange juice-egg mixture, turning to coat all sides.
5. Then dip chicken in bread crumb mixture, coating well.
6. Place chicken parts on rack to dry slightly.
7. In hot oven (400 degrees) melt butter in a 15½ x 10½ x 1 inch baking pan.

LUNCHEONS

8. Arrange coated chicken parts in the pan.
9. Turn and coat each part with melted butter; place skin side down.
10. Bake for 30 minutes at 400 degrees. Turn and bake 30 minutes more. If chicken becomes too brown, cover loosely with foil the last 10 minutes of baking.
11. Arrange on platter and garnish with watercress and wedges of orange to squeeze over each serving.

— Mrs. Melvin E. Brown

BUTTERED SPINACH SESAME

(See Page 31)

FROSTY MOULD OF CRANBERRIES

Yield: 12 Servings

This salad is delicious partially frozen. (Move from freezer to refrigerator 1 hour before serving.)

1 8½-Ounce Can Crushed Pineapple, Drained
2 3-Ounce Packages Raspberry Gelatin
2 Cups Boiling Water
2 Cups Pineapple Juice
1 8-Ounce Package Cream Cheese, Softened
2 Tablespoons Salad Dressing
1 Cup Heavy Cream, Whipped
1 Cup Walnuts, Chopped Coarsely
1 Tart Apple, Pared and Chopped
1 16-Ounce Can WHOLE Cranberry Sauce

1. Oil mould with mayonnaise or salad oil.
2. Drain fruit, reserving liquid. Add water to make 2 cups.
3. Dissolve gelatin in boiling water. Add fruit juice and chill until partially set.
4. Blend together softened cream cheese and salad dressing.

5. Gradually blend gelatin into cream cheese-salad dressing mixture. Fold in whipped cream. Set 1½ cups of this mixture aside.
6. Add drained fruit, whole cranberry sauce, nuts, and apple to remaining cheese-gelatin mixture. Pour into 12 x 7½ x 2 inch glass dish and chill until set, about 2 minutes.
7. Frost with 1½ cups of reserved whipped cream mixture. Chill for several hours.

— Mrs. Charles E. Martin

PEPPY POPOVERS

(See Page 77)

BUTTERMILK POUND CAKE

Yield: 12 Servings

1 Cup Butter
2 Cups Sugar, Granulated
4 Eggs
3 Cups Flour, Sifted
½ teaspoon Soda
½ teaspoon Salt
1 Cup Buttermilk
1 teaspoon Vanilla Extract
1 teaspoon Lemon Extract

1. Preheat oven to 350 degrees. Grease and flour a 10 inch tube pan.
2. Cream butter and sugar together until fluffy. Add eggs, one at a time, blending after each addition.
3. Mix together flour, soda and salt.
4. Add dry ingredients alternately with buttermilk, stirring the third or last portion of flour by hand so as not to overmix.
5. Add vanilla and lemon extracts. Pour into prepared tube pan, cutting through batter in several places to release air bubbles and bake for 1 hour and 15 minutes at 350 degrees.

— Mrs. R. A. Pendergrast

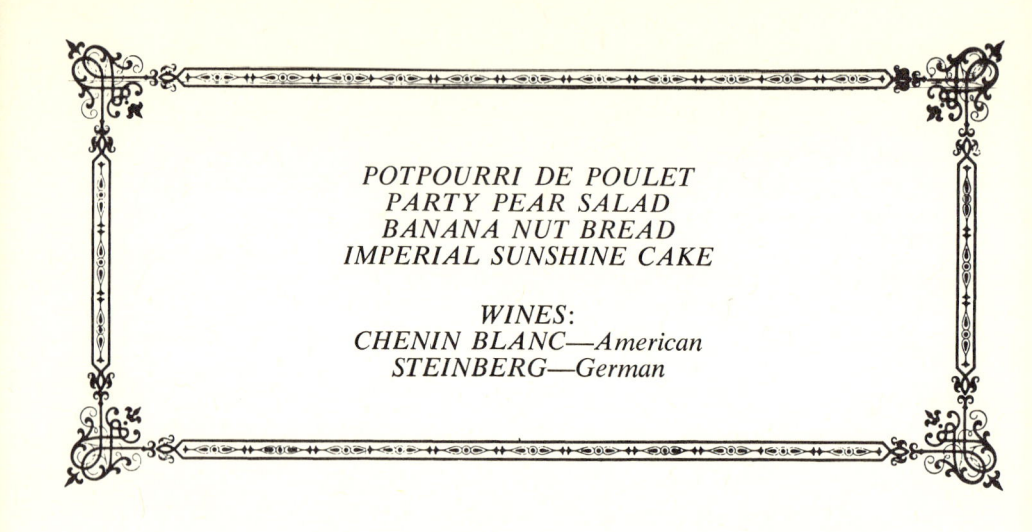

POTPOURRI DE POULET
PARTY PEAR SALAD
BANANA NUT BREAD
IMPERIAL SUNSHINE CAKE

WINES:
CHENIN BLANC—American
STEINBERG—German

POTPOURRI DE POULET

Yield: 6 Servings

2 Cups Cooked Chicken, Cubed
2 Cups Celery, Chopped
½ Cup Toasted Almonds, Chopped
½ teaspoon Salt
2 Tablespoons Onion, Grated
½ Cup Bell Pepper, Diced
½ Cup Mayonnaise
2 Tablespoons Pimiento, Diced
2 Tablespoons Lemon Juice
½ Cup Cream of Chicken Soup
½ Cup American Cheese, Grated
3 Cups Potato Chips, Crushed

1. Preheat oven to 350 degrees. Grease 1½ quart casserole.
2. Combine all ingredients except cheese and potato chips.
3. Toss lightly and place in greased casserole. Spread cheese and potato chips on top.
4. Bake uncovered until heated through and browned on top (about ½ hour).
5. Garnish with parsley.

— Mrs. Myrick Clements

PARTY PEAR SALAD

Yield: 6 Servings

2 3-Ounce Packages Cream Cheese
¼-½ Cup Pecans, Chopped
1 teaspoon Crystallized Ginger, Diced
1 teaspoon Pear Juice
2 Large Cans Pear Halves
Mint Leaves
Red Food Coloring

— 72 —

LUNCHEONS

1. Over-stuff pear half with mixture of cream cheese, pecans, ginger and juice.
2. Place other half over the stuffed half of pear. Add sprig of mint to small end.
3. Dilute red food coloring and drop on paper towel; gently rub colored towel over hump of pear.
4. Place on lettuce leaf.

— Mrs. Paul Hanes

BANANA NUT BREAD

Yield: 1 Loaf

½ Cup Shortening
1 Cup Sugar, Granulated
2 Eggs
1 teaspoon Soda
2 Cups Flour, Sifted
1 teaspoon Vanilla Extract
½ teaspoon Salt
3 Bananas, Mashed
½ Cup Pecans or Walnuts, Chopped

1. Preheat oven to 350 degrees. Grease and flour loaf pan.
2. Cream together shortening and sugar. Blend in remaining ingredients. Add bananas and chopped nuts last.
3. Pour mixture into prepared loaf pan and bake for 40 minutes at 350 degrees.

— Miss Martha Haines

IMPERIAL SUNSHINE CAKE

Yield: 10-12 Servings

1½ Cups Sugar, Granulated
½ Cup Water
7 Egg Whites, Stiffly Beaten
7 Egg Yolks, Well-Beaten
1 Cup Flour, Sifted
½ teaspoon Cream of Tartar
1 teaspoon Vanilla Extract

1. Preheat oven to 350 degrees. Place sugar in saucepan, add water and boil until it forms thin stream when dropped from spoon.
2. Add sugar mixture gradually to stiffly beaten egg whites. Beat until cool. Add well-beaten egg yolks.
3. Sift together dry ingredients. Fold dry ingredients into egg white mixture. Add vanilla extract and place in ungreased tube pan.
4. Bake about 50 minutes at 350 degrees. Invert to cool. After cooled, remove from pan.

— Mrs. Lewis Hirsch

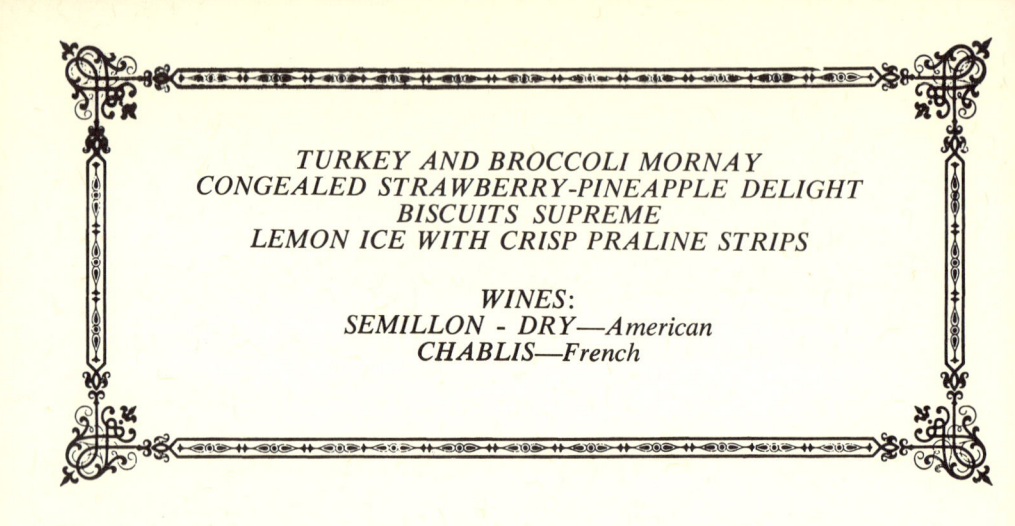

TURKEY AND BROCCOLI MORNAY
CONGEALED STRAWBERRY-PINEAPPLE DELIGHT
BISCUITS SUPREME
LEMON ICE WITH CRISP PRALINE STRIPS

WINES:
SEMILLON - DRY—American
CHABLIS—French

TURKEY AND BROCCOLI MORNAY

Yield: 8 Servings

16 Slices of Turkey (White Meat)
2 10-Ounce Packages Frozen Broccoli Spears
3 Cups Mornay Sauce
1 Cup Hollandaise Sauce (See Page 27)

1. Preheat broiler unit of range.
2. Cook broccoli according to package directions. Prepare Mornay Sauce.
3. Place 2 nice-sized spears of broccoli—with full part of each spear at opposite ends of each other—on heated plates.
4. Top with two overlapping pieces of turkey (white meat turkey rolls are ideal for this).
5. Ladle Mornay Sauce over turkey. Top with 2 Tablespoons of Hollandaise Sauce and brown under broiler.
6. Garnish plate with red spiced apple ring and sprig of parsley.

Mornay Sauce:

Yield: 3 Cups

6 Tablespoons Butter
6 Tablespoons Flour
2 Cups Milk, Heated

1 Cup Chicken Broth, Heated
2 Tablespoons Brandy
1 Pound Velveeta Cheese, Grated

1. Melt butter and add flour, cooking until bubbly.
2. Gradually add milk and chicken broth, stirring constantly until thick.
3. Add brandy and cheese, stir until well blended.

— Mrs. McNeill Stokes

CONGEALED STRAWBERRY-PINEAPPLE DELIGHT

Yield: 8 Servings

This is a terrific solution to those last two hour calls from husband who is bringing an unexpected guest home for dinner.

1 No. 303 Can Crushed Pineapple, Drained
1 6-Ounce Package Strawberry Gelatin

1. Drain juice from pineapple. Prepare gelatin according to package directions.
2. Pour gelatin solution into can with pineapple.
3. Chill until set (approximately 2 hours). Cut bottom out of can. Push out gelatin and slice. Serve on bed of curly leaf lettuce.

— Mrs. Paul Hanes

BISCUITS SUPREME

(See Page 35)

PRALINE STRIPS

Yield: 3 Dozen

24 Graham Crackers
1 Cup Butter
1 Cup Brown Sugar
1 Cup Pecans, Chopped

1. Preheat oven to 400 degrees.
2. Put graham crackers in ungreased pan.
3. In saucepan blend together butter and sugar.
4. Heat to boiling point. Reduce flame and simmer 2 minutes.
5. Add pecans and spread over crackers.
6. Bake at 400 degrees for 5 minutes.
7. Cut in strips while warm.

— Mrs. Frank Phillips

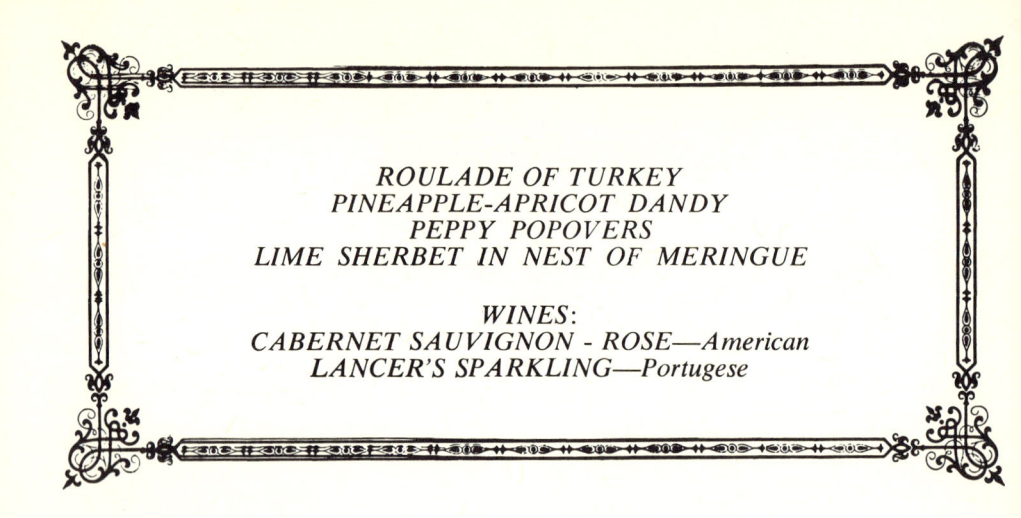

ROULADE OF TURKEY
PINEAPPLE-APRICOT DANDY
PEPPY POPOVERS
LIME SHERBET IN NEST OF MERINGUE

WINES:
CABERNET SAUVIGNON - ROSE—American
LANCER'S SPARKLING—Portugese

ROULADE OF TURKEY

Yield: 6 Servings

6 Slices Turkey, White Meat
6 Slices Ham
18 Spears Asparagus
1 Can Cream of Mushroom Soup
½ Soup-Can Milk

1. Preheat oven to 300 degrees. Grease casserole.

2. Place 1 slice of ham on top of 1 slice of turkey and add 3 spears of asparagus. Roll up and secure with pick if necessary. Place in greased casserole.

3. Cover with cream of mushroom soup, diluted with ½ soup-can of milk and bake at 300 degrees for 30 minutes.

— Mrs. William L. Holland

PINEAPPLE-APRICOT DANDY

Yield: 6 Servings

1 3-Ounce Package Orange Gelatin
1 Cup Boiling Water
1 Cup Apricot Nectar
1 3-Ounce Package Cream Cheese, Softened
1 9-Ounce Can Crushed Pineapple, Drained
¼ Cup Pecans, Chopped Finely

1. Oil moulds.
2. Dissolve gelatin in boiling water after removing it from heat.
3. Add chilled apricot nectar. Pour into oiled moulds and chill until firm.
4. Blend together softened cream cheese and crushed pineapple. Spread this mixture over unmoulded gelatin. Sprinkle chopped pecans on top.
5. Chill and serve on bed of leaf lettuce.

— Mrs. John Walter Wright, Jr.

PEPPY POPOVERS

Yield: 10-12 Each

1 Cup Flour, Sifted
¼ teaspoon Salt
2 Eggs, Well-Beaten
⅞ Cup Milk
1 Tablespoon Butter, Melted

1. Preheat oven to 450 degrees. Heavily grease muffin tins.
2. Blend together flour and salt. Beat eggs until light and add milk and butter.
3. Slowly add milk mixture to flour and blend well. Beat 1 minute with electric mixer or 2 minutes with rotary beater.
4. Heat muffin pan in oven until hot. Do NOT let butter burn.
5. Fill muffin tins ⅔ full.
6. Bake 20 minutes at 450 degrees. Reduce heat to 350 degrees and bake 10-15 minutes more.

— Mrs. Terrell Burnley

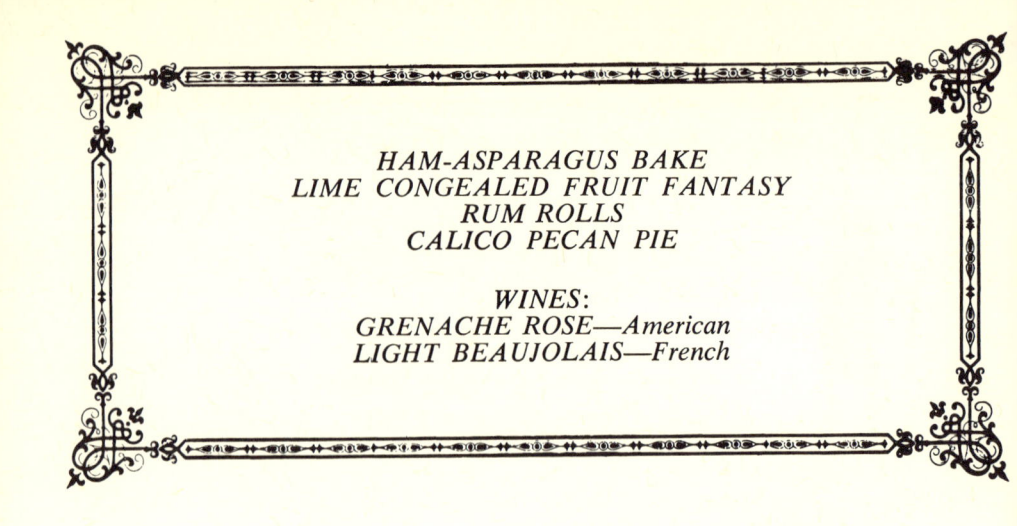

HAM-ASPARAGUS BAKE
LIME CONGEALED FRUIT FANTASY
RUM ROLLS
CALICO PECAN PIE

WINES:
GRENACHE ROSE—American
LIGHT BEAUJOLAIS—French

HAM-ASPARAGUS BAKE

Yield: 6-8 Servings

1 6-Ounce Can Evaporated Milk
2 Cups Cooked Ham, Cubed
2 Cups Rice, Cooked
½ Cup Processed Cheese, Grated
3 Tablespoons Onion, Chopped
1 Can Cream of Mushroom Soup
1 10-Ounce Package Frozen Asparagus, Cooked
½ Cup Cornflakes, Crushed
3 Tablespoons Butter, Melted

1. Preheat oven to 350 degrees.

2. Combine milk, ham, rice, cheese, onion, and soup.

3. Add liquid from cooked asparagus spears to ham mixture until very moist.

4. Place half of ham mixture in casserole. Place asparagus spears on top. Pack in rest of ham mixture. Top with crushed cornflakes, sauteed in butter.

5. Bake at 350 degrees for 25 to 30 minutes.

— Mrs. C. Christie Wilkerson

LUNCHEONS

LIME CONGEALED FRUIT FANTASY

Yield: 8 Servings

1 6-Ounce Package Lime Gelatin
2 Cups Boiling Water
1½ Cups Miniature Marshmallows
2 Cups Pineapple Juice
    (with water added if necessary)
1 Cup Heavy Cream, Whipped
1 Cup Crushed Pineapple, Drained
1 Cup Cottage Cheese
½-1 Cup Pecans, Chopped

1. Oil mould with salad oil.
2. Dissolve lime gelatin in boiling water. Add marshmallows and stir until melted.
3. Add pineapple juice and chill until partially set.
4. Remove from refrigerator and fold in whipped cream.
5. Add crushed pineapple and cottage cheese and nuts (optional).
6. Blend together and fill salad mould. Chill until set and serve.

— Mrs. M. Alexander Patton

RUM ROLLS

(See page 88.)

CALICO PECAN PIE

Yield: 8 Servings

This recipe shows off our Georgia pecans splendidly!

1 9-Inch Pastry Shell, Unbaked (See Page 39)
3 Eggs, Well-Beaten
1 Cup Pecan Halves
1 Tablespoon Butter, Melted
1 Cup Light Corn Syrup
½ teaspoon Vanilla Extract
1 Cup Sugar, Granulated
1 Tablespoon Flour

1. Preheat oven to 350 degrees. Prepare unbaked pastry shell.
2. Beat eggs until frothy. Arrange pecan halves in bottom of unbaked pastry shell.
3. Add butter, corn syrup and vanilla extract to well-beaten eggs. Blend well.
4. Combine sugar and flour and blend thoroughly with egg mixture.
5. Pour over pecan halves in pastry shell. Let stand until pecans rise to surface.
6. Bake at 350 degrees for 45 minutes. The pecans will glaze during the baking.

— Mrs. Carl E. Sanders

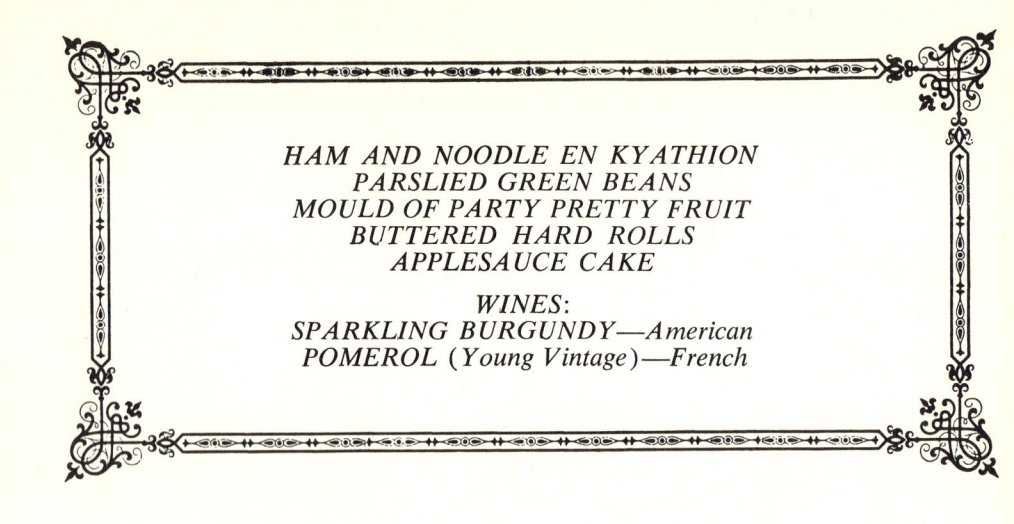

HAM AND NOODLE EN KYATHION
PARSLIED GREEN BEANS
MOULD OF PARTY PRETTY FRUIT
BUTTERED HARD ROLLS
APPLESAUCE CAKE

WINES:
SPARKLING BURGUNDY—American
POMEROL (Young Vintage)—French

HAM AND NOODLE EN KYATHION

Yield: 6 Servings

This can be prepared ahead and frozen for future guests!

4 Ounces Green Egg Noodles
⅓ Cup Onion, Chopped
⅓ Cup Bell Pepper, Chopped
½ Pound Fresh Mushrooms, Sliced
¾ Cup Butter
¾ Cup Flour, Sifted
1 teaspoon Salt
¼ teaspoon Pepper
1 Quart Milk
1 Cup Sharp Cheddar Cheese, Grated
3 Cups Cooked Ham, Cubed in Half-Inch Cubes

1. Preheat oven to 375 degrees. Grease 1½ quart casserole.
2. Cook noodles according to package directions.
3. In large, deep skillet, saute onion, bell pepper and mushrooms in butter for 5 minutes.
4. Add flour and seasonings. Stir until well blended.
5. Add milk and cheese and simmer, stirring constantly, until mixture thickens.
6. Remove from heat and stir until thoroughly blended.
7. Add noodles and ham and blend well.
8. Place about 5½ cups mixture in greased 1½ quart casserole.
9. Bake at 375 degrees for 20 to 25 minutes.

— Mrs. Marion D. Todd

MOULD OF PARTY PRETTY FRUIT

Yield: 6-8 Servings

This makes an extra special salad for buffet or seated luncheons.

1 No. 303 Can Pineapple Chunks, Drained
1 8-Ounce Jar Maraschino Cherries, Drained

1 Envelope Plain Gelatin
1 6-Ounce Package Lemon Gelatin
1 Can Peach Quarters (Dietetic), Drained
1 Cup White Seedless Grapes, Canned or Fresh

1. Drain fruit. Reserve pineapple juice and add water if necessary in order to make 2 cups of liquid.
2. Mix plain gelatin with few drops of cold water to dissolve.
3. Bring the 2 cups of pineapple juice to a boil. Add lemon gelatin and dissolved plain gelatin. Stir well and cool.
4. Arrange peach quarters in bottom of ring mould with a cherry between each slice. Cut remaining peaches into chunks.
5. Pile all fruit up sides of mould and gently on top of peaches and cherries.
6. Fill mould with liquid and chill until set.
7. Serve on bed of leaf lettuce.

— Mrs. S. M. Jordan

APPLESAUCE CAKE

Yield: 12 Servings

This is a very moist cake and melts in your mouth!

1 Cup Seedless Raisins
1 Cup Pecans or Walnuts, Chopped
1¾ Cups Flour, Sifted
½ teaspoon Salt
1 teaspoon Soda
1 teaspoon Cinnamon
½ teaspoon Cloves, Ground
1 Cup Brown Sugar
½ Cup Butter
1 Egg
1 No. 303 Can Applesauce

1. Preheat oven to 350 degrees. Grease shallow (9 x 13 inch) sheet pan.
2. Dust raisins and nuts with small part of flour.
3. Sift together flour, salt, soda, cinnamon, and cloves.
4. Cream together brown sugar and butter. Add egg and blend well.
5. Add sifted dry ingredients to butter-sugar mixture and blend thoroughly.
6. Add nuts, raisins, and applesauce.
7. Bake in greased pan at 350 degrees for 30-40 minutes. Cool.

Frosting

¼ Cup Butter
2 Cups Confectioner's Sugar
Salt
2 Tablespoons Milk
½ teaspoon Rum Extract

1. Cream together butter and sugar. Add remaining ingredients and beat on high speed until velvety smooth.

— Mrs. Andrew N. Foster

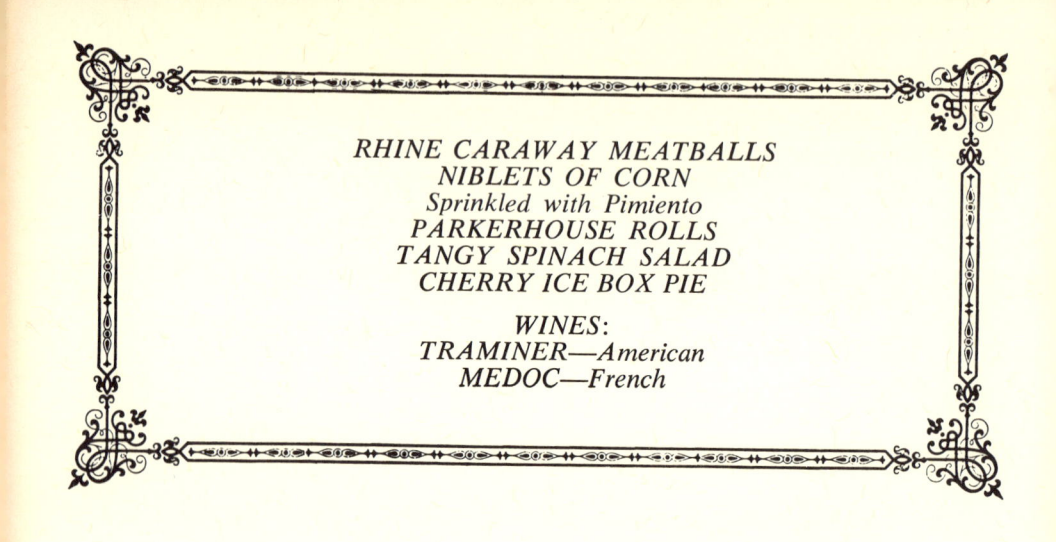

RHINE CARAWAY MEATBALLS
NIBLETS OF CORN
Sprinkled with Pimiento
PARKERHOUSE ROLLS
TANGY SPINACH SALAD
CHERRY ICE BOX PIE

WINES:
TRAMINER—American
MEDOC—French

RHINE CARAWAY MEATBALLS

Yield: 4 Servings

This good and easy recipe has only 280 calories per serving!

1 Cup Uncooked Potato, Coarsely Grated
1 Pound Round Steak, Ground
¼ teaspoon Pepper
½ teaspoon Salt
1 Tablespoon Parsley Leaves, Chopped
1 Small Onion, Minced
1 teaspoon Lemon Rind, Grated
1 Egg
2½ Cups Water
4 Beef Bouillon Cubes
2 teaspoons Cornstarch
1 Tablespoon Water
½ teaspoon Caraway Seeds
Sprigs of Parsley

1. One hour before serving, mix together potato, meat, pepper, salt, parsley, onion, lemon rind and egg.
2. Mix thoroughly and form into 12 meatballs. In a skillet, bring water to boil.
3. Dissolve bouillon cubes in water, add meatballs, cover and simmer for 30 minutes.

4. Remove meatballs from broth and place on heated platter.
5. Make paste of cornstarch and water. Add caraway seeds and stir into broth.
6. Cook until smooth and thick. Pour a bit of the sauce over meatballs and garnish with sprigs of parsley.

— Mrs. Tyrone S. Clifford

TANGY SPINACH SALAD

Yield: 3-4 Servings

Fresh Spinach
4 Bacon Slices
¼ Cup Vinegar
2 Hard-Cooked Eggs, Diced

1. Wash and drain spinach leaves. Fry bacon slices until crisp. Remove bacon from pan and add vinegar to bacon fat.
2. Place spinach leaves in a bowl. Pour Vinaigrette Sauce over them and add crumbled bacon and hard-cooked egg slices.
3. Toss and serve.

— Mrs. J. David Bansley

CHERRY ICE BOX PIE

Yield: 8 Servings

1 14½-Ounce Can Eagle Brand Milk
1 teaspoon Vanilla Extract
½ teaspoon Almond Extract
⅓ Cup Lemon Juice
1 No. 303 Can Cherry Pie Filling
½ Cup Heavy Cream, Whipped

1. Blend all ingredients together except cherry pie filling and whipped cream.
2. Fold in ½ cup whipped cream. Spread cherries on top and chill before serving.

— Mrs. M. E. Thompson, Jr.

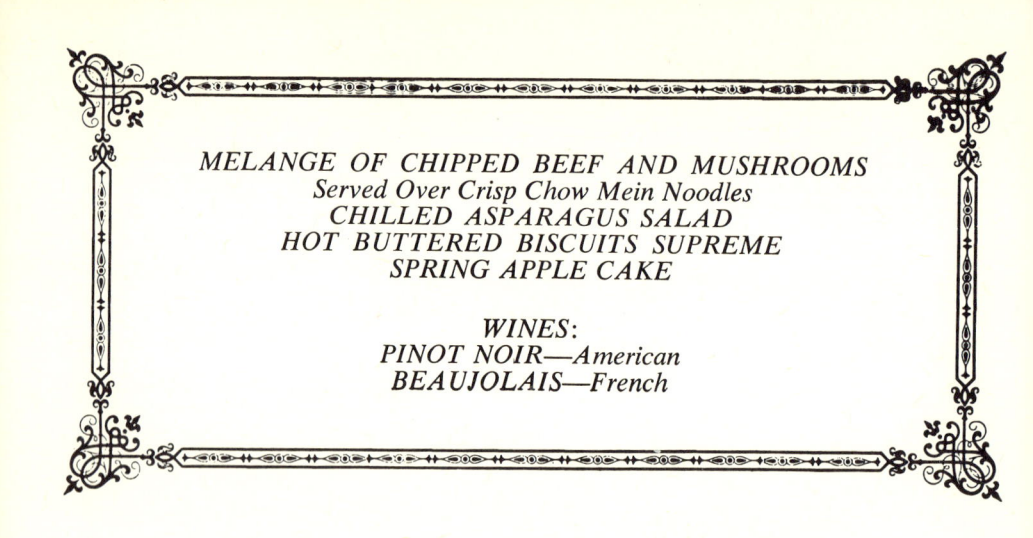

MELANGE OF CHIPPED BEEF AND MUSHROOMS
Served Over Crisp Chow Mein Noodles
CHILLED ASPARAGUS SALAD
HOT BUTTERED BISCUITS SUPREME
SPRING APPLE CAKE

WINES:
PINOT NOIR—American
BEAUJOLAIS—French

MELANGE OF CHIPPED BEEF AND MUSHOOMS

Yield: 8-10 Servings

2 Cans Cream of Mushroom Soup
2 Cans Chicken and Rice Soup
2 Packages Chipped Beef
1 Can Water Chestnuts

1. Combine all ingredients. Heat and serve over chinese noodles or rice.

— Mrs. Dan M. Hodges

CHILLED ASPARAGUS SALAD

Yield: 8-10 Servings

3 Cans Whole Green Asparagus
1 teaspoon Tarragon Leaves
1 teaspoon Garlic Salt
Black Pepper, Freshly Ground
1 Bottle Italian Dressing
½ Cup Tarragon Vinegar

LUNCHEONS

1. Drain asparagus well and layer in shallow pan. Sprinkle each layer with a few dry Tarragon leaves, freshly ground black pepper, garlic and salt.
2. Add salad dressing and vinegar, marinating asparagus overnight at room temperature.
3. Chill and serve on lettuce leaves topped with mayonnaise flavored with a little of the marinade.

— Mrs. Winthrop Rockefeller
Little Rock, Arkansas

BISCUITS SUPREME

(See page 35)

SPRING APPLE CAKE

Yield: 12 Servings

½ Cup Butter
½ Cup Shortening
2 Cups Sugar, Granulated
2 Eggs
2 Cups Cake Flour, Sifted
1 teaspoon Salt
1 teaspoon Soda
½ teaspoon Nutmeg
½ teaspoon Cinnamon
2 Large Winesap Apples, Diced
½ Cup Pecans, Chopped

1. Preheat oven to 325 degrees. Grease and flour 2 layer cake pans.
2. Cream together butter, shortening and sugar. Blend in eggs.
3. Add flour, spices and apples. Pour into baking pans, sprinkle nuts on top and bake at 325 degrees for 25 to 30 minutes.

— Mrs. A. E. Greene

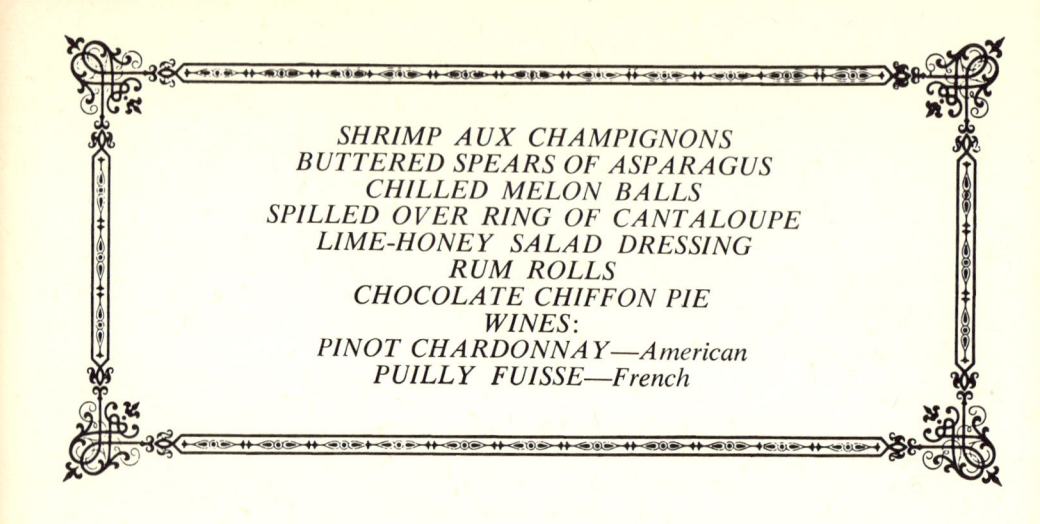

SHRIMP AUX CHAMPIGNONS
BUTTERED SPEARS OF ASPARAGUS
CHILLED MELON BALLS
SPILLED OVER RING OF CANTALOUPE
LIME-HONEY SALAD DRESSING
RUM ROLLS
CHOCOLATE CHIFFON PIE
WINES:
PINOT CHARDONNAY—American
PUILLY FUISSE—French

SHRIMP AUX CHAMPIGNONS

Yield: 4 Servings

This casserole may be made the night before and stored in refrigerator until time to bake it the next day.

1 3-Ounce Can Sliced Mushrooms
¼ Cup Butter, Melted
1½ Cups Cleaned and Deveined Shrimp, Cooked
1½ Cups American Cheese, Grated
3 Tablespoons Chili Sauce
½ teaspoon Worcestershire Sauce
½ teaspoon Salt
Dash Pepper
2 Tablespoons Pimientos, Diced
½ Cup Heavy Cream
1½ Cups Rice, Cooked
½ Cup Frito Crumbs

1. Preheat oven to 350 degrees.
2. Melt butter, add shrimp, cheese, chili sauce, Worcestershire Sauce, salt, pepper, and pimientos. Stir together carefully and add cream.
3. Layer cooked rice with shrimp mixture in a 1½ quart casserole, finishing with shrimp mixture on top. Top with Frito crumbs.
4. Bake at 350 degrees for 25 minutes.

— Mrs. Charles C. Ford

CANTALOUPE RING WITH MELON BALLS

Yield: 4 Servings

2 Large Cantaloupes
¼ Honeydew Melon
⅛ Watermelon
½ Tablespoon Sugar, Granulated
¼ Cup Lemon Juice
¼ Cup Pineapple Juice
12 Bing Cherries
Lettuce
Sprigs of Mint
Lime-Honey Salad Dressing

1. With a French ball cutter, make balls from honeydew and watermelon. Cut two slices ½ inch thick from the center of each cantaloupe and make balls from the remainder of cantaloupe. (The cantaloupe should be peeled for the slices.)
2. Add sugar to lemon juice and pineapple juice and pour over melon balls. Chill thoroughly. Drain before serving. Wrap slices of cantaloupe and chill. When arranging salad, place lettuce on plate, put melon slice on lettuce; cut in two and spread apart slightly.
3. Fill center with melon balls and garnish plate with bing cherries (with stems) and a sprig of mint. Serve with Lime-Honey Salad Dressing.

— Mrs. Charles C. Ford

Lime-Honey Fruit Salad Dresssing:

Yield: 1⅔ Cups

⅓ Cup Lime Juice
⅓ Cup Honey, Strained
1 Cup Salad Oil
½ teaspoon Paprika
½ teaspoon Prepared Mustard
½ teaspoon Salt
Grated Peel of 1 Lime

1. Combine all ingredients in a bowl. Beat with a rotary beater or a blender. Keep in a covered fruit jar. Chill before serving.

— Mrs. Charles C. Ford

BASIC SWEET DOUGH FOR RUM ROLLS

Yield: 2 Dozen

1 Cake Compressed Yeast
½ Cup Sugar, Granulated
1 teaspoon Salt
1 Cup Scalded Milk, Cooled to Lukewarm
2 Eggs, Well-Beaten
5 Cups Flour, Sifted
½ Cup Butter or Shortening, Melted
2 Tablespoons Butter, Melted
1 Cup Dark Seedless Raisins
1 Cup Brown Sugar
1 Cup Confectioner's Sugar
2 Tablespoons Hot Water
1 teaspoon Rum Extract

1. Crumble yeast into bowl, add sugar, salt, milk and eggs. Mix well.
2. Add half of flour and beat until bubbles form on surface. Add melted shortening and remainder of flour.
3. Let rise in a warm place until double. Punch down and divide into 2 parts.
4. Roll each part into rectangle ¼ inch thick. Brush with 2 Tablespoons melted butter. Combine raisins and sugar and sprinkle over dough. Roll up like jelly roll.
5. Cut into ¾-inch slices. Place in greased muffin pans. Cover and let rise in a warm place until double in bulk.
6. Bake at 400 degrees for 15 to 20 minutes. Remove rolls from muffin pans and brush with thin frosting made of 1 Cup Confectioners' Sugar, 2 Tablespoons hot water, and 1 teaspoon rum flavoring.

— Mrs. Charles C. Ford

CHOCOLATE CHIFFON PIE
With Slivered Almond Crust

Yield: 8 Servings

1 Envelope Plain Gelatin
¼ Cup Cold Water
1 1-Ounce Square Unsweetened Chocolate
½ Cup Nestle's Semi-sweet Chocolate Bits
½ Cup Water
4 Egg Yolks

½ Cup Sugar, Granulated
¼ teaspoon Salt
1 teaspoon Vanilla Extract
½ Cup Sugar, Granulated
4 Egg Whites, Stiffly Beaten
1 9-Inch Baked Pastry Shell with Slivered Almonds
1 Cup Heavy Cream
1 Tablespoon Sugar, Granulated
½ teaspoon Vanilla Extract

1. Soften gelatin in ¼ cup cold water.
2. Combine chocolates and ½ cup water. Stir over low heat until blended and thick. Remove from heat.
3. Add gelatin and stir until dissolved.
4. Beat egg yolks with ½ cup sugar until light. Add chocolate mixture, salt and vanilla extract.
5. Cool in refrigerator to room temperature. Gradually beat ½ cup sugar into beaten whites and fold into chocolate mixture. Pour into cooled pastry shell. Chill till firm. Whip together heavy cream, and vanilla and use as topping.

Slivered Almond Pastry Crust:

Yield: 1 Single Pie Crust

1 Cup Flour, Sifted
½ teaspoon Salt
⅓ Cup Shortening
2½ Tablespoons Cold Water
¼ Cup Almonds, Slivered

1. Preheat oven to 450 degrees.
2. Sift together flour and salt. Cut in shortening with a pastry blender till pieces are size of small peas.
3. Sprinkle water over this and stir with a fork until all is moistened.
4. Gather up with fingers; form into a ball and roll out on well floured wax paper. Roll to ⅛ inch thick. To transfer pastry, roll it over rolling pin, put pastry over pie plate, fitting loosely onto bottom and sides.
5. Trim ½ inch beyond edge; fold under and flute.
6. Prick bottom and sides well with a fork and press in ¼ cup slivered almonds. Bake at 450 degrees until pastry is golden brown about 8-10 minutes.

— Mrs. Charles C. Ford

SHRIMP ROCKEFELLER
CHILLED TOMATO QUARTERS
FRESH BLUEBERRY MUFFINS
FUDGE FANTASY PIE

WINES:
CHAMPAGNE BRUT—American
MOSEL (Very Dry - Young Vintage)—German

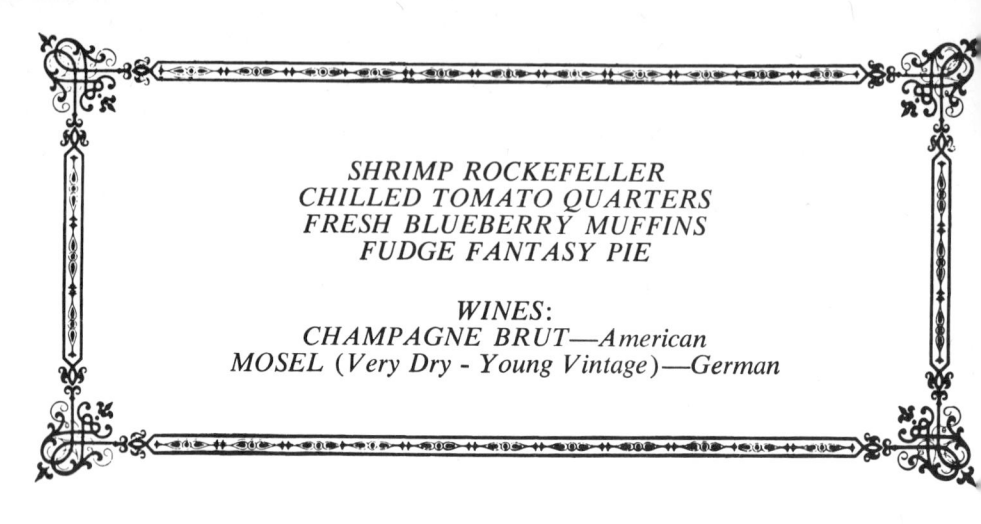

SHRIMP ROCKEFELLER

Yield: 6-8 Servings

This dish may be fixed the day before serving.

1 3-Pound Bag Frozen Shrimp
1 10-Ounce Package Chopped Frozen Spinach
1½ Tablespoons Worcestershire Sauce
2 teaspoons Anchovy Paste
2 teaspoons Salt
3 Drops Hot Pepper Sauce
1 Bunch Green Onions, Chopped
1 Head Lettuce, Chopped
1 Stalk Celery (with Leaves), Chopped
1 Clove Garlic, Pressed
½ Cup Parsley, Minced
¼ Cup Butter
½ Cup Soft Bread Crumbs
3 Tablespoons Butter, Melted
3 Tablespoons Flour
1 teaspoon Salt
1½ Cups Milk, Heated
3 Tablespoons Parmesan Cheese, Grated
¼ teaspoon Pepper, Freshly Ground
Buttered Cracker Crumbs

1. Preheat oven to 350 degrees.
2. Prepare frozen shrimp and spinach according to package directions and drain.
3. Saute Worcestershire Sauce, anchovy paste, 1 teaspoon salt, pepper sauce, green onion, lettuce, celery, garlic, and parsley in butter. Simmer 10 minutes.
4. Add bread crumbs. Spread mixture over bottom of casserole and cover with shrimp.
5. Melt butter, add flour, 1 teaspoon salt, then milk. Blend in Parmesan cheese, and pepper.
6. Pour over shrimp and sprinkle with cracker crumbs.
7. Bake at 350 degrees for 20 minutes.

— Mrs. Harry G. Haisten, Jr.

FRESH BLUEBERRY MUFFINS
Yield: 14 Muffins

2 Cups Flour, Sifted
⅓ Cup Sugar, Granulated
1 Tablespoon Baking Powder
½ teaspoon Salt
1 Cup Milk
⅓ Cup Vegetable Oil or Melted Shortening
1 Egg
1 Cup Fresh Blueberries

1. Preheat oven to 400 degrees. Grease 14 (2½ inch) muffin tins.
2. Sift flour with sugar, baking powder and salt.
3. Measure milk in 2-cup measure. Add vegetable oil and egg. Blend well.
4. Make a well in center of flour mixture. Pour in milk mixture all at once; stir quickly, with fork, just until dry ingredients are moistened. Fold in blueberries.
5. Using ¼ cup measure (not quite full), dip batter into muffin cups. Muffin cups should be slightly more than half full. Lightly sprinkle tops with granulated sugar.
6. Bake at 400 degrees for 20-25 minutes, or until muffins are golden brown.

— Miss Martha Haines

FUDGE FANTASY PIE
Yield: 8 Servings

This is my favorite dessert!

½ Cup Butter, Melted
3 1-Ounce Squares Unsweetened Chocolate
4 Eggs, Well-Beaten
3 Tablespoons Light Corn Syrup
1½ Cups Sugar, Granulated
¼ teaspoon Salt
1 teaspoon Vanilla Extract
1 9-Inch Unbaked Pastry Shell (See page 39)

1. Preheat oven to 350 degrees. Prepare pastry shell.
2. In top of double boiler melt butter and chocolate together.
3. Beat eggs until light. Blend in syrup, sugar, salt and vanilla extract with the well-beaten eggs.
4. Add the chocolate mixture, slightly cooled, to the egg mixture. Blend thoroughly and pour into an unbaked 9-inch pastry shell.
5. Bake at 350 degrees for 25 to 30 minutes until the top is crusty. The filling should remain somewhat soft inside. (Do NOT overbake. The pie should shake like a custard as it thickens when cooled).
6. Serve pie plain or with vanilla ice cream.

— Mr. Don C. Robinson

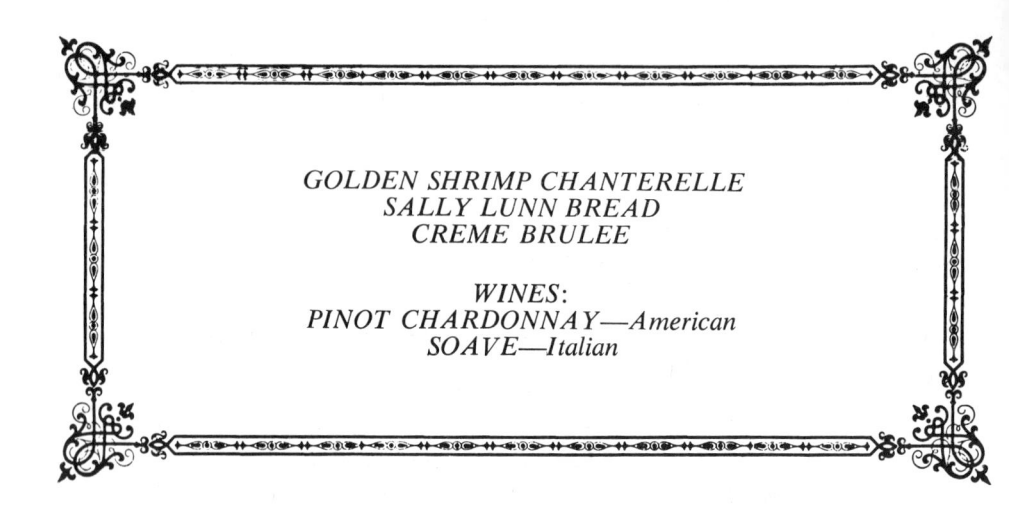

GOLDEN SHRIMP CHANTERELLE
SALLY LUNN BREAD
CREME BRULEE

WINES:
PINOT CHARDONNAY—American
SOAVE—Italian

GOLDEN SHRIMP CHANTERELLE

Yield: 6 Servings

This may be done the day before and baked the day of the party.

2 Cups Shrimp, Cooked
1 3-Ounce Can Sliced Mushrooms
6-8 Slices of Day-Old Bread, Trimmed, Buttered, and Cubed
½ Pound Sharp Cheese, Grated
3 Eggs
½ teaspoon Salt
½ teaspoon Dry Mustard
Dash Pepper
Dash Paprika
1½ Cups Milk

1. Grease 2 quart casserole.
2. Blend the following together in the casserole: shrimp, mushrooms, half of the bread cubes, and half of the cheese.
3. Top with rest of the cheese and bread cubes.
4. Blend eggs and seasonings together. Add milk and pour over all.
5. Cover and refrigerate, if prepared the day before serving.
6. Bake at 325 degrees for 45-50 minutes.

— Mrs. Curtis M. Hutchinson

SWEET AND SOUR ASPIC

Yield: 4-6 Servings

⅓ Cup Sugar, Granulated
½ Cup Water
¼ teaspoon Vinegar (Wine or Tarragon)
⅛ teaspoon Salt
1 Envelope Plain Gelatin
¼ Cup Cold Water
½ Cup Celery, Chopped
½ Cup Pecans, Chopped
1 Small Jar of Pimientos, Diced
½ Cup Asparagus Cut in One Inch Lengths
¼ Cup Lemon Juice
1 teaspoon Onion, Grated

1. In a saucepan blend together sugar, water, vinegar, and salt. Bring to a boil.

2. Soften gelatin in cold water and add to sugar-vinegar mixture.

3. Place celery, pecans, pimientos, asparagus, lemon juice and onion in shallow greased pan. Add heated mixture and chill in refrigerator until set.

4. Serve on bed of lettuce and garnish with mayonnaise and paprika.

— Miss Katharine Cutter

SALLY LUNN BREAD

Yield: 1 Large Loaf or 2 Small Loaves

This is delicious hot or cold.

1 Package Active Dry Yeast
¼ Cup Water
¾ Cup Milk, Heated and Cooled to Lukewarm
½ Cup Butter

LUNCHEONS

⅓ Cup Sugar, Granulated
3 Eggs
4 Cups Flour, Sifted
Pinch Salt

1. Dissolve yeast in water and heated milk.
2. · Cream together butter and sugar.
3. Beat eggs together and add to butter - sugar mixture. Blend well.
4. Sift flour with salt and add. Alternate with milk-yeast mixture. Let rise in warm place (will triple or more in size).
5. Punch dough down and place in one large or two small loaf pans. Let rise again before baking in a 350 degree oven for 30 minutes or until golden brown.

— Mrs. Charles Netherton

CREME BRULEE

Yeld: 4-6 Servings

1 Pint Heavy Cream
3 Tablespoons Sugar, Granulated
4 Egg Yolks, Well-Beaten
1 teaspoon Vanilla Extract
Brown Sugar
½ Cup Heavy Cream, Whipped (Optional)

1. In double boiler, heat cream to just under boiling point. Beat egg yolks until light and blend well with sugar and vanilla extract. Add to cream and stir constantly until thick.
2. • Pour into individual custard cups. Let cool thoroughly, then spread brown sugar over the top and put in broiler just long enough to melt sugar.
3. Cool. Set in refrigerator until ready to serve.
4. Serve as is or top with whipped cream.

— Mrs. Charles J. Sharitz

SHRIMP AND CRABMEAT MEDLEY
RED SPICED APPLE RING
MOULD OF AVOCADO
IMPERIAL OATMEAL BREAD
CHERRY CRUNCH PIE

WINES:
RIESLING—American
PUILLY-FUISSE—French

SHRIMP AND CRABMEAT MEDLEY

Yield: 8 Servings

Delicious and easy!

1 Bell Pepper, Chopped
1 Small Onion, Grated
1 Cup Celery, Chopped
1 Pound Flaked Crabmeat
2 Pounds Shrimp, Cooked
½ teaspoon Salt
Pepper
2 teaspoons Worcestershire Sauce
1 Cup Mayonnaise
1 Cup Bread Crumbs, Buttered

1. Preheat oven to 350 degrees.
2. Combine all ingredients, except bread crumbs and place in individual sea shells or in one large casserole.
3. Sprinkle with buttered bread crumbs and bake in oven at 350 degrees for 30 minutes.

— Mrs. J. R. Douglas, Jr.

LUNCHEONS

MOULD OF AVOCADO

Yield: 8 Servings

A mighty delicious buffet sparkler.

1 6-Ounce Package Lime Gelatin
1 Envelope Plain Gelatin
1 Cup Sour Cream
1 Cup Avocado, Mashed
Lemon Juice
1 Cup Mayonnaise
1 Tablespoon Onion, Grated
3 Cucumbers, Sliced
Sprigs of Parsley

1. Oil mould.

2. Prepare lime gelatin according to package directions. Dissolve plain gelatin in small amount of cold water.

3. Chill until partially set. Blend together rest of ingredients, except cucumbers and parsley.

4. Remove from refrigerator and fold in blended ingredients.

5. Place in oiled salad mould. Chill until set. Serve on bed of leaf lettuce and garnish with sliced cucumbers and parsley.

— Mrs. M. D. Dunlap

IMPERIAL OATMEAL BREAD

Yield: 2 Loaves

A delicious bread that keeps wonderfully well!

¾ Cup Milk, Scalded
1 Package Active Dry Yeast
1 Cup Quick-Cooking Oatmeal
1¾ Cups Boiling Water
1½ teaspoons Salt
½ Cup Dark Molasses

½ Cup Nuts, Chopped Finely
1 Tablespoon Butter
5 Cups Flour, Sifted

1. Preheat oven to 350 degrees. Grease 2 loaf pans.
2. Scald milk and cool to lukewarm. Stir in yeast.
3. Place oatmeal in large bowl. Stir in boiling water, salt, molasses, nuts, and butter.
4. Cool to lukewarm, then add flour and lukewarm yeast-milk mixture. Blend thoroughly. (Use your hands as the dough will be quite heavy.)
5. Cover bowl with a clean damp towel and set in a warm spot away from drafts until dough doubles in size (about 1½-2 hours).
6. Turn out on floured board and knead lightly for 3 minutes.
7. Divide in half, shape into two loaves, and place in greased loaf pans.
8. Let bread rise a second time until double in size.
9. Bake at 350 degrees for about 1 hour.
10. Remove from oven and brush crust with melted butter.
11. Cool slightly and remove from pans. Finish cooling process on wire rack.

— Mrs. Adolphus B. Orthwein, Jr.

CHERRY CRUNCH PIE

Yield: 8 Servings

Juice of 2 Lemons
1 Cup Sweetened Condensed Milk
½ Pint Heavy Cream
1 Can Pitted Sour Cherries, Drained
1 Cup Pecans, Chopped
¼ Cup Butter
Graham Cracker Pie Shell

1. Combine lemon juice with condensed milk; fold in whipped cream.
2. Combine cherries, nuts and butter. Add to other mixture and place in pie crust.
3. Chill for several hours.

— Mrs. Bernard P. Lyons, Sr.

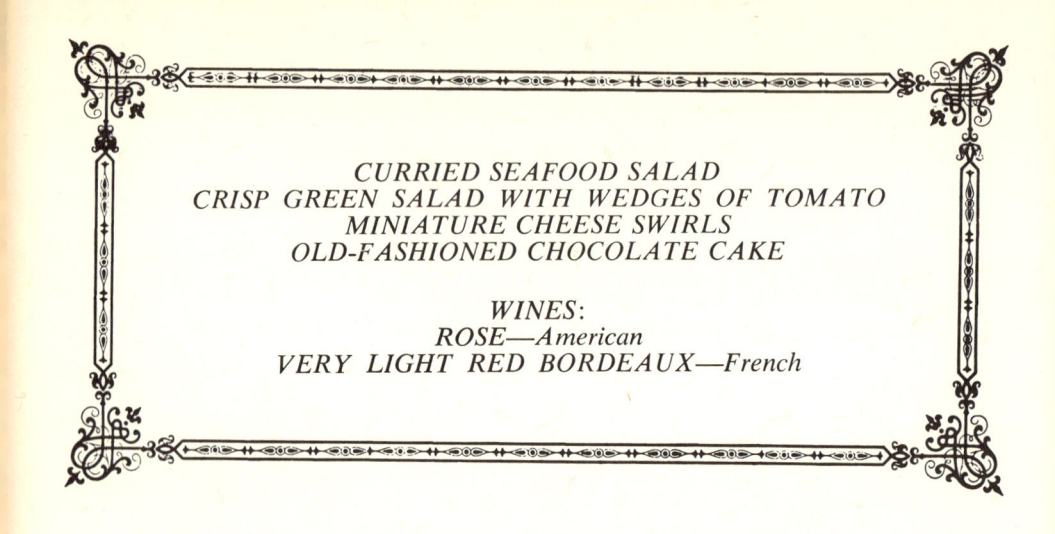

CURRIED SEAFOOD SALAD
CRISP GREEN SALAD WITH WEDGES OF TOMATO
MINIATURE CHEESE SWIRLS
OLD-FASHIONED CHOCOLATE CAKE

WINES:
ROSE—*American*
VERY LIGHT RED BORDEAUX—*French*

CURRIED SEAFOOD SALAD

Yield: 6-8 Servings

1 Pound Shrimp, Uncooked
4 Medium Potatoes
½ Pound Sea Scallops, Quartered
1 6 or 7-Ounce Can Tuna, Drained
1 6-Ounce Package Frozen Alaskan King Crabmeat, Thawed, Drained
½ Cup Mayonnaise
2 Tablespoons Lemon Juice
2 Tablespoons Curry Powder
¼ Cup Scallions, Snipped
2 Hard-Cooked Eggs

1. Shell shrimp, boil and chill.
2. Scrub potatoes, simmer covered about 30 minutes. Peel and cut into 1 inch pieces. Chill.
3. Simmer quartered scallops 5 minutes, drain, and chill.
4. Toss meat and potatoes together.
5. Combine mayonnaise, lemon juice, curry powder, and scallions.
6. Add to meat and potatoes.
7. Garnish with slices of hard-cooked eggs.

— Mrs. Elizabeth B. Morgan

MINIATURE CHEESE SWIRLS

Yield: 20 Miniature Biscuits

2 Cups Flour, Sifted
4 teaspoons Baking Powder
½ teaspoon Salt
½ teaspoon Cream of Tartar
2 teaspoons Sugar, Granulated
½ Cup Shortening
⅔ Cup Milk
½ Cup American Cheese, Grated

1. Preheat oven to 425 degrees. Grease cooky sheet.
2. Sift together dry ingredients. Cut in shortening until it resembles coarse crumbs.
3. Add milk all at once and stir until dough follows fork around bowl.
4. Turn out on lightly floured surface and knead gently for 30 seconds.
5. Pat or roll dough to ¼ inch thickness. Sprinkle with grated cheese and roll up as for jelly roll. Seal edge.
6. Cut ½ inch slices and bake cut side down on greased cooky sheet at 425 degrees for 15 minutes.

— Mrs. William Heisel

OLD-FASHIONED DARK CHOCOLATE CAKE

Yield: 12 Servings

2¼ Cups Cake Flour, Sifted
1 Tablespoon Double-Acting Baking Powder
½ teaspoon Salt
½ Cup Butter
2 Cups Sugar, Granulated
2 Eggs
4 1-Ounce Squares Unsweetened Chocolate, Melted
1½ Cups Milk
2 teaspoons Vanilla Extract
1 Cup Walnuts, Chopped

1. Preheat oven to 375 degrees. Line bottom of a 10 inch tube pan with waxed paper.
2. Sift together flour, baking powder, and salt.
3. Cream together butter and sugar.
4. Add eggs, one at a time, beating thoroughly after each addition.
5. Blend in melted chocolate. Add flour mixture and milk alternately and blend well.
6. Blend in vanilla extract and nuts.
7. Pour batter into tube pan and bake at 375 degrees for 55 to 60 minutes.
8. Cool in pan 15 minutes, then turn out on wire rack to cool completely.
9. Ice with chocolate icing or 7 minute white icing.

— Mrs. T. H. Yon

COQUILLE OF CRABMEAT MORNAY
BUTTERED SPEARS OF BROCCOLI
Topped with a Twist of Lemon
GRAPEFRUIT JUBILEE
CINNAMON CRESCENT ROLLS
FRENCH SILK PIE

WINES:
EMERALD GREEN—American
CHABLIS—French

COQUILLE OF CRABMEAT MORNAY

Yield: 8 Servings

2 6½-Ounce Cans Flaked Crabmeat
3 Cups Mornay Sauce (See Page 74)
1 Cup Hollandaise Sauce (See Page 27)
Grated Parmesan Cheese

1. Preheat broiler unit of range.

2. Remove any shells from crabmeat.

3. Prepare Mornay Sauce and gently combine with crabmeat.

4. Sterilize serving sea shells. Pile crabmeat mixture into shells and top with Tablespoon of Hollandaise Sauce.

5. Run crab-filled serving shells under broiler to lghtly brown. Sprinkle with Parmesan cheese and serve.

— Mrs. McNeill Stokes

GRAPEFRUIT JUBILEE

Yield: 8 Servings

This is a delightful ladies' luncheon favorite dish!

1 3-Ounce Package Cherry Gelatin
1 3-Ounce Package Lemon Gelatin
2 Grapefruit
3 Cups of Liquid (from juices - add water if necessary)
1 Can Crushed Pineapple

1. Cut grapefruit in halves (you can scallop edges in "V" shape cuts for added decoration as you separate the halves.) Remove fruit pulp and juice.
2. Mix gelatin as per package directions. Add fruit and partially chill in the refrigerator.
3. Pour partially chilled gelatin and fruit mixture into grapefruit shells.
4. Refrigerate until completely set and cut in half again before serving.

— Mrs. Willis A. Haines

CINNAMON CRESCENT ROLLS

Yield: 8 Servings

2 Packages Crescent Rolls
6 Tablespoons Butter, Melted
Cinnamon Sugar

1. Preheat oven to 375 degrees.
2. Place triangles of dough on ungreased cooky sheet.
3. Make paste of cinnamon sugar and butter.
4. Brush dough with cinnamon sugar paste. Roll up dough and brush again.
5. Bake at 375 degrees for 10-12 minutes. Serve piping hot.

— Mrs. Charles C. Ford

FRENCH SILK PIE

Yield: 8 Servings

What a marvelous quick, easy and delicious treat this is!

3 Egg Whites
⅛ teaspoon Salt
¼ teaspoon Cream of Tartar
¾ Cup Sugar, Granulated
½ Cup Pecans or Walnuts, Chopped Finely
½ teaspoon Vanilla Extract
1 4-Ounce Package Sweet Cooking Chocolate
3 Tablespoons Water
1 Tablespoon Brandy
2 Cups Heavy Cream

1. Preheat oven to 300 degrees. Lightly grease 8-inch pie pan.
2. In mixing bowl blend together egg whites until foamy. Add salt and cream of tartar.
3. Add sugar gradually and continue beating until very stiff peaks form.
4. Fold in nuts and vanilla extract.
5. Pile into lightly greased pie pan forming a nest by building up a half inch rim around the edge of the pie pan. Do not extend over the rim.
6. Bake at 300 degrees for 50 minutes. Cool.
7. In a double boiler place chocolate and water. Stir until melted. Cool.
8. Add brandy to chocolate mixture.
9. Whip 1 cup of heavy cream. Fold into chocolate mixture.
10. Pile into meringue shell and chill 2-3 hours before serving.
11. Whip rest of heavy cream, piling high on top of pie. Garnish with bits of shaved chocolate and serve!

— Mrs. McNeill Stokes

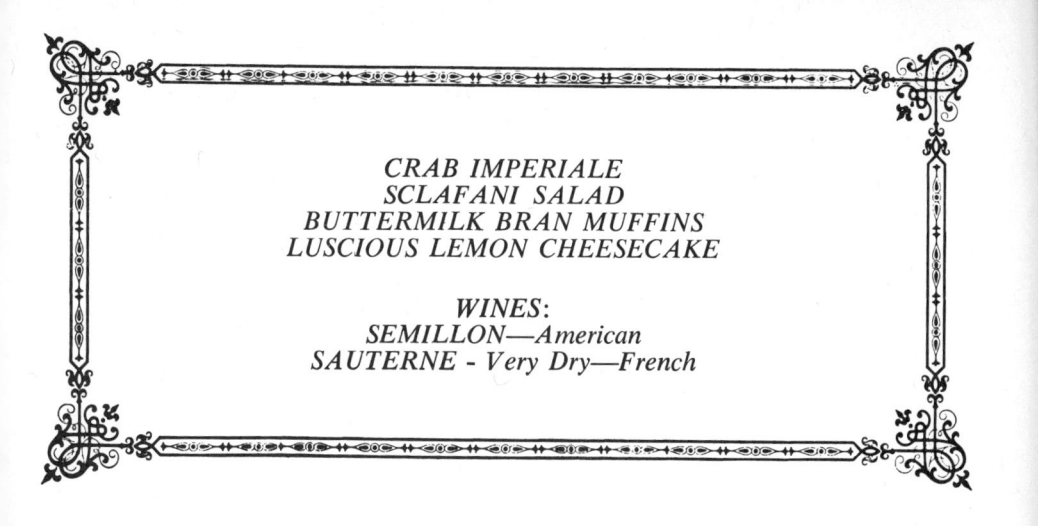

CRAB IMPERIALE
SCLAFANI SALAD
BUTTERMILK BRAN MUFFINS
LUSCIOUS LEMON CHEESECAKE

WINES:
SEMILLON—*American*
SAUTERNE - Very Dry—*French*

CRAB IMPERIALE

Yield: 4-6 Servings

3-4 Tablespoons Butter, Melted
¼ teaspoon Salt
¼ teaspoon Cayenne Pepper
¼ teaspoon Celery Seed
1 Pound Flaked Crabmeat
1 Tablespoon Prepared Mustard
1 teaspoon Dry Mustard
3½ Tablespoons Mayonnaise
Snipped Parsley
3½ Tablespoons Bell Pepper, Chopped
½ teaspoon Lemon Juice

1. Preheat oven to 350 degrees.
2. Blend together melted butter, salt, Cayenne pepper and celery seed.
3. Add crabmeat, mustards, mayonnaise, parsley, Bell pepper and lemon juice.
4. Place in sterilized sea shells. Top with melted butter and sprinkle with paprika.
5. Bake 20 to 30 minutes at 350 degrees or until top is golden brown.
6. If mixture seems a bit dry, add a small amount of cream before placing in shells.

— Miss Diane Love

LUNCHEONS

SCLAFANI SALAD

Yield: 6 Servings

2 Large Wooden Bowls
1 Clove Garlic
1 Hard-Cooked Egg, Sliced
3 Anchovy Fillets
4 Heads Different Varieties of Lettuce, Coarsely Chopped
1 Bunch Watercress
1 Bunch Parsley
1 Cup Celery, Chopped
1 Cup Radishes, Sliced
1 Medium Onion, Sliced
½ Cup Chives, Diced
1 Cup Bell Pepper, Chopped
4 Medium Tomatoes, Cubed
1 Pound Shrimp, Cooked

1. Rub garlic clove in wooden bowl. Add anchovy fillets and egg.
2. Add small amount of dressing.
3. Place some of chopped greens into above bowl and toss with more dressing.
4. Add remaining ingredients and serve.

Salad Dressing:

Yield: 1½ Quarts

1 Quart Salad Oil
6 Eggs
1 6-Ounce Lea and Perrin's Sauce
1 14-Ounce Bottle Catsup
1 8-Ounce Jar Hot Prepared Mustard
1 teaspoon Tabasco Sauce
6 Anchovy Fillets
4 Cloves Garlic, Minced
2 Tablespoons Salt
1. Tablespoon Pepper
1 Cup Wine Vinegar

1. Place salad oil in deep pot; add eggs and whip until thick.
2. Add remainder of ingredients and whip for 5 minutes.
3. Store dressing in refrigerator. Do NOT freeze.

— Mrs. Richard H. Pretz

BUTTERMILK BRAN MUFFINS

Yield: 1 dozen

1 Cup Flour, Sifted
2 teaspoons Baking Powder
¾ teaspoon Salt
½ teaspoon Soda
1 Cup Milk
3 Cups Whole-Bran Cereal
½ Cup Seedless Raisins
⅓ Cup Shortening
½ Cup Sugar, Granulated
1 Egg

1. Preheat oven to 400 degrees. Grease muffin pan.
2. Sift together flour, baking powder, salt, and baking soda. Add whole-bran cereal and raisins; mix.
3. Cream together shortening and sugar until light and fluffy. And egg and blend.
4. Add flour mixture alternately with buttermilk, stirring with fork until dry ingredients are moistened. Do not beat. (Batter will be lumpy.) Quickly fill muffin pan ⅔ full and bake at 400 degrees for 20-25 minutes.

— Miss Martha Haines

LUSCIOUS LEMON CHEESECAKE

Yield: 8 Servings

1 8-Ounce Package Cream Cheese, Softened
2 Cups Milk
1 Package Jell-o Lemon Instant Pudding
1 8-Inch Graham Cracker Crust

1. Blend cream cheese until soft. Add ½ cup of the milk and blend well.
2. Add rest of milk and pudding mix.
3. Beat slowly, about 1 minute.
4. Pour into crust, top with graham cracker crumbs and chill 1 hour.

— Mrs. T. J. Gavin

*HOT CRAB SALAD
CURRIED FRUIT CASCADE
BUTTERED PARKERHOUSE ROLLS
CHOCOLATE MERINGUE PIE*

*WINES:
CHAMPAGNE - EXTRA DRY—American
CHAMPAGNE - EXTRA DRY—French*

HOT CRAB SALAD

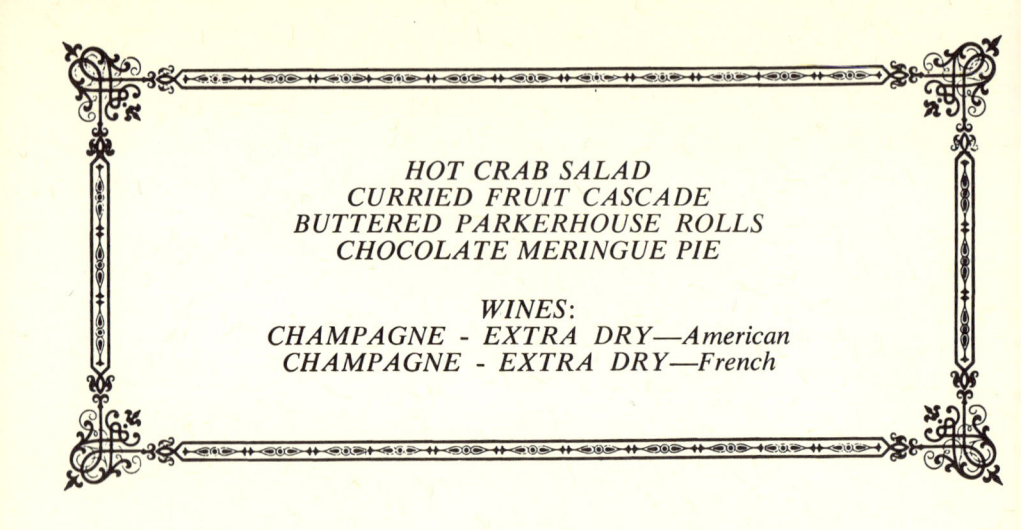

Yield: 8 Servings

This salad is a real guest pleaser.

1 Pound Flaked Crabmeat
1 Bell Pepper, Minced
1 Small Onion, Minced
1 Cup Mayonnaise
½ teaspoon Salt
⅛ teaspoon Pepper
1 teaspoon Worcestershire Sauce
1 Cup Bread Crumbs
¼ Cup Buttered Bread Crumbs

1. Preheat oven to 375 degrees. Grease casserole(s).

2. Combine everything in greased casserole(s) except the buttered bread crumbs.

3. Bake at 375 degrees 10 to 15 minutes for small shells. Top with buttered bread crumbs. Bake for 25 minutes for individual casseroles and 35 to 40 minutes for large casserole.

— Mrs. William Heisel

LUNCHEONS

CURRIED FRUIT CASCADE

Yield: 8-10 Servings

2 Cups Dried Apricots, Cut in Eighths
1½ Cups Water
1 Cup Sugar, Granulated
½ teaspoon Salt
1 Tablespoon Lemon Juice
1 Tablespoon Butter
Maraschino Cherries
½ teaspoon Curry Powder
1 No. 303 Can Sliced Peaches, Diced

1. Blend together all ingredients except curry powder and diced peaches. Simmer 15 minutes.
2. Add diced peaches, stir in curry powder, and chill overnight.

— Mrs. J. Lee Edwards

CHOCOLATE MERINGUE PIE

Yield: 8 Servings

3 Egg Yolks
1 Cup Sugar, Granulated
1 1-Ounce Square Baker's Semi-Sweet Chocolate
1 Tablespoon Butter
2 Tablespoons Flour
1 Cup Milk, Lukewarm
1 teaspoon Vanilla Extract
1 Baked Pastry Shell (See Page 39)
3 Egg Whites, Stiffly Beaten
3 Tablespoons Sugar, Granulated

1. Preheat oven to 350 degrees. Prepare baked pastry shell.
2. Beat egg yolks and sugar together until creamy.
3. In top of double boiler, melt chocolate and butter. Add chocolate mixture and flour to egg yolk mixture.
4. Add milk and blend well. Add vanilla extract and blend. Cook mixture in top of double boiler until quite thick, stirring often.
5. While chocolate mixture is cooking, prepare meringue: Beat egg whites until frothy. Add 3 Tablespoons sugar slowly and continue beating until stiff peaks are formed.
6. Pour chocolate mixture into baked pastry shell.
7. Spoon meringue over chocolate, spreading well to all edges of pie shell.
8. Bake at 350 degrees for 10 to 15 minutes.

— Mrs. J. David Bansley

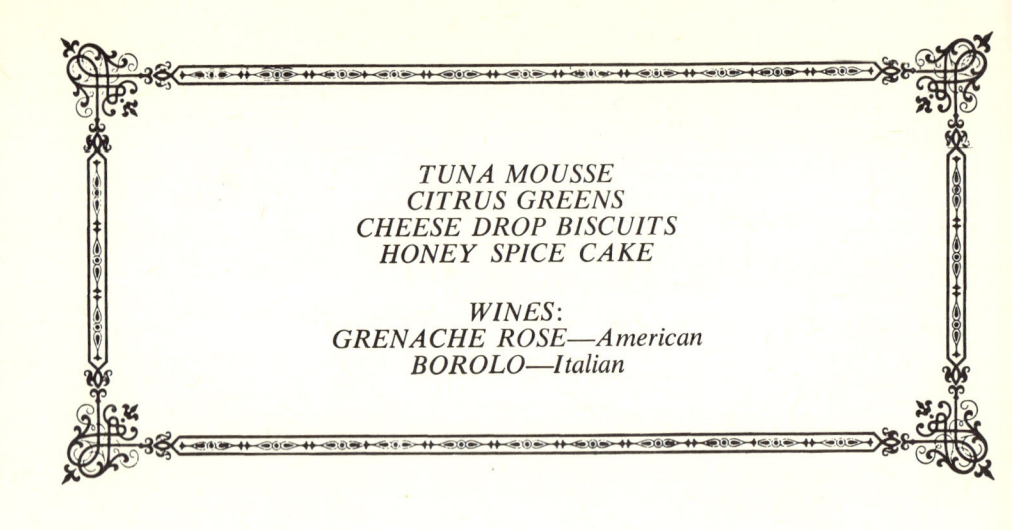

TUNA MOUSSE
CITRUS GREENS
CHEESE DROP BISCUITS
HONEY SPICE CAKE

WINES:
GRENACHE ROSE—*American*
BOROLO—*Italian*

TUNA MOUSSE

Yield: 4 Servings

1 Envelope Plain Gelatin
¼ Cup Cold Water
2 6½-Ounce Cans Tuna (Albacore)
2 Tablespoons Lemon Juice
½ Cup Mayonnaise
3 Tablespoons Green Onion Tips, Chopped
1 Cup Sour Cream
1 Tablespoon Horseradish

1. Soften plain gelatin in cold water. Blend together all ingredients.

2. Turn into attractive fish mould. Chill until set.

3. Garnish with strips of pimiento and watercress.

— Mrs. Don Bomgardner

CITRUS GREENS

Yield: 4 Servings

¼ Head Escarole
¼ Head Romaine
¼ Head Bibb Lettuce
¼ Head Leaf Lettuce
2 Number 303 Cans Grapefruit Sections
Olive Oil
Freshly Ground Black Pepper

1. Wash and drain all lettuce. Break into bite-size pieces.
2. Toss citrus sections with salad greens, olive oil, and freshly ground black pepper.
3. No vinegar is necessary as the citrus sections provide plenty of zip.

— Miss Blanche Thebom

CHEESE DROP BISCUITS

(See Page 51)

HONEY SPICE CAKE

Yield: 12 Servings

½ Cup Butter
½ Cup Pecans or Walnuts, Chopped
1 Cup Brown Sugar
2½ No. 303 Cans Sliced Cling Peaches, Drained
1 Package Betty Crocker Honey Spice Cake

1. Preheat oven to 350 degrees.
2. Blend together butter, nuts and brown sugar. Spread ⅔ of sugar-nut mixture into 9 inch cake pan.
3. Arrange half of peach slices over sugar-nut mixture.
4. Prepare cake batter according to package directions. Pour half of cake batter over peaches and half in 8 inch cake pan.
5. Bake at 350 degrees for 35 minutes.
6. Turn 9 inch cake into dish with peach side up. Top with 8 inch cake and place remainder of peaches on top.
7. Sprinkle with rest of sugar mixture. Run under broiler until sugar melts.

— Mrs. G. T. Chappelle

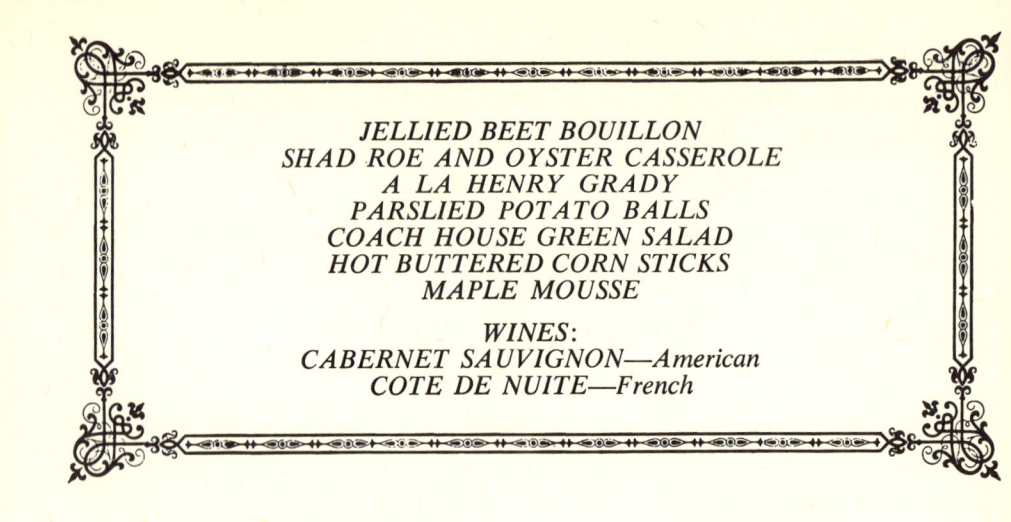

JELLIED BEET BOUILLON
SHAD ROE AND OYSTER CASSEROLE
A LA HENRY GRADY
PARSLIED POTATO BALLS
COACH HOUSE GREEN SALAD
HOT BUTTERED CORN STICKS
MAPLE MOUSSE

WINES:
CABERNET SAUVIGNON—American
COTE DE NUITE—French

JELLIED BEET BOUILLON

Yield: 8 Servings

4 Whole Fresh Beets, Diced

1 Quart Beef Bouillon

1½ Envelopes Plain Gelatin

⅓ Cup Sherry

1 Tablespoon Lemon Juice

Pinch Salt

8 teaspoons Sour Cream

1. Cook beets in enough water to yield 1 cup beet juice and add beet juice to beef bouillon. Simmer.

2. Dissolve gelatin in sherry and add to bouillon mixture.

3. Add lemon juice and salt. Pour into bouillon cups and chill until firm.

4. Top with 1 teaspoon sour cream.

— Mrs. Julia Black Wellborn

SHAD ROE AND OYSTER CASSEROLE A LA HENRY GRADY

Yield: 8 Servings

2 Pints Oysters
2 Shad Roe (Fresh or Canned)
2 Pounds Fresh Mushrooms
2 Pints Thick Cream Sauce
    (Made with Heavy Cream)
Bread Crumbs

1. Preheat oven to 325 degrees.
2. Heat oysters, drain off juice (using some juice in cream sauce) Blend all ingredients except bread crumbs together well, but gently. Place in large casserole.
3. Cover with bread crumbs, dot with butter and bake for 30 minutes at 325 degrees.

— Mrs. Julia Black Wellborn

COACH HOUSE GREEN SALAD

Yield: 8 Servings

2 Pounds Fresh Spinach
2 Heads Chicory
1 Bunch Watercress
Salt
1 Clove Garlic
2 Tablespoons Lemon Juice
6 Tablespoons Olive Oil
Black Pepper, Freshly Ground
2 Hard-Cooked Eggs, Cut into Wedges
½ Red Onion, Sliced Thinly
6 Slices Crisp Bacon, Crumbled

1. Wash spinach well in several changes of clear water. Using scissors, cut away tough stems and discard.
2. Prepare chicory and watercress and tear greens into bite-size pieces.
3. Sprinkle bottom of salad bowl with salt and rub with garlic.
4. Add lemon juice and olive oil. Chill bowl.
5. When ready to serve, add greens, sprinkle wtih pepper, garnish with egg wedges, onion slices and bacon. Toss lightly.

— Mrs. Julia Black Wellborn

LUNCHEONS

CORN STICKS

Yield: 8 Servings

¾ Cup Flour, Sifted
Pinch Salt
1 Tablespoon Baking Powder
2 Tablespoons Sugar, Granulated
¾ Cup Cornmeal
1 Egg, Well-Beaten
2-3 Tablespoons Butter, Melted
¾ Cup Milk

1. Preheat oven to 425 degrees. Grease corn stick pans.
2. Sift together flour and salt, baking powder and sugar. Add cornmeal and mix.
3. Blend together egg, butter and milk. Add to dry ingredients, stirring briskly.
4. Heat corn stick pans and fill with batter.
5. Bake for 25 minutes at 425 degrees.

— Mrs. Julia Black Wellborn

MAPLE MOUSSE

Yield: 8 Servings

2 Cups Maple Syrup, Heated
8 Egg Yolks, Well-Beaten
1 Quart Heavy Cream
¼ Cup Maple Syrup
2 Tablespoons Sugar, Granulated
Pinch Salt

1. Heat 2 cups maple syrup in double boiler. When hot, add well-beaten egg yolks, stirring slowly for about 1 minute.
2. Cool thoroughly. Whip heavy cream with the ¼ cup of maple syrup, sugar and salt. Add to egg yolk mixture.
3. Pour into melon mould and freeze.
   To serve, unmold onto platter and decorate with maple candy leaves and whipped cream.

— Mrs. Julia Black Wellborn

CHILLED VICHYSOISSE
QUICHE LORRAINE
MOULD OF BROCCOLI AND EGG SUPREME
CHERRY SURPRISE

WINES:
GEWURTZTRAMINER—American
SWISS WINE (WHITE and LIGHT)—Switzerland

CHILLED VICHYSOISSE

Yield: 8 Servings

2 10½-Ounce Cans Frozen Cream of Potato Soup
2 13¾-Ounce Cans Chicken Broth
2 12-Ounce Cartons Sour Cream
2 teaspoons Onion, Minced
Chopped Chives

1. Blend together all ingredients except chives.
2. Pour into soup cups and chill for several hours.
3. Sprinkle with abundance of chopped chives just before serving.

— Mrs. Adolphus B. Orthwein, Jr.

QUICHE LORRAINE

Yield: 8 Servings

1 9-Inch Unbaked Pastry Shell, Chilled
   (See Page 39)
1 Tablespoon Butter, Softened
10 Slices Crisp Bacon, Crumbled
1 Cup Imported Swiss Cheese, Grated
1 Tablespoon Flour
Salt

LUNCHEONS

Pepper
Pinch Nutmeg
6 Eggs Plus 2 Extra Egg Yolks
1 Cup Milk
1 Cup Heavy Cream
¼ Cup Parmesan Cheese, Grated
2 Tablespoons Butter, Melted and Lightly Browned

1. Preheat oven to 450 degrees.
2. Spread softened butter on bottom of unbaked pastry shell.
3. Sprinkle crumbled bacon and grated Swiss cheese over butter. Sift dry ingredients together.
4. Add eggs, egg yolks, milk and heavy cream to dry ingredients and stir until mixed, but not frothy.
5. Pour egg mixture over cheese and bacon in pastry shell and bake at 450 degrees for 10 minutes.
6. Reduce heat to 325 degrees and bake 20-25 minutes longer. Remove from oven and sprinkle with Parmesan cheese and dot with lightly browned butter.
7. Return to oven and bake at 325 degrees for 10 minutes. Cut into wedges and serve hot.

— Mrs. Adolphus B. Orthwein, Jr.

MOULD OF BROCCOLI AND EGG SUPREME

Yield: 8 Servings

This may double for a colorful cold vegetable or a congealed salad.

2 10-Ounce Packages Chopped Frozen Broccoli
2 Hard-Cooked Eggs, Chopped
1 Can Beef Bouillon
1 Tablespoon Lemon Juice
2 Envelopes Plain Gelatin
¼ teaspoon Salt
1 Tablespoon Worcestershire Sauce
Dash Tabasco Sauce
Dash Pepper
½ Cup Mayonnaise

1. Cook broccoli 3 to 5 minutes. Drain.
2. Soften gelatin in ¼ cup cold bouillon.
3. Simmer remaining bouillon and add lemon juice, gelatin and seasonings.
4. Cool and add other ingredients. Grease mould(s) with mayonnaise and chill.
5. Serve on bed of lettuce and garnish with strip of pimiento.

— Mrs. L. W. Taylor

CHERRY SURPRISES

Yield: 4 Dozen Tiny Muffins

2 Cups Pecans, Chopped
½ Cup Brown Sugar
¼ Cup Sugar, Granulated
½ Cup Butter
2 Egg Yolks, Well-Beaten
1 teaspoon Vanilla Extract
1 Cup Cake Flour, Sifted
¼ teaspoon Baking Powder
2 Egg Whites, Stiffly Beaten
48 Maraschino Cherries

1. Preheat oven to 350 degrees.
2. Grease tiny muffin tins and sprinkle chopped pecans in bottom of tins.
3. Cream together brown sugar, granulated sugar and butter.
4. Add egg yolks and vanilla extract and blend.
5. Sift flour and baking powder together and add, blending well.
6. Fold in stiffly beaten egg whites.
7. Place 1 teaspoon batter on top of nuts and press a whole Maraschino cherry into center.
8. Bake at 350 degrees for 10 minutes and, while still warm, roll in Confectioner's sugar.

— Mrs. Robert B. Ansley, Jr.

SPINACH CASSEROLE SUPREME
Served on Toasted English Muffins

WHITE FRUIT SALAD

WHIPPED CREAM CAKE

SPINACH CASSEROLE SUPREME

Yield: 8 Servings

Bottom Layer:

    2 10-Ounce Packages Chopped Frozen Spinach
    1 Tablespoon Butter, Browned
    1 Tablespoon Flour
    ½ Cup Spinach Water
    Salt and Pepper

1. Prepare spinach according to package directions.
2. Make cream sauce from remaining ingredients listed and blend with cooled spinach.

Second Layer:

    3 Large Bermuda Onions, Chopped
    ½ Cup Butter

1. Saute onions in butter.

Third Layer:

    2 3-Ounce Cans Sliced Mushrooms
    ¼ Cup Butter

1. Saute mushrooms in butter. Add a few pieces of chopped onion for flavor.

LUNCHEONS

Fourth Layer:

    4 Firm Medium Tomatoes
    Flour or Egg-Bread Crumb Mixture

1. Slice tomatoes thick. Dip in flour or egg-bread crumb mixture.
2. Fry slightly using same skillet throughout to maintain the blending of flavors.

Top with bacon strips or poached eggs and serve on a toasted English Muffin. Run under broiler to heat before serving.

WHITE FRUIT SALAD

Yield: 8-10 Servings

1 No. 2 Can Crushed Pineapple, Drained
1 Envelope Plain Gelatin
½ Jar White Cherries
½ Cup Almonds, Chopped
2 Tablespoons Confectioner's Sugar
6 Tablespoons Mayonnaise
4 Large Marshmallows
¾ Cup Heavy Cream, Whipped
Few Maraschino Cherries

1. Oil mould with salad oil. Reserve juice from fruit and add water to make 2¼ cups.
2. Soak gelatin in ¼ cup of fruit juice. Heat 1 cup of fruit juice.
3. Whip heavy cream while gelatin is soaking.
4. Dissolve softened gelatin in remaining 1 cup hot fruit juice. Cool.
5. Add fruit, nuts, mayonnaise and whipped cream.
6. Place in oiled mould and chill until set.
7. Serve on bed of curly leaf lettuce.

— Mrs. M. Alexander Patton

LUNCHEONS

WHIPPED CREAM CAKE

Yield: 12 Servings

This yummy good recipe makes four layers (9 inch pans), and I use more whipped cream and more almonds to make it even more yummy.

3 Cups Flour, Sifted
¼ teaspoon Salt
2 Cups Sugar, Granulated
¾ Cup Butter
6 Egg Yolks
6 Egg Whites, Stiffly Beaten
¾ Cup Lukewarm Water
1 Tablespoon Baking Powder
1 teaspoon Vanilla Extract

1. Preheat oven to 350 degrees.
2. Sift flour and salt together twice.
3. Sift sugar twice to eliminate lumps.
4. Cream together butter and 1 cup of sugar.
5. Mix remaining cup of sugar with egg yolks and add to creamed mixture.
6. Add flour, one cup at a time, following each cup with ⅓ of water.
7. Add baking powder to last cup of flour and mix well.
8. Fold in stiffly beaten egg whites.
9. Add vanilla extract.
10. Bake 15 to 20 minutes at 350 degrees.

Whipped Cream Cake Filling

1 Pint Heavy Cream, Whipped
¼ Cup Sugar, Granulated
½ Pound Almonds, Blanched and Ground

1. Mix together and spread on top and sides of cake.
2. KEEP FINISHED CAKE IN REFRIGERATOR!

— Mrs. A. Thomas Bradbury

HOSTESS' NOTES

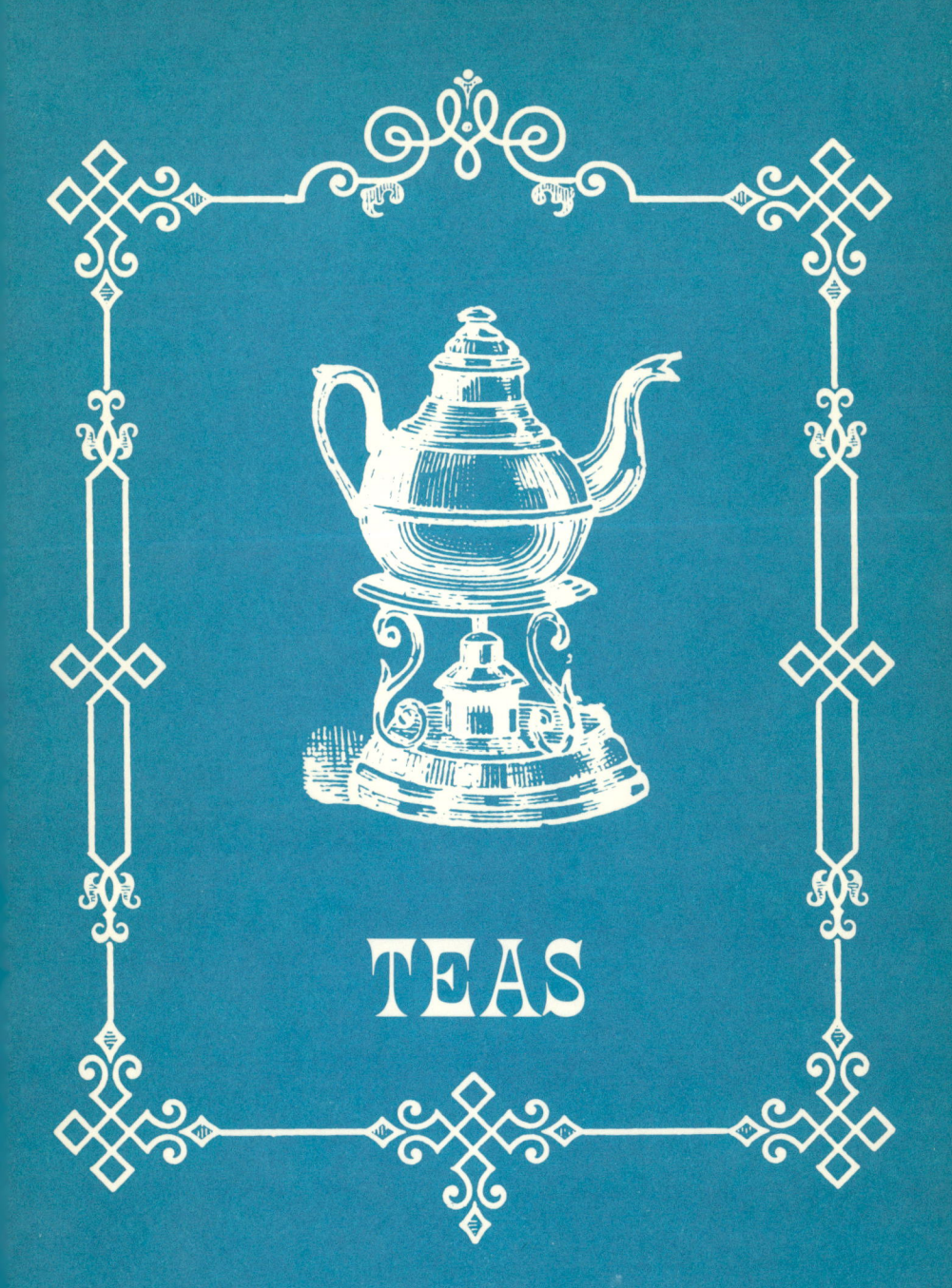

TEAS

TEAS

The highlight of any morning or afternoon can be the pleasant tradition of morning coffees or afternoon teas. Atlanta hostesses are still rightly proud of this heritage and delight in parties such as these.

If you're a "top of the morning" person, a coffee might be convenient for you; but, if the idea of rushing to get things tidy by ten bothers you, then consider a tea. Whatever the hour, you'll find a coffee or tea a fitting way to entertain friends of varied interests and ages.

MORNING COFFEES

Usually, six to twenty-five friends form a congenial group for coffee at ten o'clock. Because of the flexibility of a morning coffee, the budget-minded will find this an inexpensive way to entertain. However, a coffee party can be as elegant as the hostess wishes. (See page 123 for service).

INVITATIONS

One Atlanta hostess sent a daisy-printed invitation reading, "Daisies won't tell," announcing wedding plans and a coffee party honoring a bride-to-be. A matching centerpiece of white daisies and blue bachelor buttons in a gigantic coffee pot brightened the serving table.

CENTERPIECES

For the easiest-to-fix centerpieces ever, try a bowl of fresh fruit, a basket of Georgia peaches, or three cartons of strawberries in their original containers. Luxurious floral displays are grand, but during winter scarcity, or when your garden is going through a temporary lull, you'll be amazed at the effectiveness of a china rooster, a few fresh eggs, and dried pine needles for a casual setting.

Decorate a styrofoam ball with flowers, fall leaves, Christmas holly, or other seasonal foliage; hang it from the ceiling or light fixture in the entrance or some other archway in the room to add a festive touch, especially when honoring a guest. Those little favors you find in party shops could be tucked into the arrangement to carry out a particular theme.

Gardenias or magnolias afloat in a shallow dish with three or more small sprays scattered judiciously down the center of the table provide a lovely reminder of Atlanta coffees and teas of long ago.

AFTERNOON TEAS

As a social event, afternoon tea follows the highest traditions of Southern hospitality. Characterized by charm and graciousness, the tea party can be given on a shoestring. The little extras that make a tea enjoyable do not have to be extravagant.

In the household account book of one of Atlanta's Victorian hostesses, the tea guests list always numbered between one hundred and three hundred

TEAS

persons. Moreover, she gave three or four teas a year. You may not wish to be quite so ambitious, but your accommodations for a tea would determine the number of guests you invite. Written invitations are usually a necessity for large teas, while telephoning is desirable for small occasions.

CENTERPIECES

A captivating air is achieved with a silver bowl of flowers, fresh buds and leaves in a porcelain compote, or colorful fruits on a crystal epergne. For a small tea, a rosebud in a tiny vase adds daintiness to the tea tray or coffee table. Silver candlesticks or candelabra will give your room a soft glow, especially in the fall and winter if your draperies are drawn.

PARTY IDEA

Nestle fresh flowers in a spring basket to set the pace for tea on May Day. Give each guest a wee basket lined with a paper lace doily and a flower tied to the handle with pastel ribbon. Each person can hang the basket on her arm to be filled with delectables from the tea table.

SERVICE AND SETTING

Spread the dining table with your prettiest organdy, lace or embroidered cloth as a worthy background for your fine china and silver. At one end of the table, place the tea tray. Toward the front of the tray, arrange a pot of steaming tea, a pitcher of boiling water, a bowl of lump sugar, the creamer, and a plate of lemon slices. Have all handles pointing toward the pourer. Around the back and side of the tray, arrange cups on saucers with the spoons at the right of the cups. The extra cups and saucers may be placed on a side table. Set up one cup, saucer and spoon ready for the first guest.

At the other end of the table, place a similar tray for coffee or punch. You may want to have a pot of tea and a pot of coffee on one end and a cold punch on the other. In the summer, particularly, it will be most refreshing if you substitute punch for the coffee or tea. Your punch will not be diluted from melting ice if you mix a small portion of punch beforehand and freeze it in ice rings. Use the individual ice ring for keeping the punch cold while serving. As the ring melts, it will add to the supply of punch while maintaining the original flavor.

Consider these elegant touches to give a lift to your tea party. Drift a fresh flower in a slice of lemon, lime or orange in your punch bowl. Pull the stem of the flower through a hole in the center of the slice, poking through just enough to stabilize the flower to keep it from tilting.

Arrange frosted grapes to drape over the edge of a punch bowl. To frost grapes, dip small clusters into egg whites and then into granulated sugar. The egg whites will absorb the coating of sugar, giving it that snowy effect. Completely cover the grapes with sugar so they will be pure white. Dry frosted grapes on a wire rack before using to decorate the punch bowl.

Pouring

The hostess pours at a small tea. For a larger tea it is customary to ask two friends to pour while the hostess mingles with the guests and takes care of other arrangements. An idea that you might borrow from the Victorian hostess who gave large parties is to have someone designated in each room to insure that all guests feel especially welcomed.

Remember the most important thing on the menu is good tea. Be sure it is hot, not lukewarm. Another option, besides coffee and punch, is a decanter of sherry. As you leaf through the menus, you will find many recipes for your tea or coffee tray.

The warmth and graciousness of sharing tea is a time-honored practice in Atlanta homes and will never lose its place in Southern households.

PARTY - PRETTY SANDWICHES

PREPARATION:
1. For a shortcut to party-pretty sandwiches, freeze bread and cut and spread bread while frozen.
2. Spread tiny shapes of frozen bread to outermost edges with softened butter to prevent sogginess.

STORAGE:
1. For advance preparation of sandwiches, wrap in foil or waxed paper and a damp towel and refrigerate until served the following day.
2. For advance preparation up to two weeks ahead, freeze foil-wrapped sandwiches and store at 0 degrees. (Allow three hours for thawing.)
3. Fillings that freeze well: American cheese, sliced or ground meat, peanut butter, fish, chicken, turkey.
4. Fillings to avoid freezing: mayonnaise, lettuce, tomatoes, celery, carrots, egg salad.

MORNING COFFEE

AMANDINE CHICKEN SANDWICHES
TOMATO-EGG SANDWICHES   SUNNY LEMON TRIANGLES
PASTEL MINTS   CHEESE BACON PUFFS
SWEDISH ROSE COOKIES
DATE-NUT KRISPIES   COFFEE CAKE SQUARES
FROSTY MOCHA PUNCH

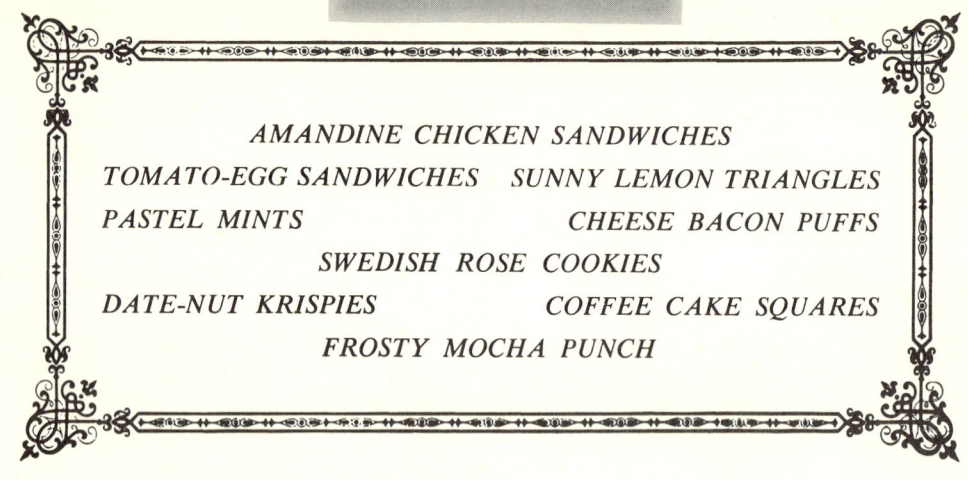

AMANDINE CHICKEN SANDWICHES

Yield: 4 Dozen

2 Cups White Meat of Chicken, Ground
½ Cup Blanched Almonds, Chopped
Mayonnaise
Salt and Pepper
Curry Powder (Optional)
4-5 Dozen Semi-Circles of White Bread

1. Blend together chicken and almonds and moisten with mayonnaise.
2. Season to taste with salt and pepper.
3. Add pinch of curry powder, if desired.
4. Spread on semi-circle of white bread and garnish with small strip of pimiento.

— Miss Martha Haines

TOMATO-EGG SANDWICHES

Yield: 4 Dozen

20 Small Ripe Tomatoes
4 Dozen Rounds of Rye Bread
20 Hard-Cooked Eggs
Mayonnaise
Sprigs of Parsley

1. Place thin slice of tomato on round of rye bread cut the same size as tomato.
2. Top with slice of hard-cooked egg, and rosette of mayonnaise. Add sprig of parsley.

— Miss Martha Haines

TEAS

SUNNY LEMON TRIANGLES

Yield: 4 Dozen

2 Cups Dark Seedless Raisins
1 Cup Pecans, Chopped Finely
2 Lemon Rinds, Grated
2 Eggs
2 Cups Sugar, Granulated
2 Cups Mayonnaise
4 Dozen Triangles of Whole Wheat Bread

1. Grind raisins, nuts and lemon rind together. Blend all ingredients together with mayonnaise.
2. Cook in double boiler for 10 minutes. Spread on small triangles of whole wheat bread.

— Mrs. Paul Hanes

PASTEL MINTS

Yield: 5 Dozen

6 Cups Confectioner's Sugar, Sifted
6½ Tablespoons Water
¾ teaspoon Wintergreen Extract
Few Drops Food Coloring

1. In top of double boiler, combine all ingredients.
2. Cook over hot, NOT BOILING, water for 2½ to 3 minutes.
3. Drop by teaspoon onto a sheet of waxed paper and let harden.
4. Store in refrigerator, one layer at a time.

— Mrs. Paul Hanes

CHEESE BACON PUFFS

Yield: 6 Dozen

6 Eggs, Well-Beaten
3 Cups Cheddar Cheese, Grated
2 Tablespoons Onion, Grated
1½ teaspoons Dry Mustard
18 Slices White Bread, Trimmed
72 (1-inch) Bacon Squares, Uncooked

TEAS

1. Preheat oven to 375 degrees.
2. In small bowl, beat eggs with fork. Blend in grated cheese, onion and dry mustard.
3. Cut each slice of bread into quarters to make 72 squares. Arrange in shallow baking pan. Spoon heaping teaspoonful of cheese mixture on center of each bread square. Top with a one-inch piece of bacon.
4. Bake 15 minutes at 375 degrees or until bread is toasted and topping is slightly puffed.

— Mrs. John C. Hopkins, Jr.

SWEDISH ROSE COOKIES

1½ Pounds Butter, Softened
1½ Cups Sugar, Granulated
6 Cups Flour, Sifted
Red Jelly or Jam

1. Preheat oven to 357 degrees.
2. Cream together butter and sugar.
3. Add flour gradually and blend well. Chill until easy to handle.
4. Form dough into very small balls making a depression in each. Fill small depression with jelly.
5. Bake on ungreased baking sheet at 375 degrees for 18 minutes.

— Miss Irene Burba

DATE-NUT KRISPIES

Yield: 5 Dozen

¼ Cup Butter, Melted
2 Cups Dates, Cut and Pitted
2 Cups Sugar, Granulated
4 Eggs
6 Cups Rice Krispies
1 Cup Pecans, Chopped
Confectioner's Sugar

1. In heavy skillet, blend together melted butter, dates, sugar and eggs. Cook over low heat until well blended, stirring constantly, until mixture reaches soft ball stage (234-238 degrees). Cool slightly.

2. Stir in Rice Krispies, and nuts. Blend well.
3. Lightly sprinkle confectioner's sugar on waxed paper.
4. Shape mixture into 4 rolls. Wrap in the waxed paper. Chill and slice thinly.

— Mrs. W. Troy Gaunt

COFFEE CAKE SQUARES

Yield: 5 Dozen Small Squares

1 Cup Butter, Softened
2 Cups Sugar, Granulated
4 Eggs
2 Cups Sour Cream
1½ teaspoons Soda
3 Cups Flour, Sifted
1 Tablespoon Baking Powder
2 teaspoons Vanilla Extract

1. Preheat oven to 350 degrees. Grease two 8 x 11 inch square pans.
2. Cream together butter and sugar. Add eggs and blend well.
3. Blend together sour cream and soda and add to egg-sugar mixture.
4. Add flour, baking powder and vanilla extract. Blend thoroughly.

Topping:

½ Cup Sugar, Granulated
2 Tablespoons Cinnamon
1½ Cups Walnuts, Chopped

1. Pour half of batter into two 8 x 11 inch greased square pans.
2. Combine all ingredients for topping. Sprinkle half of topping on batter. Pour last half of batter over nut mixture and top with rest of topping.
3. Bake at 350 degrees for 30-35 minutes. Cut into small squares and serve warm.

— Mrs. Robert S. Grady

FROSTY MOCHA PUNCH

Yield: 110 4-Ounce Servings

38 16-Ounce Bottles of Sparkoffee
3½ Gallons and 1 Quart Vanilla or Mocha Ice Cream

1. Pour Sparkoffee over Ice Cream and serve.

— Mrs. Willis A. Haines

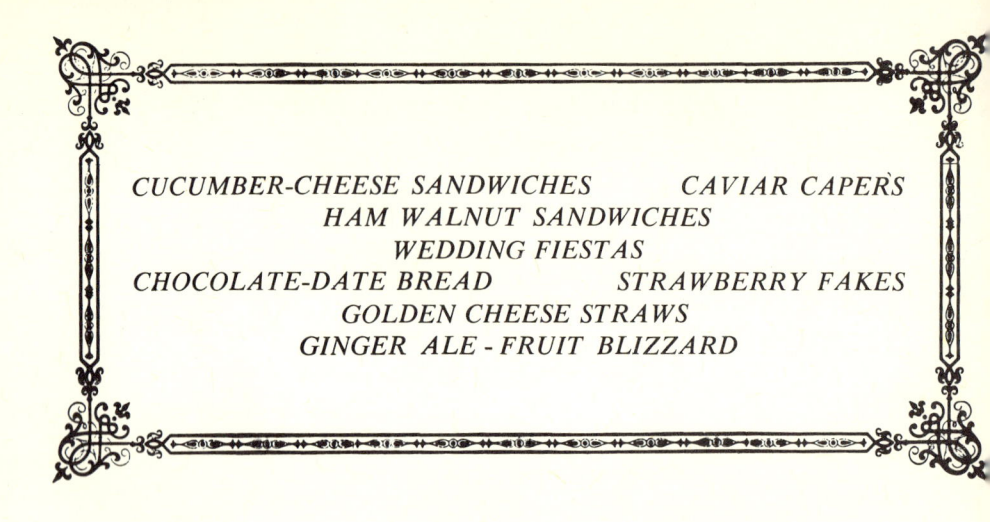

CUCUMBER-CHEESE SANDWICHES   CAVIAR CAPERS
HAM WALNUT SANDWICHES
WEDDING FIESTAS
CHOCOLATE-DATE BREAD   STRAWBERRY FAKES
GOLDEN CHEESE STRAWS
GINGER ALE - FRUIT BLIZZARD

CUCUMBER-CHEESE SANDWICHES
Yield: 4-5 Dozen

1½ Cups Cottage Cheese
½ Cup Cucumber, Seeded and Diced
¼ Cup Parsley, Minced
4-5 Dozen Triangles of Bread (White and/or Whole Wheat)

1. Blend first three ingredients together and spread on triangles of bread.
2. Garnish with tiny wedge of cucumber or gherkin fan.

— Miss Martha Haines

CAVIAR CAPERS
Yield: 5 Dozen

This is extra specially pretty.

Butter, Softened
Caviar (Red or Black)
5 Dozen Toast Strips
Lemon Juice
20 Hard-Cooked Eggs

1. Blend together softened butter and caviar. Spread caviar mixture on toast strips and sprinkle with lemon juice.
2. Garnish with riced hard-cooked egg white and yolk.

— Mrs. McNeill Stokes

HAM-WALNUT SANDWICHES

Yield: 5 Dozen

2 Cups Cooked Ham, Ground
½ Cup Walnuts, Chopped Finely
Salt and Pepper
Mayonnaise
5 Dozen Ovals of White Bread

1. Blend together ham and chopped walnuts. Season with salt and pepper and moisten with mayonnaise.
2. Spread on oval of bread and serve. Garnish with parsley or watercress.

— Mrs. Willis A. Haines

WEDDING FIESTAS

Yield: 6 Dozen

2 Cups Butter
½ Cup Confectioner's Sugar
5 Cups Cake Flour, Sifted
2 Tablespoons Vanilla Extract
2 Cups Almonds, Chopped

1. Preheat oven to 350 degrees.
2. Cream together butter and Confectioner's sugar. Add flour and blend well.
3. Blend in vanilla extract and chopped nuts. Chill overnight and shape into crescents.
4. Bake 20 minutes at 350 degrees. Roll in Confectioner's sugar while warm and serve.

— Mrs. J. P. Ashmore, Sr.

CHOCOLATE DATE BREAD

Yield: 6 Dozen

4 Cups Flour, Sifted
2½ Tablespoons Baking Powder
2 teaspoons Salt

1⅓ Cups Sugar, Granulated
1 Cup Pitted Dates, Diced
2 6-Ounce Packages Semi-sweet Chocolate Chips
2 Cups Strong Coffee
¼ teaspoon Soda
2 Eggs, Well-Beaten
¼ Cup Vegetable Oil

1. Preheat oven to 375 degrees. Grease and flour 9 x 5 x 3 inch pan. Into large bowl sift together flour, baking powder, salt and sugar. Add dates and chocolate chips. Blend together well.
2. Stir in coffee, soda, eggs and vegetable oil. Pour into greased pan and let stand 20 minutes. Bake at 375 degrees for 60 minutes.
3. Cool 20 minutes in pan, then remove to wire rack to finish cooling. When cool, wrap in foil and chill. Arrange small slices on platter and serve. Garnish platter with camellias or single magnolia blossom. (Note introductory pages of Tea section).

— Miss Martha Haines

STRAWBERRY FAKES

Yield: 5-6 Dozen

2 Cans Sweetened Condensed Milk
6 3-Ounce Packages Strawberry Gelatin
2 Cups Pecans, Chopped
2 Cans Angel Flake Coconut
2 Packages Red Sugar
2 Packages Slivered Almonds
Green Food Coloring
1 Tablespoon Water

1. Blend together condensed milk, gelatin, pecans and coconut.
2. Chill in refrigerator for 2 days. Roll dough into shape of strawberries. Roll "strawberries" into red sugar.
3. Soak almond slivers in 3 drops green food coloring and 1 Tablespoon water.
4. Use green almond slivers for strawberry stems.

— Mrs. Frank Phillips

GOLDEN CHEESE STRAWS

Yield: 5-6 Dozen

2 Cups Butter
1 Pound Sharp Cheese, Grated
4 Cups Flour, Sifted
2 teaspoons Salt
Cayenne Pepper

1. Preheat oven to 350 degrees. Grease baking sheet.

2. Blend butter and cheese together until creamy. Add flour, salt and Cayenne pepper to taste. Blend well.

3. Roll dough to ¼ inch thickness and cut into strips or other shapes.

4. Bake 8 to 10 minutes at 350 degrees.

— Miss Winnie Mobley

GINGER ALE-FRUIT BLIZZARD

Yield: 90 4-Ounce Servings

1 Quart Orange Juice
1 Quart Grapefruit Juice
1 Quart Pineapple Juice
1 Cup Lemon Juice
1 Cup Lime Juice
Sugar to Taste
8 Quarts Ginger Ale (Room Temperature)

1. Blend together all fruit juices and sugar. Freeze into ice cubes or fruit ring garnished with strawberries and/or cherries and sprigs of mint.

2. Pour room temperature ginger ale over frozen fruit and serve.

— Mrs. Benjamin Dysart, III

FLAKED CRABMEAT DIAMONDS   CARROT-OLIVE STRIPS
PINEAPPLE RIBBON SANDWICHES
CHEESE WHEELS
COCONUT KISSES   GINGERBREAD GEMS
PASTEL PETIT FOURS
CRANBERRY-ORANGE CRUSH

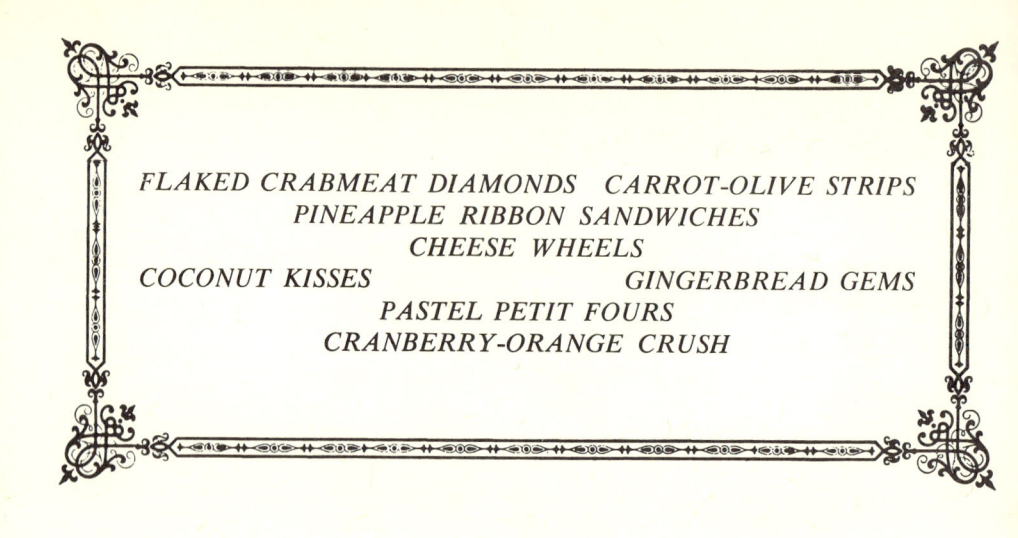

FLAKED CRABMEAT DIAMONDS

Yield: 5 Dozen

2 6-Ounce Cans Flaked Crabmeat
2 Cups Celery, Diced
Mayonnaise
Lemon Juice
5 Dozen Diamonds of Whole Wheat Bread
Pimiento

1. Combine flaked crabmeat with diced celery.
2. Moisten with mayonnaise, adding lemon juice to taste.
3. Spread on diamonds of whole wheat bread and garnish with miniature diamond-shaped pimientos.

— Mrs. Ogden Stokes

PINEAPPLE RIBBON SANDWICHES

Yield: 5 Dozen

5 8-Ounce Packages Cream Cheese
5 Cans Crushed Pineapple, Drained
15 Slices Whole Wheat Bread, Trimmed
10 Slices of White Bread, Trimmed

1. Blend together crushed pineapple and cream cheese.
2. Stack 3 slices of whole wheat bread and 2 slices white bread alternately with pineapple-cheese mixture between each slice.
3. Press together firmly and trim crusts.
4. Wrap each stack in foil and chill for several hours.
5. Cut in half-inch slices and cut each slice in thirds.

— Mrs. Solon P. Patterson

CARROT OLIVE STRIPS

Yield: 5 Dozen

4 Cups Carrots, Finely Grated
1 Cup Celery, Minced
2 Cups Ripe Olives, Chopped
6 Tablespoons Onion, Minced
1 teaspoon Salt
1 Cup Mayonnaise or Salad Dressing
5 Dozen Thin Strips of White Bread, Trimmed

1. Combine first six ingredients and chill.
2. Spread on strips of trimmed white bread.
3. Garnish with carrot curls or fans of ripe olives.

— Mrs. Robert B. Ansley, Jr.

CHEESE WHEELS

Yield: 5 Dozen

5 Dozen Rounds of White Bread
Butter
Parmesan Cheese

1. Cut rounds of bread.
2. With a smaller cutter, take circles from the center of each round.
3. Toast the original round and spread with butter.
4. Spread "wheel" heavily with parmesan cheese.
5. Toast again, and serve hot or cold.

— Mrs. Ogden Stokes

COCONUT KISSES

Yield: 6 Dozen

8 Egg Whites, Stiffly Beaten
Dash Salt
4 Cups Sugar, Granulated
2 teaspoons Vanilla Extract
8 Cups Corn Flakes
4 3½-Ounce Cans (5 Cups) Coconut, Flaked
2 Cups Walnuts, Chopped
Melted Chocolate (optional)

1. Preheat oven to 350 degrees. Grease baking sheet.
2. Beat egg whites with salt until foamy. Gradually add sugar and beat until soft peaks form. Add vanilla extract.

3. Fold in corn flakes, coconut and walnuts.
4. Drop from teaspoon onto greased baking sheet and bake at 350 degrees for 20 minutes.
5. Remove cookies immediately. Dribble with melted chocolate if desired.

— Mrs. John C. Hopkins, Jr.

GINGERBREAD GEMS

Yield: 4-5 Dozen

½ Cup Butter
½ Cup Sugar, Granulated
½ Cup Dark Molasses
1 Egg
2½ Cups Flour, Sifted
½ teaspoon Baking Powder
1 teaspoon Ginger
1 teaspoon Cloves, Ground
1 teaspoon Cinnamon
½ teaspoon Salt

1. Preheat oven to 350 degrees. Grease baking sheet.
2. Cream together butter and sugar. Blend in molasses and add egg. Blend well.
3. Sift dry ingredients together, add to molasses mixture, and blend well.
4. Drop onto greased baking sheet and bake at 350 degrees for 10-12 minutes.

— Mrs. Andrew N. Foster

CRANBERRY-ORANGE CRUSH

Yield: 110 4-Ounce Servings

½ teaspoon Cinnamon
½ teaspoon Nutmeg
½ teaspoon Allspice
4 Quarts Cranberry Juice Cocktail
3 Pints Orange Juice
5 Quarts Ginger Ale, Chilled

1. Combine all ingredients except ginger ale.
2. Blend together well and bring to a boil. (Strain through cheesecloth, if desired.)
3. Chill. Add ginger ale just before serving.
4. If desired, float a frozen fruit ring in punch.

— Mrs. Paul Hanes

DEVILED HAM CORNUCOPIAS
CHECKERBOARD DANDIES   HERBED PARTY TRIANGLES
SPICY ORANGE BITES
CHOCOLATE CHARMERS   ACCORDION TREATS
DATE-NUT CORONETS
COOL MINT CRUSH

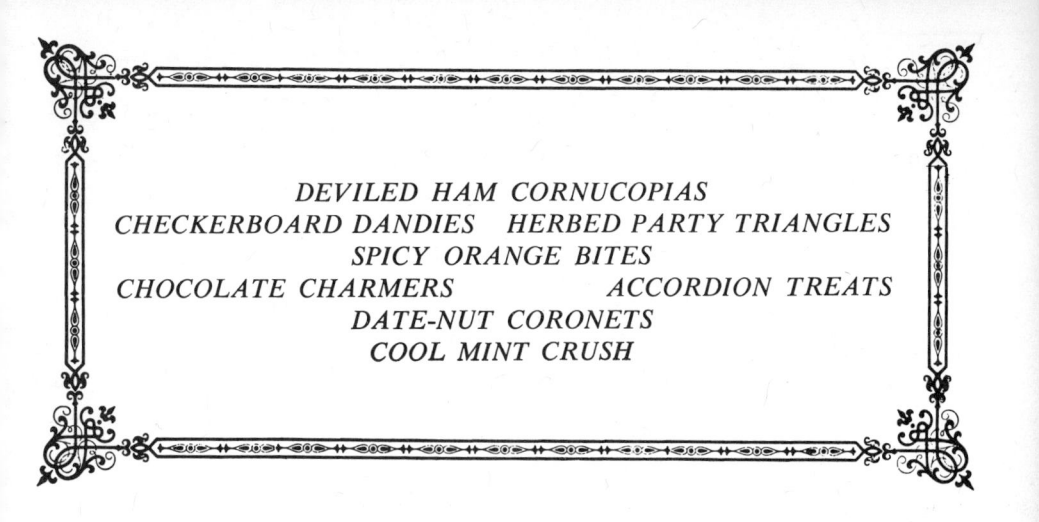

DEVILED HAM CORNUCOPIAS

Yield: 5 Dozen

60 Thin Slices of White Bread
Mayonnaise
Deviled Ham Filling

1. Preheat oven to 350 degrees.
2. Using round cooky cutter, cut circle from each slice of bread.
3. Flatten circles with rolling pin and spread both sides with mayonnaise.
4. Roll up to form cornucopia and fasten with pick. Bake on ungreased cooky sheet at 350 degrees for 12-15 minutes until lightly browned. Remove picks.

Deviled Ham Filling:

½ Cup Mayonnaise
3 4½-Ounce Cans Deviled Ham
6 Hard-Cooked Eggs
3 Tablespoons Prepared Mustard

1. Combine all ingredients. Chill. Fill each cornucopia with 1 teaspoon of filling. (You may want to be fancy and use a pastry tube to fill).
2. Sprinkle with parsley or paprika. Garnish tray with tomato roses and serve.

— Mrs. John C. Hopkins, Jr.

HERBED PARTY TRIANGLES

Yield: 4-5 Dozen

1 8-Ounce Package Cream Cheese, Softened
¾ Cup Almonds Chopped
¼ Cup Bell Pepper, Chopped
¼ Cup Onion, Chopped
3 Tablespoons Pimiento, Chopped
1 Tablespoon Catsup
¾ teaspoon Salt
¾ teaspoon Pepper
4-5 Dozen Triangles of Rye Bread

1. Blend together all ingredients, and spread on triangles of Rye bread.

— Mrs. Benjamin Dysart, III

CHECKERBOARD DANDIES

Yield: 4-5 Dozen

Whole Wheat Bread, Trimmed
White Bread, Trimmed
1 Cup Butter, Softened
¼ Cup Capers, Minced
Mayonnaise

1. Stack alternately 2 slices whole wheat bread and 2 slices white bread and spread with butter-caper mixture.
2. Wrap in waxed paper and damp cloth. Chill.
3. Cut each stack of bread in ½ inch slices. Place 3 alternating slices together (white strip over whole wheat strip). Spread with mayonnaise or softened butter between slices. Wrap and chill.
4. Slice ½ inch thick in checkerboard slices and serve.
Garnish platter with crisp watercress and radish roses.

— Mrs. Harry I. Talbert

SPICY ORANGE BITES

Yield: 5 Dozen Small Squares

1 Tablespoon Flour
¼ Cup Brown Sugar
½ teaspoon Cinnamon
2 Cups Flour, Sifted
2 teaspoons Baking Powder
¼ teaspoon Soda
1 teaspoon Salt
½ Cup Sugar, Granulated
Rind of 1 Large Orange, Grated
⅔ Cup Orange Juice
½ Cup Butter, Melted
2 Eggs
1 Tablespoon Butter, Melted

1. Preheat oven to 350 degrees. Grease a 9 inch cake pan.
2. In small bowl combine 1 Tablespoon flour, brown sugar and cinnamon.
3. In large bowl combine 2 cups flour, baking powder, soda, salt, granulated sugar and orange rind. Add all at once, orange juice, ½ cup melted butter and eggs. Stir until just blended.
4. Spread batter in pan. Into brown-sugar mixture stir 1 Tablespoon melted butter. Sprinkle this mixture on top of batter. Bake 30 minutes at 350 degrees.
5. Cut into bite-size squares and serve.

— Miss Martha Haines

CHOCOLATE CHARMERS

Yield: 5-6 Dozen

1 Cup Butter
1 Cup Sugar, Granulated
3 Eggs
3 1-Ounce Squares Semi-Sweet Chocolate
1½ teaspoons Vanilla Extract
3½ Cups Flour, Sifted
2 teaspoons Baking Powder
¼ teaspoon Soda

TEAS

1. Preheat oven to 400 degrees. Grease baking sheet.
2. Cream together butter and sugar. Add eggs and blend well.
3. In top of double boiler, melt chocolate. Cool and add vanilla extract.
4. Sift dry ingredients together and blend in well.
5. Using a teaspoon, drop onto greased baking sheet and bake at 400 degrees for 8-10 minutes.

— Mrs. Dewey Weaver

ACCORDION TREATS

Yield: 4-5 Dozen

1½ Cups Butter
1½ Cups Sugar, Granulated
4 Eggs
2 teaspoons Vanilla Extract
2½ Cups Flour, Sifted
½ teaspoon Salt

1. Preheat oven to 325 degrees.
2. Cream together butter and sugar. Add eggs and vanilla extract.
3. Sift flour and salt together and add to sugar-egg mixture. Blend well.
4. Take piece of aluminum foil one yard long and fold in half, making two thicknesses.
5. Fold in 1 inch folds like an accordion. Pull folds out a little, dropping teaspoon of dough in creases, two on one crease, then one on the next.
6. Bake at 325 degrees for 25 minutes.
7. When you have baked cookies on one side of foil, turn foil over and use the other side.

— Mrs. A. E. Green

DATE-NUT CORONETS

Yield: 5 Dozen

1 Cup Butter
2 Cups Brown Sugar
1 teaspoon Salt
2 Packages Coconut
2 Eggs
2 8-Ounce Packages of Pitted Dates, Chopped
2 Cups Pecans, Chopped
2 Cups Rice Krispies
2 teaspoons Vanilla Extract

1. In a double boiler, blend together butter, brown sugar, salt, eggs and dates. Cook until thickened (approximately 10 minutes).
2. Cook slightly and add nuts, Rice Krispies and vanilla extract.
3. Form into small balls or fingers and roll in shredded coconut or Confectioner's sugar.

— Miss Winnie Mobley

COOL MINT CRUSH

Yield: 100 4-Ounce Servings

This would be especially pretty with a fruited ice ring garnished with forsted mint. (Note introductory pages to Tea section).

4 Cups Sugar, Granulated
1 Quart Water
Juice of 12 Lemons
Juice of 4 Oranges
2 Handfuls Fresh Mint, Crushed
11 Quarts Ginger Ale

1. Boil sugar and water together for 5 minutes. Pour hot syrup over fruit juice and mint. Chill.
2. Add chilled ginger ale to punch bowl.

— Mrs. McNeill Stokes

SHRIMP - CUCUMBER ROUNDS   POPPY SEED SQUARES
DEVILED DIAMONDS
CHEESE PUFFS
FRUIT CAKE COOKIES   PECAN DELIGHTS
CHOCOLATE BUTTER CREAM CUPS
ORANGE FROST

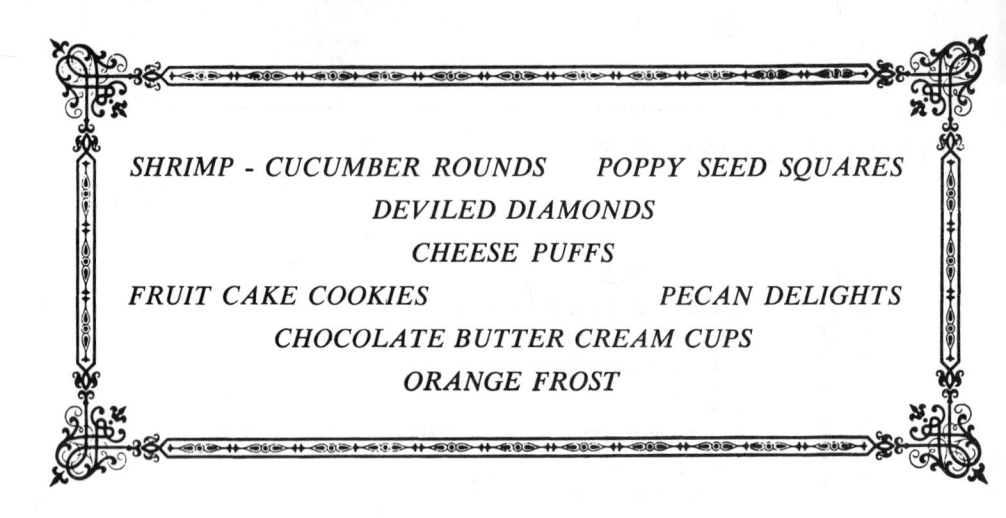

SHRIMP - CUCUMBER ROUNDS

Yield: 5 Dozen

5 Dozen Rounds of Whole Wheat Bread
1¼ Cups Cream Cheese, Whipped
5 Dozen Slices Cucumber
5 Dozen Small Shrimp, Cooked

1. Cut slices of bread into rounds, using three rounds per slice.
2. Spread each round with 1 teaspoon whipped cream cheese. Top with slice of cucumber and small cooked shrimp. (You may want to add a small amount of cream cheese to the top of the cucumber slice to secure the shrimp.)

— Mrs. William Heisel

POPPY SEED SQUARES

Yield: 5 Dozen

1 Pound Cheddar Cheese
1 Cup Butter, Softened
Poppy Seed
5 Dozen Toast Squares

1. Preheat oven to 300 degrees. Grease baking sheet.
2. Cream cheese and butter together well. Spread on toast squares.
3. Sprinkle with poppy seed and heat in oven at 300 degrees.

— Miss Janet Barnes

TEAS

DEVILED DIAMONDS

Yield: 5 Dozen

5 Dozen Diamonds of White Bread
5 Tablespoons Butter, Softened
Canned Deviled Ham
Mayonnaise
Stuffed Olives

1. After bread is cut into diamond shapes (2 diamonds per slice of bread), spread softened butter over each diamond lightly.

2. Moisten deviled ham with mayonnaise and spread on each diamond. Garnish with sliced stuffed olives.

— Mrs. I. J. W. Johnston

CHEESE PUFFS

Yield: 5 Dozen

5 Dozen Rounds of White Bread
2 Cups Mayonnaise
1 Cup Cheddar Cheese, Grated

1. Preheat broiler unit of range.

2. Top rounds of bread with mixture of mayonnaise and cheese. Broil several inches from broiler unit until golden brown. Serve hot. (Tiny rounds of meat or shrimp may be added as garnishes.)

— Mrs. Frank Briggs

FRUIT CAKE COOKIES

Yield: 4 Dozen

½ Pound Almonds, Chopped
½ Pound Pecans, Chopped
1 Package Dates, Chopped
1 Cup Dark Seedless Raisins
½ Pound Citron, Chopped

TEAS

    4 Slices Pineapple
    1 Pound Candied Cherries
    1 Can Coconut, Shredded
    1 Cup Sherry

1. Combine all ingredients and marinate overnight.

Cooky Dough:

    3 Eggs
    1½ Cups Brown Sugar
    ⅔ Cup Butter, Melted
    1 teaspoon Soda
    1 teaspoon Buttermilk
    1 teaspoon Vanilla Extract
    3 Cups Flour, Sifted
    1 teaspoon Cloves
    2 teaspoons Cinnamon
    1 teaspoon Nutmeg

1. Preheat oven to 350 degrees. Grease baking sheet.

2. Blend together eggs, brown sugar and melted butter. Combine soda and buttermilk and add to egg-sugar mixture.

3. Blend in vanilla extract. Sift together flour, cloves, cinnamon, and nutmeg. Add dry ingredients to wet ingredients.

4. Blend in marinated fruit. Drop onto greased baking sheet and bake at 350 degrees for 10-15 minutes.

— Mrs. A. E. Greene

PECAN DELIGHTS

Yield: 3 Dozen

    6 Egg Whites, Stiffly Beaten
    1 Pound Brown Sugar, Sifted
    2 Cups Cake Flour, Sifted

Dash Salt
1 teaspoon Baking Powder
3 Cups Walnuts, Chopped
1 Tablespoon Vanilla Extract

1. Preheat oven to 275 degrees. Grease and flour square cake pan.
2. Beat egg whites until stiff peaks form and fold in sifted brown sugar. Sift together flour, salt and baking powder and add to egg white-sugar mixture. Reserve part of the flour to dredge walnuts.
3. Lightly dust chopped walnuts with flour and add with vanilla extract. Pour into greased and floured square pan.
4. Bake at 275 degrees for 45 minutes to 1 hour. Cut into fingers. When cooled, ice with Confectioner's icing.

— Mrs. John C. Hopkins, Jr.

CHOCOLATE BUTTER CREAM CUPS

Yield: 4 Dozen

24 Ounces Semi-sweet Chocolate Chips
½ Cup Butter

1. In top of double boiler, melt and blend together chocolate chips and butter. Pour into miniature baking cups and spread over the sides.
2. Chill in muffin tins. Fill with butter cream frosting, ice cream, custard or fresh fruit pieces.

— Mrs. Steve J. Dixon

ORANGE FROST

Yield: 100 4-Ounce Servings

3 12-Ounce Cans Frozen Orange Juice, Diluted
8 Quarts Ginger Ale, Chilled
2 Quarts Orange Sherbet

1. Combine orange juice and ginger ale and pour over orange sherbet.
2. Float slices of orange, sprigs of mint and Maraschino cherries in punch bowl for colorful garnishes.

— Mrs. Everett P. Bean

AFTERNOON TEA

CORNUCOPIAS ALOHA   PARSLEY PINWHEELS
MINIATURE BASKETS OF CHICKEN SALAD
MOCHA BOURBON BALLS
COFFEE CRUMB CAKES   ORANGE BLOSSOMS
PECAN SANDIES
SPARKLING CATAWBA

CORNUCOPIAS ALOHA

Yield: 5 Dozen

60 Slices White Bread, Trimmed
2 8-Ounce Packages Cream Cheese, Softened
½ Can Crushed Pineapple, Drained
Ripe Olives, Pitted

1. Spread trimmed slices of bread with softened cream cheese and pineapple mixture.
2. Roll into cornucopia shape. Chill, seam side down.
3. Garnish with petals of ripe olive.

— Mrs. Thomas I. Sangster

PARSLEY PINWHEELS

Yield: 4-5 Dozen

1 Loaf Unsliced Whole Wheat Bread, Trimmed
½ Cup Butter, Softened
3 Tablespoons Parsley, Chopped
1 teaspoon Lemon Juice
Stuffed Green Olives

1. Cut trimmed loaf of whole wheat bread in ¼ inch slices, lengthwise. Spread with mixture of butter, parsley, and lemon juice.
2. Line up row of stuffed green olives near end of each slice and roll up. Wrap and chill.
3. Place seam against cutting board and cut in ⅜ inch slices.

— Mrs. Louie Lathem

CHICKEN SALAD BASKETS

Yield: 5 Dozen

60 Slices White Sandwich Bread, Trimmed
Melted Butter
2 Cups Chicken Salad
Sprigs of Parsley

1. Preheat oven to 300 degrees. Grease small muffin tins.
2. Brush trimmed pieces of bread with melted butter. Place in small muffin tins so that the 4 corners protrude above muffin tins.
3. Toast in 300 degree oven.
4. Fill with chicken salad and garnish with sprigs of parsley.

— Mrs. Robert Sasser

MOCHA BOURBON BALLS

Yield: 5 Dozen

1 Pound Vanilla Wafers, Crushed
2 Cups Walnuts, Chopped
2 Tablespoons Cocoa
2 Cups Confectioner's Sugar
3 Tablespoons Light Corn Syrup
4 1-Ounce Jiggers Bourbon or Rum

1. Blend together crushed wafers, chopped nuts, cocoa and sugar.
2. In separate bowl, mix corn syrup and bourbon together. Gradually add to crumb mixture.
3. Shape into balls the size of small walnuts and roll in Confectioner's sugar.
4. Chill overnight.

— Mrs. Benjamin Dysart, III

COFFEE CRUMB CAKE

Yield: 4 Dozen Small Squares

This truly melts in your mouth!

⅔ Cup Brown Sugar
¼ Cup Biscuit Mix
¼ Cup Instant Coffee
2 teaspoons Cinnamon
¼ Cup Butter
½ Cup Walnuts, Chopped
2⅔ Cups Biscuit Mix
1 Cup Sugar, Granulated

TEAS

    6 Tablespoons Shortening
    2 Eggs
    4 teaspoons Instant Coffee
    ½ Cup Milk
    1 Cup Milk
    2 teaspoons Vanilla Extract

1. Preheat oven to 350 degrees. Grease and flour two 8 inch square pans.
2. Blend together brown sugar, ¼ cup biscuit mix, ¼ cup instant coffee, and cinnamon.
3. Cut in butter. Add nuts and reserve as topping.
4. Combine 2⅔ cups biscuit mix, sugar, shortening, eggs, 4 teaspoons instant coffee, ½ cup milk. Blend one minute until batter is smooth.
5. Stir in 1 cup milk and vanilla extract. Blend one minute longer.
6. Pour into greased and floured 8 inch square pans. Sprinkle topping evenly on batter and bake at 350 degrees for 40 minutes.
7. Cut into bite-size pieces and serve warm.

                — Mrs. Tyrone S. Clifford

ORANGE BLOSSOMS

                Yield: 5-6 Dozen

    6 Eggs
    Few Drops of Yellow Food Coloring
    2⅔ Cups Sugar, Granulated
    1 Tablespoon Baking Powder
    1 teaspoon Salt
    1 Cup Warm Water
    3 Cups Flour, Sifted
    2 teaspoons Vanilla Extract

1. Preheat oven to 400 degrees. Grease small muffin tins.
2. Blend together eggs and coloring. Add sugar and rest of ingredients.
3. Place about 1 teaspoon batter in each muffin tin. (These are to be very small).
4. Bake at 400 degrees for 10 minutes.

Dipping:

    4 Cups Sugar, Granulated
    4 teaspoons Lemon Rind, Grated
    4 teaspoons Orange Rind, Grated

Juice of 4 Oranges
Juice of 4 **Lemons** (If juice runs short you can add frozen, undiluted orange juice).
Few Drops Yellow Food Coloring.

1. Combine all ingredients. Dip muffins into mixture and place on rack to drip.
2. Decorate with slivers of red or green candied cherries.

— Mrs. Rogers MacLeslie

PECAN SANDIES

Yield: 6 Dozen

2 Cups Butter
¼ Cup Confectioner's Sugar
4 teaspoons Vanilla Extract
2 Tablespoons Water
4 Cups Flour, Sifted
2 Cups Pecans, Chopped
Confectioner's Sugar

1. Preheat oven to 300 degrees.
2. Cream together butter and sugar. Add vanilla extract and stir in water and flour. Blend well.
3. Fold in nuts. Form into small (1½ inch) crescents.
4. Place on ungreased baking sheet and bake at 300 degrees for 20 minutes.
5. Remove from oven and dust with Confectioner's sugar while hot.

— Mrs. Benjamin Dysart, III

SPARKLING CATAWBA

Yield: 125 4-Ounce Servings

6 46-Ounce Cans Pineapple Juice
3 Quart Bottles Ginger Ale
6 6-Ounce Cans Frozen Lemonade
3 Quart Bottles Sparkling Catawba White Grape Juice

1. Chill and combine all ingredients. Float fresh strawberries in punch bowl and garnish with frosted grapes. (See Introductory pages of Tea Section).

— Mrs. McNeill Stokes

CAVIAR BITES   TOMATO WHEELS
       MAPLE NUT SANDWICHES
            CHEESE TIDBITS
PERSHING POINT COOKIES   PECAN SPICE SQUARES
          FROSTY BANANA MIST
      Garnished with Whole Fresh Strawberries

CAVIAR BITES

Yield: 5 Dozen

5 Dozen Triangles of Toast
1 8-Ounce Package Cream Cheese, Softened
Salt and Pepper
Parsley, Minced
Caviar

1. Spread triangles of toast with seasoned cream cheese.
2. Sprinkle minced parsley on outer edges. Place red or black caviar in center.

— Mrs. Homer L. Sangster

TOMATO WHEELS

Yield: 5 Dozen

These are sheer delights!

5 Dozen Rounds of White Bread
5 Dozen Thick Tomato Slices
30 Hard-Cooked Eggs
Mayonnaise
Parsley
Chives, Minced

1. Rice whites of hard-cooked eggs. Rice yellows separately.
2. Spread mayonnaise on one side of round (rounds may be toasted if desired) and top with tomato.
3. Remove tomato seeds and fill spaces with:
    1) Riced whites of hard-cooked eggs
    2) Parsley
    3) Riced yellow of hard-cooked eggs
    4) Minced chives

— Mrs. Adolphus B. Orthwein, Jr.

MAPLE NUT SANDWICHES

Yield: 5 Dozen

4½ Cups Maple Sugar, Crushed
6 Tablespoons Butter
¾ Cup Evaporated Milk
1½ Cups Walnuts, Chopped
5 Dozen Strips of Whole Wheat or White Bread

1. Roll maple sugar with rolling pin until fine. Cream together butter and crushed maple sugar until stiff.
2. Add evaporated milk and sufficient maple sugar to obtain a stiff, creamy mixture. Blend in chopped nuts and spread on thin strips of buttered whole wheat or white bread.

— Mrs. Everett P. Bean

CHEESE TIDBITS

Yield: 6 Dozen

1 Cup Butter, Softened
2 Small Jars English Cheese
3 Cups Flour, Sifted
1 teaspoon Salt
80 Stuffed Olives, Drained

1. Preheat oven to 400 degrees. Grease baking sheet.
2. Cream together butter, English Cheese, flour, and salt. Roll into walnut-sized balls and stuff olive into each center.
3. Chill overnight. Bake 15-20 minutes in 400 degree oven on greased baking sheet. Serve warm.

— Mrs. Jack Staton

PERSHING POINT COOKIES

Yield: 6 Dozen

2 Cups (12 Ounces) Chocolate Chips
4 Eggs, Stiffly Beaten
Dash Salt
1 Cup Sugar, Granulated
1 teaspoon Vanilla Extract
1 teaspoon Vinegar
½ Cup Almonds, Chopped (Optional)
1 Cup Coconut, Shredded

1. Preheat oven to 350 degrees. Grease baking sheet.

TEAS

2. In top of double boiler, melt chocolate chips.
3. Beat together egg whites and salt until foamy. Gradually add sugar and beat until stiff peaks form.
4. Blend in vanilla extract and vinegar. Fold in melted chocolate, chopped nuts and coconut.
5. Drop onto greased baking sheet and bake at 350 degrees for 10 minutes.

— Mrs. William Rowell

PECAN SPICE SQUARES

Yield: 4-5 Dozen Tiny Squares

4 Eggs
1 Box Brown Sugar
2½ Cups Flour, Sifted
2 teaspoons Baking Powder
2 Cups Pecans, Chopped
1 teaspoon Vanilla Extract

1. Preheat oven to 325 degrees. Grease two 9 inch square pans.
2. Beat eggs until frothy and add sugar. Cook in double boiler for 15 minutes, stirring constantly. Cool until warm.
3. Add flour, nuts and vanilla extract. Pour batter into two pans and bake for 65 minutes at 325 degrees.
4. Cool, cut into tiny squares and serve.

— Mrs. Linton D. Baggs, Jr.

FROSTY BANANA MIST

Yield: 60 4-Ounce Servings

6 Cups Sugar, Granulated
3 Gallons Water
10 Bananas, Mashed
Juice of 10 Oranges
Juice of 4 Lemons
2 Quarts Pineapple Juice
6-8 Quarts Ginger Ale

1. Combine sugar and water and bring to a boil.
2. Blend together rest of ingredients and add to sugar-water mixture.
3. Freeze in ice cube trays, if desired. Crush before serving. Add ginger ale until desired consistency is obtained.
4. Garnish with whole fresh strawberries and sprigs of fresh mint.

— Mrs. Robert B. Ansley, Jr.

CHANTERELLE SANDWICHES
HAWAIIAN NUT SANDWICHES   HERBED FLOWERPOTS
HOT HAM PUFFS
JIM JAM SURPRISES
CHOCOLATE CONFETTI   CHERRY WINKS
PARTY PEACH PUNCH

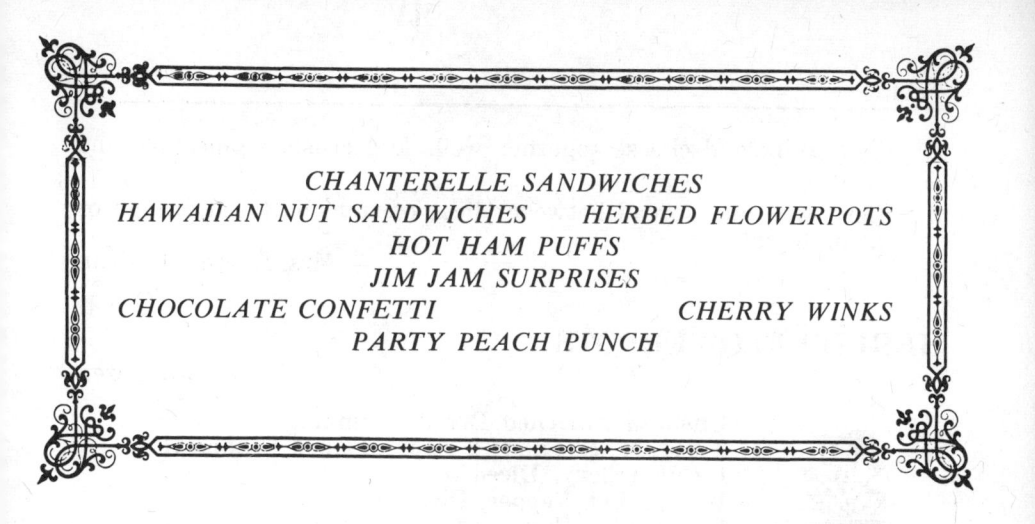

CHANTERELLE SANDWICHES

Yield: 5-6 Dozen

6 Tablespoons Butter, Melted
2 Tablespoons Onion, Minced
¼ Cup Flour
1 Cup Milk
2 Tablespoons Cheddar Cheese, Grated
2 Cups Chicken, Ground
2 Cups Mushrooms, Minced
Salt and Pepper
5-6 Dozen Triangles of Buttered Toast
Grated Parmesan Cheese

1. Preheat oven to 300 degrees.
2. Saute minced onion in melted butter until tender. Add flour and cook until bubbly.
3. Blend in milk and grated cheese. Add chicken, mushrooms, and season to taste. Blend together well.
4. Spread on toasted buttered triangles of bread and sprinkle with grated Parmesan cheese. Heat in oven at 300 degrees and serve hot.

— Mrs. Steve J. Dixon

HAWAIIAN NUT SANDWICHES

Yield: 4-5 Dozen

¼ Cup Evaporated Milk
2 8-Ounce Packages Cream Cheese, Softened
1 Cup Pineapple, Crushed and Drained
¼ Cup Pecans, Chopped

— 151 —

TEAS

1. Blend milk and cheese together well. Add crushed pineapple and nuts.
2. Blend well and spread between slices of thin, buttered orange or raisin bread.

— Mrs. Everett P. Bean

HERBED FLOWERPOTS

Yield: 4-5 Dozen

Unsliced Enriched Bread, Trimmed
2 6½-Ounce Cans (2 Cups) Flaked Crabmeat
1 Cup Celery, Diced
½ Cup Bell Pepper, Diced
½ teaspoon Salt
Dash Pepper
2 Tablespoons Lemon Juice
⅔ Cup Mayonnaise or Salad Dressing
Sprigs of Parsley

1. Cut bread into 1 inch slices. Freeze.
2. Cut circles in frozen slices with one inch round cutter. Scoop out centers leaving bottom and sides ¼ inch thick.
3. Blend all ingredients, except parsley, together well. Chill.
4. Pile filling into flowerpots and garnish with sprig of parsey.

— Miss Irene Burba

HOT HAM PUFFS

Yield: 4-5 Dozen

4 4½-Ounce Cans Deviled Ham
2½ Tablespoons Burgundy
Dash Pepper
4-5 Dozen Rounds of White Bread

1. Blend all ingredients together well. Spread on small rounds of white bread.

Topping:

4 Egg Whites, Stiffly Beaten
¾ Cup Mayonnaise
4 teaspoons Spicy Mustard Sauce

1. Preheat broiler unit or range.
2. Combine all ingredients of topping and spoon onto ham mixture. Place under broiler until golden brown.

— Miss Edith Ogden

TEAS

JIM JAM SURPRISES

Yield: 5 Dozen

1 Cup Butter, Softened
6 Tablespoons Sugar, Granulated
1 teaspoon Vanilla Extract
3 Cups Flour, Sifted
Red Jelly
Pecan Halves
Confectioner's Sugar

1. Preheat oven to 325 degrees. Grease baking sheet.
2. Cream together butter and sugar. Add vanilla extract and flour.
3. Roll dough into balls. Make depression in center of each ball.
4. Place jelly in depression and top with pecan half.
5. Bake at 325 degrees for 20 minutes or until done. Sift Confectioner's sugar over hot surprises and serve!

— Mrs. Everett P. Bean

CHOCOLATE CONFETTI

Yield: 6 Dozen

2 Packages Confectioner's Sugar
1 Cup Butter, Melted
1 Can Eagle Brand Milk
1 Pound Walnuts, Chopped
1 Can Coconut, Shredded
1 12-Ounce Package Semi-Sweet Chocolate Chips
1 Individual Cake of Paraffin

1. Combine sugar, butter, milk, walnuts and coconut.
2. Roll into small balls and chill. Keep well chilled until ready to dip.
3. In double boiler, melt chocolate and paraffin together.
4. Use picks to dip balls into chocolate-paraffin mixture. After dipping, slowly turn balls (for just a few seconds) so chocolate will not drip off.

— Mrs. Albert W. Boam

CHERRY WINKS

Yield: 5 Dozen

⅔ Cup Shortening
1 Cup Sugar, Granulated
2 teaspoons Lemon Rind, Grated
2 teaspoons Vanilla Extract

— 153 —

TEAS

    2 Eggs
    ¼ Cup Milk
    2 Cups Flour, Sifted
    1 teaspoon Baking Powder
    ½ teaspoon Soda
    ½ teaspoon Salt
    1 Cup Seedless Raisins
    1 Cup Walnuts, Chopped
    3 Cups Wheat Flakes, Slightly Crushed
    Candied Cherries

1. Preheat oven to 400 degrees. Grease baking sheet.
2. Cream together shortening and sugar. Add grated lemon rind and vanilla extract and blend well.
3. Add eggs and milk. Blend thoroughly.
4. Sift together dry ingredients and add to sugar-milk mixture. Blend well and fold in raisins.
5. Drop by teaspoons onto crushed wheat flakes and toss lightly to coat.
6. Place on greased baking sheet about 2 inches apart.
7. Top each with candied cherry half.
8. Bake at 400 degrees for 12 minutes and cool slightly before removing from pan.

— Mrs. Dewey Weaver

PARTY PEACH PUNCH

Yield: 100 4-Ounce Servings

This is truly a taste of Georgian hospitality!

    24 12-Ounce Cans Peach Concentrate
    1½ Gallons Water
    2 Quarts Champagne (Optional)
    2 Quarts Ginger Ale
    1½ Pints Orange Juice
    1⅓ Cups Lemon Juice
    1½ Quarts Fresh Peach Halves and Slices

1. Use canned concentrate of Georgia Peaches. (If concentrate is not available, prepare a puree of fresh ripe peaches, using an electric blender to achieve a satin-smooth consistency).
2. Mix all ingredients, except champagne, ginger ale and peach halves. Chill.
3. Add champagne, ginger ale and peach halves before serving.

— Mrs. Carl E. Sanders

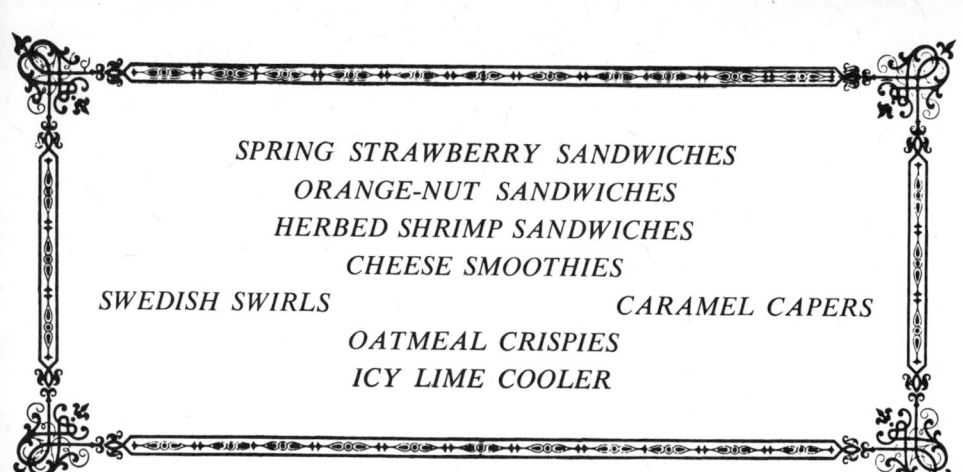

SPRING STRAWBERRY SANDWICHES
ORANGE-NUT SANDWICHES
HERBED SHRIMP SANDWICHES
CHEESE SMOOTHIES
SWEDISH SWIRLS   CARAMEL CAPERS
OATMEAL CRISPIES
ICY LIME COOLER

SPRING STRAWBERRY SANDWICHES

Yield: 4 Dozen

68 Slices White Bread, Trimmed
Butter
Mayonnaise
1½ Pints Fresh Strawberries, Blended with Sugar
(or 1 Can Frozen Strawberries, Drained)

1. Stack 4 slices of white bread together. Butter inside of both outside slices of bread. Spread mayonnaise on inside slices.
2. Spread with strawberry-sugar mixture. Wrap sandwiches in waxed paper and a damp cloth. Chill and cut into slices to serve.

— Mrs. John H. Harland

ORANGE-NUT SANDWICHES

Yield: 4 Dozen

2-8 Ounce Packages Cream Cheese
¼ Cup Orange Rind, Grated
1 Cup Dark Seedless Raisins, Chopped
½ Cup Pecans, Diced
½ Cup Orange Juice
4 Dozen Ovals of Whole Wheat Bread

1. Blend together all ingredients.
2. Spread on ovals of whole wheat bread.

— Mrs. Byford E. Wagstaff

HERBED SHRIMP SANDWICHES

Yield: 5 Dozen

2 Pounds Shrimp, Cooked and Diced
2 Tablespoons Onion, Minced
2 teaspoons Celery, Minced
2 teaspoons Bell Pepper, Minced
4 teaspoons Lemon Juice
1 teaspoon Lemon Rind, Grated
½ teaspoon Salt
8-10 Drops Tabasco Sauce
Dash Pepper
1½ Cups Mayonnaise
5 Dozen Triangles of White Bread

1. Combine shrimp with rest of ingredients. Season to taste. Spread on triangles of white bread.

— Mrs. Everett P. Bean

CHEESE SMOOTHIES

Yield: 5-6 Dozen

1 Cup Butter
2 5-Ounce Jars Sharp Cheese Spread
1½ Cups Pancake Mix
½ teaspoon Caraway Seed

1. Preheat oven to 375 degrees. Grease baking sheet.

2. Cream butter and cheese together until smooth and light.

3. Add pancake mix and caraway seed. Blend well.

4. Roll into small balls and place on greased baking sheet. Chill several hours.

5. Bake at 375 degrees for 10 minutes and serve piping hot.

— Mrs. Linton D. Baggs, Jr.

SWEDISH SWIRLS

Yield: 4 Dozen

1 Cup Shortening
½ Cup Brown Sugar
2 Egg Yolks
2 Cups Flour, Sifted
¼ teaspoon Almond Extract
Granulated or Brown Sugar
Pecan or Walnut Halves

1. Preheat oven to 375 degrees. Grease baking sheet.
2. Cream together shortening and sugar; add egg yolks and blend well.
3. Blend in flour and add almond extract.
4. Form in balls the size of small walnuts. Roll in granulated or brown sugar. Press pecan or walnut half on top. Bake on greased baking sheet for 12 to 15 minutes at 375 degrees.

— Mrs. Homer L. Sangster

CARAMEL CAPERS

Yield: 4 Dozen

1 Cup Butter
2 Cups Brown Sugar
2 Eggs
2 teaspoons Vanilla Extract
2 Cups Flour, Sifted
2 teaspoons Baking Powder
2 Cups Almonds, Chopped

1. Preheat oven to 350 degrees. Grease two 9 inch square pans.
2. Cream together butter and sugar.
3. Add eggs and vanilla extract to butter-sugar mixture.

TEAS

4. Sift together flour and baking powder; add to egg mixture and blend well.
5. Fold in chopped nuts. Place in two greased square pans and bake at 350 degrees for 15 minutes. Cut in squares and serve.

— Miss Winnie Mobley

OATMEAL CRISPIES

Yield: 4 Dozen

1 Cup Butter
1 Cup Brown Sugar
1 Cup Sugar, Granulated
2 Eggs, Well-Beaten
1 teaspoon Vanilla Extract
3 Cups Oatmeal
1½ Cups Flour, Sifted
1 teaspoon Soda
1 teaspoon Salt

1. Preheat oven to 350 degrees.
2. Cream together butter, brown sugar and granulated sugar.
3. Add eggs, vanilla extract and oatmeal, blending thoroughly.
4. Sift together flour, soda and salt. Add to egg-sugar mixture.
5. Roll dough into long cylinders 1½ inches in diameter. Chill. Slice and place on ungreased baking sheet.
6. Bake at 350 degrees for 10 minutes.

— Mrs. Evelyn Riley

ICY LIME COOLER

Yield: 110 4-Ounce Servings

24 10-Ounce Bottles 7-Up
3½ Gallons + 1 Quart Lime Sherbet

1. Chill 7-Up and pour over lime sherbet to serve.

— Miss Martha Haines

BACON-CHEESE SANDWICHES
OLIVE AND EGG SANDWICHES
CRAB CANAPES   CHINESE CHEWS
OATMEAL-COCONUT CORONETS   DATE-NUT DELIGHTS
CHRISSIE'S CHEEZITS
HOT SPICED APPLE CIDER
Bobbing with Clove-Spiked Oranges

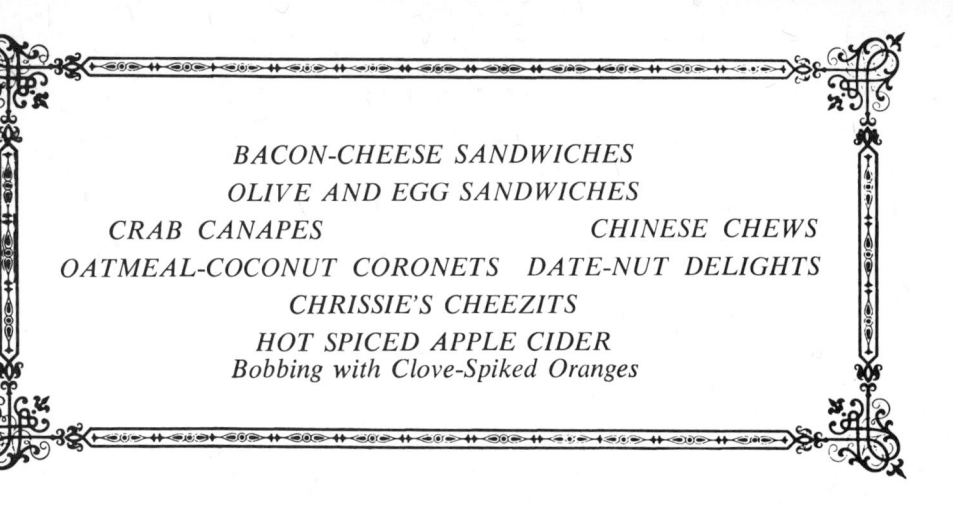

BACON-CHEESE SANDWICHES

Yield: 5 Dozen

1½ Cups American or Swiss Cheese, Grated
1½ Cups Crisp Bacon, Crumbled
3 Tablespoons Dill Pickle, Minced
9 Tablespoons Mayonnaise
Few Drops Onion Juice
Salt and Pepper
5 Dozen Toasted Rounds of White Bread

1. Blend all ingredients together and spread on toasted circles of bread.
2. Garnish with bits of parsley and serve.

— Mrs. Willis A. Haines

OLIVE AND EGG SANDWICHES

Yield: 5 Dozen

30 Hard-Cooked Eggs, Chopped
1½ Cups Stuffed Olives, Chopped
Salad Dressing
Paprika

1. Blend together hard-cooked eggs and olives with sufficent salad dressing to moisten well. Season to taste and spread on triangles of buttered oatmeal bread. Sprinkle with paprika.
2. Garnish platter with tomato roses. (See page 245).

— Mrs. Everett P. Bean

TEAS

CRAB CANAPES

Yield: 5 Dozen

4 teaspoons Horseradish
2 Tablespoons Mayonnaise
2 teaspoons Lemon Juice
Salt and Pepper
2 6½-Ounce Cans Flaked Crabmeat
1 Cup Sharp Cheese, Grated
5 Dozen Toast Strips

1. Blend together horseradish, mayonnaise and lemon juice. Season well.
2. Combine cheese and crabmeat. (You may want to add a little cream for greater spreading consistency.)
3. Spread crab mixture on toast strips and sprinkle with more grated cheese. Serve.

— Mrs. Solon P. Patterson

CHINESE CHEWS

Yield: 4-5 Dozen

2 Cups Sugar, Granulated
1½ Cups Flour, Sifted
2 teaspoons Baking Powder
1 teaspoon Salt
2 Cups Pitted Dates, Diced
2 Cups Pecans, Chopped
4 Eggs, Well-Beaten

1. Preheat oven to 350 degrees. Grease two 9 inch square pans.
2. Mix dry ingredients together. Add dates and nuts and fold in well-beaten eggs. Pour into greased pans.
3. Bake at 350 degrees for 15 minutes. While still warm, cut into tiny squares and sprinkle with Confectioner's sugar.

— Miss Katharine Cutter

OATMEAL COCONUT CORONETS

Yield: 6-7 Dozen

2 Cups Shortening
2 Cups Brown Sugar
2 Cups Sugar, Granulated

TEAS

    4 Eggs
    4 Cups Flour, Sifted
    2 teaspoons Soda
    1 teaspoon Baking Powder
    1 teaspoon Salt
    2 Cups Coconut, Shredded
    4 Cups Oatmeal, Quick-cooking
    2 teaspoons Vanilla Extract

1. Preheat oven to 350 degrees. Grease baking sheet.
2. Cream together shortening, brown sugar and granulated sugar. Add eggs and blend well.
3. Sift together dry ingredients and add to sugar-egg mixture.
4. Blend in coconut, oatmeal and vanilla extract.
5. Drop onto greased baking sheet and bake at 350 degrees for 15-20 minutes or until done.

                      — Mrs. A. E. Greene

DATE-NUT DELIGHTS

Yield: 6-7 Dozen

    1 Cup Butter
    1 Cup Sugar, Granulated
    1 Cup Brown Sugar
    3 Eggs
    4 Cups Flour, Sifted
    1 teaspoon Soda
    1 teaspoon Vanilla Extract

1. Cream together butter, granulated sugar and brown sugar. Add eggs and blend well.
2. Sift flour and soda together and add. Blend in vanilla extract.
3. Roll cooky dough into long rectangle ¼ inch thick.

Filling:

    1 Pound Dates, Chopped
    ½ Cup Sugar, Granulated
    ½ Cup Water
    1 Cup Walnuts, Chopped

TEAS

1. Combine ingredients for filling except nuts and cook until thick. Cool and fold in nuts.
2. Spread date mixture on dough and roll as for jelly roll. Chill overnight.
3. Slice chilled, rolled dough and bake at 350 degrees for 15-20 minutes or until done.

— Mrs. A. E. Greene

CHRISSIE'S CHEEZITS

Yield: 200-250 Each

½ Cup Butter
¼ Pound Old English Cheese
1¼ Cups Flour, Sifted
½ teaspoon Salt
½ Cup Pecans, Ground
½ teaspoon Cayenne Pepper

1. Cream together butter and cheese. Add other ingredients and blend well.
2. Form rolls of dough ½ inch in diameter. Roll in waxed paper and chill thoroughly.
3. Preheat oven to 300 degrees. Slice rolls thin and place on greased baking sheet.
4. Bake at 300 degrees until slightly browned (15-20 minutes).

— Mrs. Ray B. Vaughters

HOT SPICED APPLE CIDER

Yield: 100 4-Ounce Servings

This is marvelous for those chilly, blustery days!

9 46-Ounce Cans Apple Juice
2 teaspoons Cinnamon
2 teaspoons Nutmeg
2 teaspoons Allspice
2 teaspoons Cloves, Ground

1. Blend all ingredients together and heat thoroughly.
2. Pour into punch bowl and bob oranges spiked with cloves in the autumn brew.
3. For an added touch, use cassia sticks as individual stirrers for each punch cup.

— Mrs. McNeill Stokes

CORNED BEEF ROLL-UPS   HERBED EGG SANDWICHES
CAVIAR CHEESE TRIANGLES
TINY JAM TARTS
DIVINITY DREAMS   DATE DELIGHTS
GINGER SPICE DROPS
HOT RUSSIAN TEA

CORNED BEEF ROLL-UPS

Yield: 100 Each

4 Cups Cheddar Cheese, Grated
2 Large Cans Corned Beef
1 Small Jar Mustard
¼ Cup Butter, Melted
50 Thin Slices of White Bread, Trimmed

1. Blend first four ingredients together and spread mixture on thin slices of white bread.
2. Roll up each slice of bread; anchor with a pick and cut into 2 small pieces. Chill overnight.
3. Allow cornucopias to reach room temperature before toasting slowly (at 250 degrees).
4. For an added flair, small corned beef roll-ups could be "tied" with a small strip of pimiento after toasting.

— Mrs. John H. Stone, III

HERBED EGG SANDWICHES

Yield: 4-5 Dozen

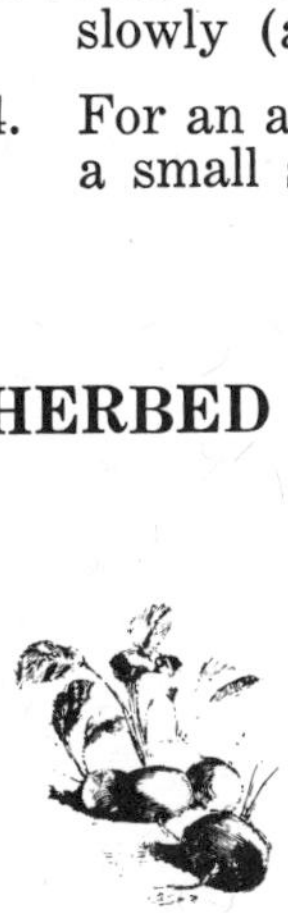

6 Hard-Cooked Eggs, Chopped
½ Cup Radishes, Minced
½ Cup Cucumber, Minced
¼ Cup Parsley, Chopped
¼ Cup Sweet Pickle, Chopped
2 Tablespoons Chives, Minced
Salt and Pepper
Mayonnaise or Salad Dressing
4-5 Dozen Strips of Whole Wheat Bread

TEAS

1. Blend together all ingredients and spread on strips of whole wheat bread.
2. Garnish with tiny gherkin fan or small radish rose.

— Mrs. Harry I. Talbert

CAVIAR-CHEESE SANDWICHES

Yield: 4-5 Dozen

1 8-Ounce Package Cream Cheese, Softened
1 Cup Ripe Olives, Chopped
1 Tablespoon Caviar (Red or Black)
1 Tablespoon Lemon Juice
Heavy Cream
4-5 Dozen Triangles of Toast
Mayonnaise
Stuffed Olives, Sliced

1. Combine first 4 ingredients and moisten with enough cream for spreading consistency.
2. Spread toast triangles with mayonnaise and cover with a thin layer of the caviar mixture.
3. Garnish with a slice of stuffed olive.

— Mrs. Solon P. Patterson

TINY JAM TARTS

Yield: 4 Dozen Tarts

This recipe allows you to use your favorite pastry recipe with a new variation at tea time.

2 Recipes for Double Crust Unbaked Pastry
Choice of Jams or preserves -
Blackberry, Damson, Strawberry

1. Preheat oven to 450 degrees.
2. Roll and cut your pastry with a round biscuit cutter. Press pastry into small bite-size muffin tins.
3. Bake at 450 degrees until slightly browned.
4. Remove from oven and fill with jams of your choice.
5. Return to oven for several minutes to melt preserves. Cool and serve.

— Mrs. Thomas L. Johns, Jr.

DIVINITY DREAMS

Yield: 6 Dozen

8 Cups Sugar, Granulated
2 Cups Light Corn Syrup
2 Cups Hot Water
1 teaspoon Salt
8 Egg Whites, Stiffly Beaten
4 teaspoons Vanilla Extract

1. In a large saucepan combine sugar, corn syrup, water and salt.
2. Cook and stir until sugar dissolves and mixture comes to a boil.
3. Cook to hard ball stage (250 degrees) without stirring.
4. Pour hot syrup very slowly over stiffly beaten egg whites, beating constantly at high speed with electric mixer for about five minutes.
5. Add vanilla extract and continue beating until mixture forms soft peaks and begins to lose its gloss.
6. Drop by teaspoons onto waxed paper.
7. Swirl each candy to a peak.

— Miss Edith Ogden

DATE DELIGHTS

Yield: 4-5 Dozen

2 Cups Sugar, Granulated
3 Cups Flour, Sifted
2 Tablespoons Baking Powder
6 Eggs
2 teaspoons Vanilla Extract
2 Packages Pitted Dates, Chopped
2 Cups Walnuts, Chopped
Confectioner's Sugar

1. Preheat oven to 350 degrees. Grease two 9 inch square pans.
2. Stir together sugar, flour and baking powder. Add eggs and vanilla extract. Blend well.
3. Fold in dates and nuts. Place in two greased pans.
4. Bake at 350 degrees for 30 to 40 minutes.
5. While warm, cut into tiny bars and dust with Confectioner's sugar.

— Mrs. Marvin Gregory, Jr.

GINGER SPICE DROPS

Yield: 6 Dozen

½ Cup Shortening
1 Cup Sugar, Granulated
2 Eggs
⅔ Cup Molasses
4 Cups Flour, Sifted
1 teaspoon Salt
1 teaspoon Soda
2 teaspoons Ginger
½ teaspoon Cinnamon
1 teaspoon Cloves, Ground
1 Cup Water
Pecan Halves

1. Preheat oven to 400 degrees. Grease baking sheet.
2. Cream together shortening and sugar. Add eggs and molasses.
3. Sift together dry ingredients and add alternately with water.
4. Drop by teaspoon and place 2 inches apart on greased baking sheet.
5. Bake at 400 degrees for eight minutes or until done.
6. While slightly warm, frost with Confectioner's icing. (Note directions on package).
7. Top with pecan halves.

— Miss Janet Barnes

HOT RUSSIAN TEA

Yield: 130 4-Ounce Servings

1 7-Ounce Jar of Tang
½ Cup Instant Tea
1¼ Cup Sugar, Granulated
1 teaspoon Cloves, Ground
1 teaspoon Cinnamon
Dash Salt

1. Blend all ingredients together well.
2. Use heaping teaspoon of blended ingredients per cup of boiling water.
3. Garnish with clove-spiked slices of lemon with or without fresh mums piercing the center of each lemon slice. (Note introductory pages to Tea section.)

— Mrs. Jeremiah Luxemburger

HOSTESS' NOTES

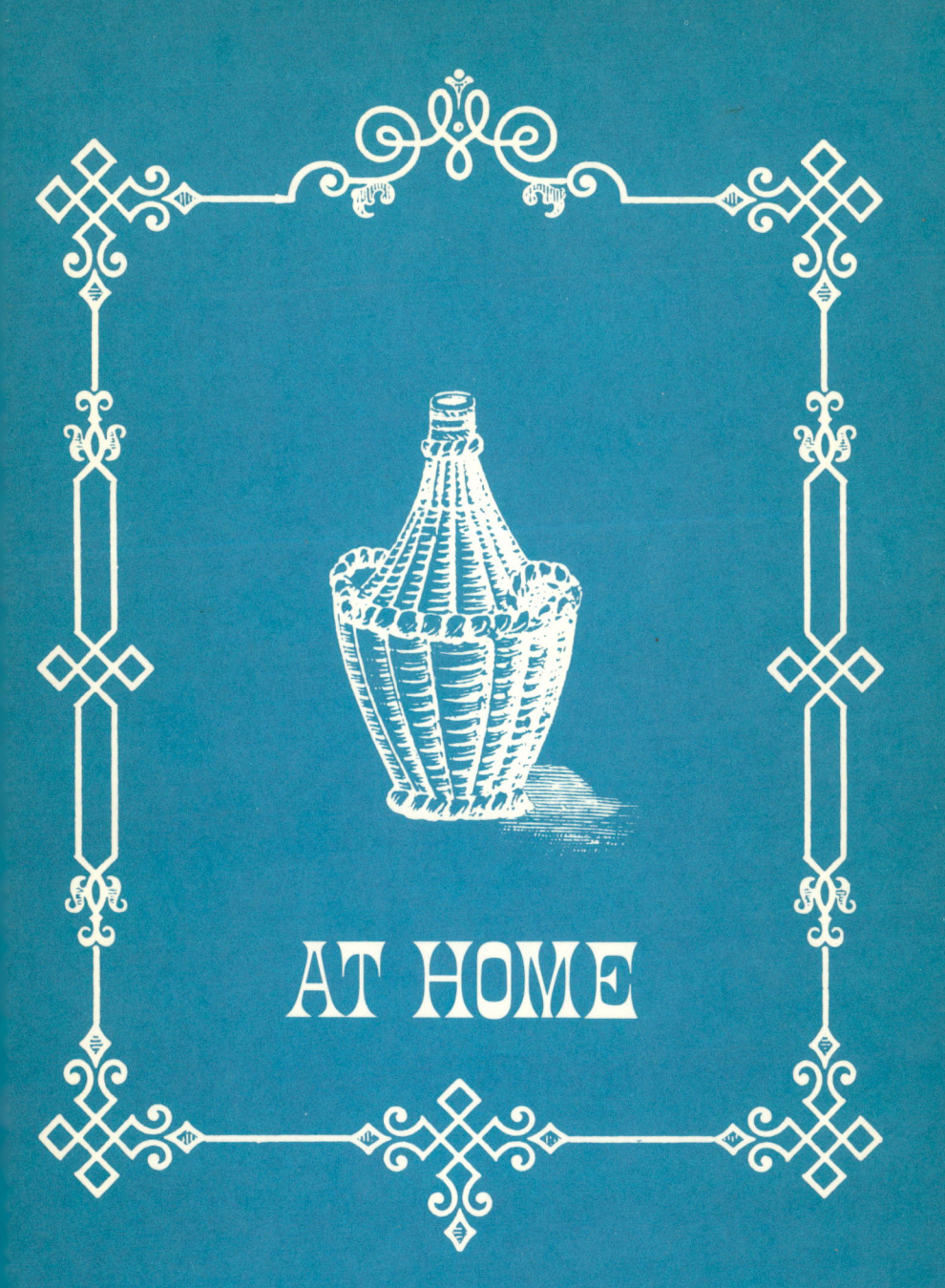

AT HOME

AT HOME

Whether gathered 'round a flickering fireplace on a wintry night with a few friends, or entertaining on a grand scale at a cocktail party, open house or reception, being At Home with friends is an old fashioned custom in Atlanta.

At Home parties are very flexible and can serve many social purposes. In 1877, President Rutherford B. Hayes, the first office-holding president to pay Atlanta a visit, was honored at a reception. A large, relatively good-humored crowd at the Markham House listened to the messenger of good-will trying to establish a friendly feeling between the North and South. President and Mrs. Hayes were also entertained at a brilliant reception at the Executive Mansion by Governor and Mrs. Colquitt.

At Home guest lists may include as few as ten or may be expanded to the limits of available space. Because an At Home party is a stand-up affair in the dining and living room, as well as porch and/or patio, more people can be accommodated. At Home parties may be limited in time with guests stopping by during the hours of late afternoon and early evening. A written note that corresponds with the special occasion is an appropriate invitation.

Receiving Line

If you have guests of honor, the traditional receiving line is in order. For more casual occasions, the host and hostess should circulate most of the time.

Before the turn of the century, elaborate receptions were synonymous with long receiving lines. Fifty Atlanta ladies received with Mrs. Inman, when the Inman Home was the scene of a reception for the financier, Jay Gould in 1891.

A reception can be held just about anywhere. When Labor leader Eugene B. Debs was in town in 1894, he held a reception on the stage of the Columbia Theatre (the old De Gives' Opera House). An impromptu reception was cast for William Jennings Bryan after his arrival in town. Mr. Bryan was taken to the Kimball House; and, as he stepped off the elevator, the dancers of the Nine O'Clocks German Club attending the ball completely surrounded him.

Serving

The dining table is excellent for serving and should be in the center of the dining area so that guests may be served from either side. For an especially large occasion, two serving tables would be most satisfactory. At informal gatherings, lighter snacks may be conveniently spread in small bowls around the entire entertaining area. A fun way to serve hors d'oeuvres at informal cocktail parties is to use garden variety baskets with sturdy handles. The dining table may be covered with your prettiest cloth, or left uncovered, if highly polished. Candelabra or candlesticks cast a genial glow

AT HOME

on your party room. Use your best silver, china and crystal serving dishes for attractively presenting refreshments. Silver flatware is not necessary since only finger foods should be served. At one end of the table, place the punch bowl and cups. A brightly-hued flower tied to the punch ladle will add to the party mood. Improvise, if you find yourself in the predicament of not having a punch bowl. Grandmother's antique washbowl will not only be serviceable, but also a nice conversation piece. A hollowed-out pumpkin or watermelon coated with paraffin provides a unique bowl for a cold punch if the occasion is an informal affair.

A few days in advance of the party, ask friends to serve punch with two or more relief servers. Another friend should be asked to replenish the punch as needed.

CENTERPIECES

In the late 1890's, one Atlanta hostess created a fan on her white cloth with red satin streamers. At the end of each streamer was a full-blown rose and at the confluence of the streamers was the foliage of the roses.

You might enjoy tying bows here, there and everywhere to silver candelabra holding candles of the same shades and set on a lace tablecloth, rippling with rows of narrow satin ribbon.

Single flowers with stems cut short and chased with leaves and fern scattered about the apron of the tablecloth add a gay note to the party fare.

For a captivating focal point, highlight the table with a compote overflowing with lacy petals and luscious grapes centered with translucent plastic rain spraying as gracefully as a celestial fountain.

A silver or china cake basket blossoming with nosegays of fresh violets tied with different shades of pastel ribbon lends a delicate air of formality. You may prefer white roses spotlighted in a silver champagne cooler with silver glitter pasted along the edges of the roses.

For a resplendent arrangement, select pink carnations and fragrant peach blossoms or invert a compote and place a Revere bowl on top, filled with flowers. There is a surprisingly large assortment of tiered compotes and epergnes in shops that can be used in various ways. Arrange with flowers, nosegays, fruits or berries for a rather dramatic setting.

When Governor and Mrs. James M. Smith gave a reception for the legislature in the 1880's at the Mansion, the cakes became the center of attraction. One was a crescent, another a star, while the masterpiece was a tremendous cake embossed with the Georgia Coat of Arms. An anniversary or birthday cake may be decorated in a special way and surrounded with greens or flowers for extra festiveness.

Party Ideas

Before the days of cars in Atlanta, young men enjoyed drives up and down Peachtree in sleek buggies and always ended their outings at the Piedmont Driving Club with mint juleps. Tom Payne often remarked that "the saddest sound in all the world was the suck of the straw in the last drop of the julep." You might enjoy frosty mint juleps at your next party (See page 185).

If you need an extra serving space at your party, convert your ironing board into a bar by making a cover-all of vinyl coordinated with the party's motif. Glue colorful cut-outs of felt to the cloth. By gluing on the designs, different designs may be applied for future parties. You may also cover large pasteboard boxes with brightly-colored contact paper for added serving space.

A geographical-go-round can be fun for those who enjoy traveling. The mood of this party is first set when the guests receive their invitation in the form of a travel ticket or luggage check. For instant atmosphere, you might choose colorful maps and travel posters, small souvenirs grouped for a centerpiece, or place mats and runners made from foreign fabrics. Serve guests Bacardi Cocktail from Cuba, Vermouth Cassis from France, Gimlet from Hong Kong, Planter's Punch from Jamaica, Singapore Gin Sling from Singapore, or a Frozen Daiquiri from Puerto Rico. A wine tasting in lieu of a cocktail party may be especially elegant. Accent your decor with a wealth of grapes and provide a selection of several white and red wines. Decant the white wines first, then the red. Have trays of cheese and fruit with crackers and rounds of pumpernickel bread, followed with a light dessert and sweet wine.

Whatever the reason, whatever the size, At Home parties are fun and merriment electrified by your own personal touch. Share with others a delight in living. Be truly hospitable and have an At Home party soon!

SMOKED TURKEY FINGERS   SLIVERS OF COUNTRY HAM
MARINATED ARTICHOKE HEARTS
AVOCADO APPETEASERS   SWEET POTATO CRISPIES
PARSLIED PECAN CHEESE BALL
CRAB DIP DIVINE   ANCHOVY DIP
CRISP VEGETABLE FLOWERS
TWENTY-FOUR HOUR COCKTAILS

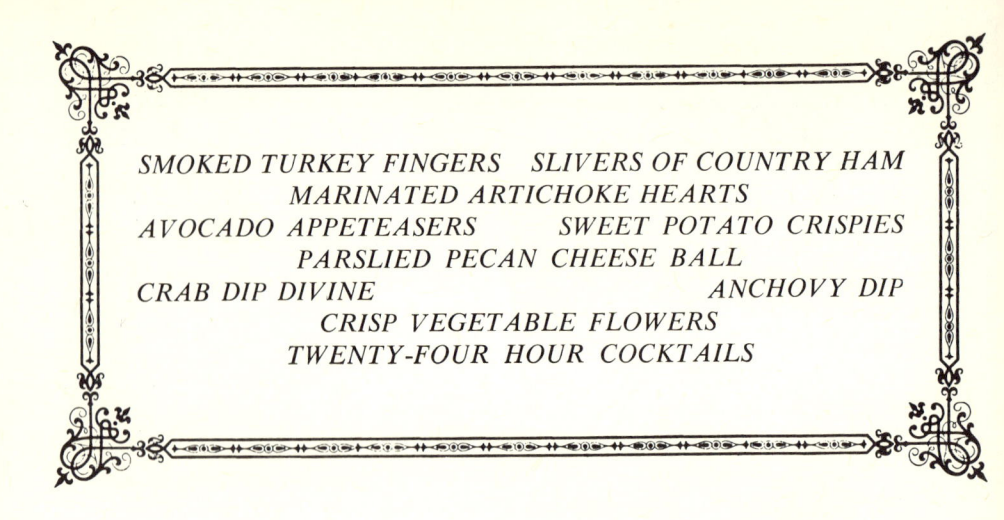

SMOKED TURKEY FINGERS

Yield: 100 each

100 Thin Slices Smoked Turkey
1 8-Ounce Package Cream Cheese
Watercress

1. Spread thin slices of smoked turkey with cream cheese. Roll up each slice and tuck watercress into one end. Sprinkle with paprika and serve.

— Mrs. E. E. Paschal, Jr.

BEATEN BISCUITS

Yield: 6 Dozen Tiny Biscuits

6 Cups Flour, Sifted
⅔ Cup Butter
1 teaspoon Sugar, Granulated
2 Cups Cold Water
1 teaspoon Salt

1. Preheat oven to 325 degrees.
2. Blend together all ingredients. Knead for 15 minutes.
3. Beat vigorously until dough is soft.
4. Roll dough to ½ inch thickness on lightly floured board. Cut dough with miniature biscuit cutter.
5. Pierce biscuits with fork and bake on ungreased baking sheet at 325 degrees for 30 minutes.
6. Serve with slivers of country ham.

— Mrs. Terrell Burnley

GOLDEN HAM SAUCE

Yield: 2 Cups

2 Cups Mayonnaise
3 Tablespoons Prepared Mustard

1. Blend ingredients together and serve with baked ham and slices of party rye bread or miniature beaten biscuits.

— Mrs. Steve J. Dixon

MARINATED ARTICHOKE HEARTS

Yield: 60 Servings

20 Packages (9 Ounces Each) Frozen Artichoke Hearts
10 Envelopes (5/8 ounce) Parmesan Salad Dressing Mix
2 1/4 Cups Lemon Juice
5 Cups Salad Oil

1. Cook artichokes according to package directions. Drain and chill.
2. Combine Dressing Mix, lemon juice, and salad oil.
3. Pour over artichokes and chill at least 2 hours. Serve with individual picks.

— Mrs. Thomas I. Sangster

AVOCADO APPETEASERS

Thin Slices of Avocado
Lemon Juice
Curry Powder

1. Chill and marinate avocado slices in lemon juice.
2. Sprinkle with curry powder and serve with frilly picks.

— Mrs. Robert B. Ansley, Jr.

SWEET POTATO CRISPIES

Yield: 5-6 Dozen

5 Pounds Sweet Potatoes
6 Tablespoons Butter
Salt
1/4 Cup Orange Juice
Cornfakes, Crushed

1. Preheat deep fat fryer to 365 degrees.
2. Scrub and boil potatoes. Peel and mash. Add other ingredients.
3. When cool, shape into small balls. Roll in crushed cornflakes and fry in deep fat at 365 degrees for 3 to 4 minutes or until crisp.

— Mrs. Everett P. Bean

AT HOME

PARSLIED PECAN CHEESE BALL

Yield: 2 Cheese Balls

2 Pounds New York Sharp Cheese, Grated
1 Pound Roquefort Cheese
3 8-Ounce Packages Cream Cheese
4 Cloves Garlic, Minced
¼ Cup Worcestershire Sauce
1 Cup Pecans, Ground
Snipped Parsley

1. Grate New York Sharp Cheese into large bowl and add other cheeses.

2. Let soften an hour or so. Add garlic and Worcestershire Sauce. Blend well and shape into ball.

3. Place ground pecans on waxed paper. Just before serving, roll ball in ground pecans until cheese ball is completely coated.

4. Then roll in finely chopped parsley until it is a colorful green ball.

5. Serve surrounded by crackers of varying shapes.

— Mrs. Ben Y. Cooper

CRAB DIP DIVINE

Yield: 3 Cups

1 12-Ounce Bottle Catsup
1 12-Ounce Bottle Chili Sauce
¼ Cup Horseradish
Juice of 1 Lemon
Dash Tabasco
Dash Worcestershire Sauce
2 6½-Ounce Cans Flaked Crabmeat

1. Blend together all ingredients. Chill. Serve in pineapple shell with crisp crackers or similar foundations.

— Miss Marjorie Chisholm

AT HOME

ANCHOVY DIP

Yield: 2 Cups

1 Cup Mayonnaise
1 8-Ounce Package Cream Cheese, Softened
3 Tablespoons Anchovy Paste
⅓ Cup Parsley Leaves, Minced
3 Tablespoons Chives, Frozen
1 Clove Garlic, Pressed
1 Tablespoon Lemon Juice
3 Tablespoons Tarragon Vinegar
Salt and Pepper

1. Blend together well mayonnaise and softened cream cheese.
2. Add other ingredients and blend well. Serve with crisp vegetable flowers.

— Mrs. John C. Hopkins, Sr.

CRISP VEGETABLE FLOWERS

Radish Flowers
Cauliflowerets
Carrot Curls
Scored Cucumber Slices
Celery Curls

1. Place each of the above in iced water and chill for several hours until crisp.
2. Serve tucked in crushed ice in large crystal bowl.
3. Serve with anchovy dip.

— Mrs. John C. Hopkins, Sr.

TWENTY-FOUR HOUR COCKTAIL

Yield: 100 4-Ounce Servings

5 Dozen Lemons, Juice, Seeds and Rind
2¼ Cups Sugar, Granulated
1 Gallon Iced Tea
1 Gallon Whiskey

1. Dissolve sugar in tea. Add whiskey, lemon juice, seeds and grated rind. Chill 24 hours.
2. Strain and serve in wine glasses over chipped ice or dilute with water and serve as cocktail.

— Mrs. C. A. Rogers

MEATBALLS EXTRAORDINAIRE SHERRIED CLAMS
DANISH OPEN-FACE APPETIZERS
BACON WRAPPED TIDBITS CUCUMBER BITES
CARAWAY MOUND OF CHEESE
DOUBLE DIPPER CHEESE GREEN GODDESS DIP
PEPPERY SPICED NUTS
SHANGRI-LA

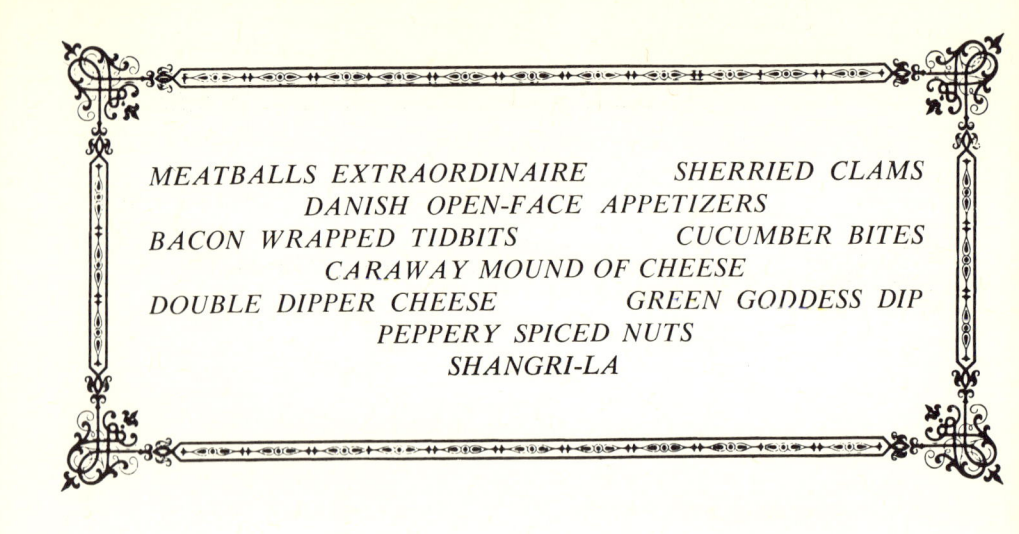

MEATBALLS EXTRAORDINAIRE

Yield: 100 Each

4 Pounds Ground Beef
1 Egg, Slightly Beaten
1 Large Onion, Grated
Salt
1 12-Ounce Bottle Chili Sauce
1 12-Ounce Jar Grape Jelly
Juice of 1 Lemon

1. Blend together meat, egg, onion, and salt. Form into 100 small meatballs.
2. Combine chili sauce, jelly, and lemon juice. Pour over meatballs and simmer in electric skillet for one hour.
3. Serve in heated chafing dish.

— Mrs. James DeSando

SHERRIED CLAMS

Yield: 3 Cups

2 Small Onions, Diced
2 Medium Bell Peppers, Diced
2 Tablespoons Butter
2 7½-Ounce Cans Minced Clams, Drained
½ Pound Mild Cheese, Grated
½ Cup Catsup
2 Tablespoons Dry Sherry
Dash Cayenne Pepper

1. Saute onion and Bell pepper in butter until lightly browned.
2. Add remaining ingredients and simmer over medium heat until cheese melts completely. Serve in scalloped sea shell.
3. Garnish center with sprig of parsley and serve on crackers of varying shapes.

— Miss Marjorie Chisholm

DANISH OPEN-FACE APPETIZERS

This is one appetizer that your own imagination is used to great advantage!

White, Whole Wheat, Pumpernickel or Rye Bread, Sliced
Smoked Salmon
Baked Ham, Sliced
Tai-Tai Shrimp
Turkey, Sliced
Cream Cheese
Hard-Cooked Eggs
Radishes
Carrot Curls
Parsley
Bleu Cheese
Pickles
Pitted Ripe Olives

1. Vary the shapes of bread that are used, i.e. triangles, strips, rounds, hearts, etc. Place each suggestion on different breads for more variety.
2. Smoked salmon may be combine with hard-cooked egg slices, ripe olives or radish fans and garnished with parsley.
3. Ham may be used in combination with pickle slices and Swiss cheese or carrot curls.
4. Spread other canapes with butter or cream cheese and cover with tiny Tai-Tai shrimp. A simple sprig of parsley as a garnish is sufficient. A bit of black caviar would also be grand.
5. Sliced turkey is an attractive color and taste combination with some of the darker breads. Top with Bleu Cheese, radish and ripe olive slices.
6. To serve, arrange on platter with bowl of cherry tomatoes nestled in bed of fresh parsley.

— Mrs. McNeill Stokes

AT HOME

BACON WRAPPED TIDBITS

Cooked Shrimp
Oysters
Stuffed Olives
Pickled Onions
Sauteed Chicken Livers

1. Preheat broiler unit of range.
2. Select any of these tidbits. Wrap in thin strip of bacon. Secure with picks. Broil under moderate heat until bacon is crisp.

— Mrs. Thomas I. Sangster

CUCUMBER BITES

Yield: 4 Dozen

4 Large Cucumbers (Peeled if desired)
4 Cups Mayonnaise
2 Cups Sour Cream
1 Cup Carrots, Shredded
¾ Cup Radishes, Diced
¼ Cup Parsley, Chopped
Salt and Pepper

1. Slice cucumber into ½ inch horizontal slices and hollow out ¼ inch, horizontally. Chill.
2. Chop pulp and combine with remaining ingredients. Fill slices with mixture.
3. Remainder may be used as dip.

— Mrs. John C. Hopkins, Jr.

CARAWAY MOUND OF CHEESE

Yield: 2 Cheese Mounds

This is a zippy cheese spread your company will always remember!

2 Cups Butter, Softened
12 Ounces Cream Cheese
2 teaspoons Prepared Mustard
2 teaspoons Paprika
2 Tablespoons Caraway Seed

AT HOME

1. Combine all ingredients until smooth. More paprika may be added if desired. Mould and serve.

— Mrs. Harry G. Haisten, Jr.

DOUBLE DIPPER CHEESE

Yield: 2 Cups

⅔ Cup Roquefort Cheese
4 3-Ounce Packages Cream Cheese
2 Tablespoons Parsley, Chopped
¼ Cup Green Onions, Chopped
Dash Cayenne Pepper
Dash Worcestershire Sauce
4 Heaping Tablespoons Mayonnaise
½ Cup Sour Cream
½ teaspoon Horseradish
Salt

1. Blend cheeses together.
2. Add remaining ingredients and blend well. Set aside and do NOT refrigerate.
3. Serve with potato chips or other crisp foundations.

— Mrs. John C. Hopkins, Jr.

GREEN GODDESS DIP

Yield: 2 Cups

Pretty to serve in flower of red cabbage surrounded by other crisp fresh vegetables such as squash, carrots, cucumbers, radishes, cauliflower and celery.

2 Soft, Ripe Avocados
2 Cups Sour Cream
½ Cup Mayonnaise
1 teaspoon Salt
1 Cup Parsley, Minced
½ Cup Green Onions, Diced

AT HOME

1. Mash avocados well. Add sour cream, mayonnaise and salt. Blend well.
2. Fold in minced parsley and diced green onions.
3. Serve with sliced raw vegetables as mentioned above.

— Mrs. Thomas I. Sangster

PEPPERY SPICED NUTS

Yield: 4 Cups

2 Tablespoons Butter, Melted
1 Pound Pecan or Walnut Halves
2 teaspoons Worcestershire Sauce
Dash Hot Pepper Sauce
½ teaspoon Salt
⅛ teaspoon Pepper

1. Preheat oven to 325 degrees.
2. In skillet saute pecan or walnut halves in butter until hot. Add remaining ingredients.
3. Arrange nuts in shallow pan and bake at 325 degrees for 20 minutes.

— Mrs. E. E. Paschal, Jr.

SHANGRI-LA

Yield: 100 4-Ounce Servings

3 Gallons Dry Red Wine, Chilled
1 Dozen Lemons, Sliced
2 Dozen Oranges, Sliced
3 Cups Sugar, Granulated
1 Gallon Sparkling Water, Chilled

1. Slice lemon and oranges and place in punch bowl.
2. Pour sugar over fruit and let stand one hour.
3. When ready to serve, add wine and sparkling water. Add ice and serve.

— Miss Martha Haines

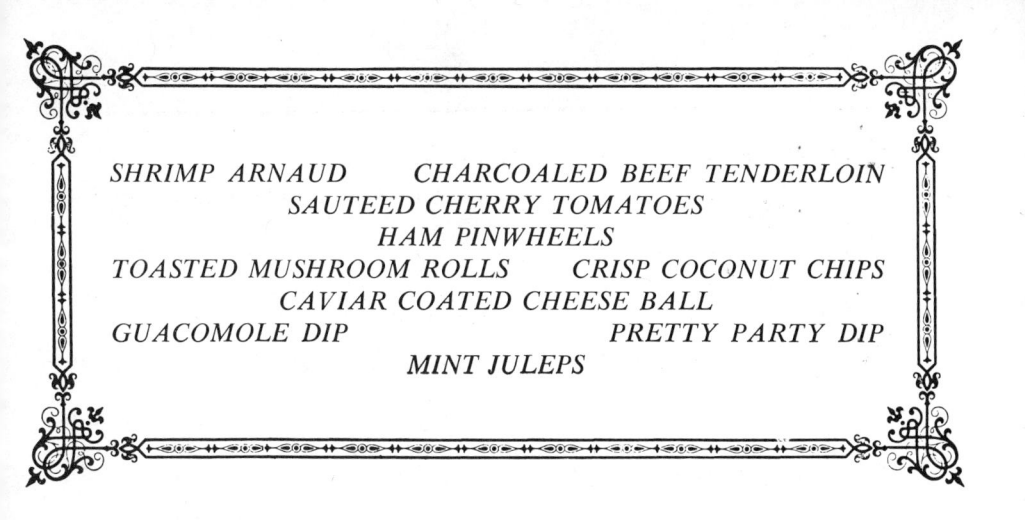

SHRIMP ARNAUD   CHARCOALED BEEF TENDERLOIN
SAUTEED CHERRY TOMATOES
HAM PINWHEELS
TOASTED MUSHROOM ROLLS   CRISP COCONUT CHIPS
CAVIAR COATED CHEESE BALL
GUACOMOLE DIP   PRETTY PARTY DIP
MINT JULEPS

SHRIMP ARNAUD

Yield: 60 Servings

1½ Cups Vinegar
1½ Cups Salad Oil
1½ Cups Chili Sauce
1½ teaspoons Garlic Salt
2 Tablespoons Prepared Mustard
6 Pounds Shrimp, Cooked (30 per pound)

1. Blend together vinegar, salad oil, chili sauce, garlic salt and mustard.
2. Add shrimp and toss lightly to coat with sauce. Chill in marinade overnight.
3. Serve in giant scalloped sea shell with individual picks.

— Mrs. Thomas I. Sangster

CHARCOALED BEEF TENDERLOIN

Yield: 100 Servings

4 Whole Fillets of Beef (2-3 Pounds Each)
¼ Cup Worcestershire Sauce
¼ Cup Wine Vinegar
½ Cup A-1 Sauce
¼ Cup Brown Sugar
⅔ Cup Catsup
2 teaspoons Accent
Dash Cayenne Pepper

AT HOME

1. Blend all ingredients together well.
2. Pour marinade over fillets wrapped in heavy duty aluminum foil. Chill overnight.
3. For an added delicacy, place foil-wrapped fillets on grill over low coals and hickory smoke, covered for 10-12 minutes for rare beef. Baste with marinade in foil occasionally.
4. Slice thinly and garnish platter with fresh mushroom caps and parsley.

— Mrs. Al Jennings

SPICY BEEF SPREAD

Yield: 1½-2 Cups

1 8-Ounce Package Cream Cheese, Softened
½ Cup Butter, Softened
¼ Cup Mayonnaise
¼ Cup Horseradish

1. Blend cream cheese and butter together until light and fluffy.
2. Blend in mayonnaise and horseradish. Serve with party rounds and roasted beef.

— Mrs. Charles C. Ford

SAUTEED CHERRY TOMATOES

This is a delightful treat for that extra special party.

Cherry Tomatoes
¼ Cup Butter
   (per Small Basket of Cherry Tomatoes)
Salt

1. Rinse a small basket of cherry tomatoes, drain well and remove stems.
2. Saute tomatoes in skillet with butter. Shake (do NOT stir) skillet vigorously until the tomato skins are slightly wrinkled.
3. Season to taste and serve.

— Mrs. Dewey Weaver

HAM PINWHEELS

Yield: 10 Dozen

1 Pound Roquefort Cheese
2 8-Ounce Packages Cream Cheese
1 Cup Butter
16 Slices Broiled Ham

1. Blend together Roquefort cheese, cream cheese and butter the day before serving.
2. Spread each slice of ham with cheese mixture and roll as for jelly roll.
3. Wrap in waxed paper and chill.
4. Just before serving, slice ham rolls thinly crosswise.
5. Arrange one pinwheel on each round of bread.

— Mrs. Paul Hanes

TOASTED MUSHROOM ROLLS

Yield: 13-14 Dozen

Mushroom lovers delight! These are true delicacies and can be made far in advance to freeze for future use.

2 Pounds Fresh Mushrooms, Diced
1 Cup Butter
¾ Cup Flour
1 Tablespoon Salt
1 teaspoon Accent
4 Cups Light Cream
2½ Tablespoons Chives, Minced
4 teaspoons Lemon Juice
4 Sandwich Loaves of White Bread, Trimmed

1. Peel mushrooms and dice. Saute for five minutes in butter.
2. Blend in flour, salt and accent. Stir in light cream and simmer until thick.
3. Add minced chives and lemon juice. Blend well.
4. Remove crusts from bread and roll slices thin. Spread with mixture and roll up.
5. Pack and freeze if desired.
6. When ready to serve, defrost, cut each roll in half and toast on all sides in 400 degree oven for about 20 minutes.

— Mrs. J. David Bansley

CRISP COCONUT CHIPS

Fresh Coconut, Sliced Thinly
Melted Butter
Salt

AT HOME

1. Preheat broiling unit of range.
2. Slice fresh coconut into thin chips and toss lightly with melted butter.
3. Place chips on baking sheet and broil golden brown.
4. Sprinkle lightly with salt and serve warm.

— Mrs. Jordan Stokes, III

CAVIAR COATED CHEESE BALL

Yield: 2 Cheese Balls

2 Pounds Cheddar Cheese, Grated
3 8-Ounce Packages Cream Cheese
4 Jars Pimiento Cheese
2 teaspoons Cayenne Pepper
2 Onions, Grated
2 Cloves Garlic, Minced
2 Tablespoons Lea and Perrin's Sauce
2 Tablespoons Prepared Mustard
6 Tablespoons Durkees' Dressing
Salt
Black Caviar

1. Oil moulds. Blend all ingredients except caviar together.
2. Place mixture in 2 oiled moulds and chill well.
3. Spread moulds with black caviar and serve.

— Mrs. David Grundpest, Jr.

GUACOMOLE DIP

4 Ripe Avocados
2 teaspoons Onion Juice
2 Ripe Tomatoes, Diced and Drained
2 teaspoons Lemon Juice
French Dressing
Salt
Cayenne Pepper

1. Sieve avocado. Add remaining ingredients.
2. Add French dressing until desired consistency is obtained. Serve with crisp crackers, potato chips or similar foundations.

— Mrs. Byford E. Wagstaff

AT HOME

PRETTY PARTY DIP

Yield: 1½ Cups

1 8-Ounce Package Cream Cheese
2 Tablespoons Light Cream
2 Tablespoons French Dressing
⅓ Cup Catsup
1 Tablespoon Onion, Grated
¼ teaspoon Salt

1. Blend together cream cheese and cream until smooth.
2. Add French dressing, catsup, onion, and salt.
3. Blend well and serve with your choice of foundations.

— Mrs. Donavan N. Staton

MINT JULEPS

Yield: 1 Serving

Deep in the heart of Dixie!

Confectioner's Sugar
4 Sprigs of Mint
½ teaspoon Sugar, Granulated
Dash of Water
3 Ounces Bourbon
Maraschino Cherries with Stems

1. Place Mint Julep Cups in freezer to frost. Ring top with Confectioner's sugar.
2. Crush 4 sprigs of mint with puddler and place in frosted Mint Julep Cup.
3. Add granulated sugar and dash of water.
4. Pack Mint Julep Cup with shaved ice and add 3 ounces of Bourbon.
5. Garnish with fresh sprigs of mint and stemmed Maraschino cherry. Add straw for sipping Southern style.

- - Mr. Byford E. Wagstaff

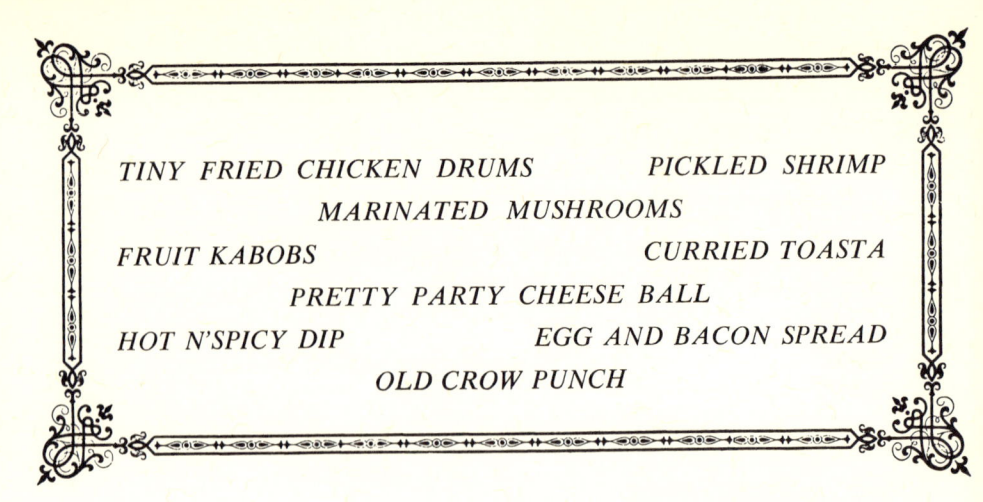

TINY FRIED CHICKEN DRUMS   PICKLED SHRIMP
MARINATED MUSHROOMS
FRUIT KABOBS   CURRIED TOASTA
PRETTY PARTY CHEESE BALL
HOT N'SPICY DIP   EGG AND BACON SPREAD
OLD CROW PUNCH

TINY FRIED CHICKEN DRUMS

Yield: 150 Each

This is Southern Fried Chicken turned elegante!

150 Plump Part of Chicken Wings (Chicken Drums)
Eggs
Evaporated Milk
Seasoned Flour
Vegetable Oil

1. Preheat oil in deep fat fryer to 360 degrees.
2. Blend together well 2 eggs for every 13 ounce can of evaporated milk. Dip chicken pieces in egg-milk mixture.
3. Dredge chicken with flour and repeat process once more.
4. Place in 365 degree oil and fry until golden brown.
5. Drain and serve in heated chafing dish.

— Mrs. McNeill Stokes

PICKLED SHRIMP

Yield: 120-150 each

4 to 5 Pounds Fresh or Frozen Shrimp in Shells (30 Shrimp per Pound)
1 Cup Celery Leaves
½ Cup Mixed Pickling Spices
2 Tablespoons Salt
4 Cups Onion, Sliced
14 Bay Leaves
3 Cups Vegetable Oil

AT HOME

	1½ Cups White Vinegar
	6 Tablespoons Capers and Juice
	5 teaspoons Celery Seed
	1 Tablespoon Salt
	Few Drops Hot Pepper Sauce
(Optional)	Bell Pepper Pieces
(Optional)	Pineapple Chunks

1. In a large kettle, cover shrimp with boiling water. Add celery leaves, pickling spices and salt.
2. Cover and simmer for five minutes. Drain, peel and devein shrimp under cold water.
3. Alternate shrimp and onion in large shallow dish.
4. Combine bay leaves, vegetable oil, vinegar, capers and juice, celery seed, salt and hot pepper sauce. Blend together well and pour over cooked shrimp.
5. Cover and chill at least 24 hours, spooning marinade over shrimp occasionally. Serve individually or as appetizer kabobs by spearing a shrimp, a piece of Bell pepper, and a pineapple chunk.

— Miss Emily Stevens

MARINATED MUSHROOMS

Yield: 120 Each

120 Fresh Button Mushrooms
20 Lemons (5 Cups Lemon Juice)
2½ Cups Olive Oil
Salt and Pepper

1. Wash and peel mushrooms.
2. Place 24 button mushrooms per shallow dish and pour the juice of 4 lemons and ½ cup olive oil over them.
3. Marinate for at least 2 hours.
4. Drain and serve with individual cocktail picks.

— Miss Janet Barnes

FRUIT KABOBS

Fresh or Frozen Melon Balls
Whole Strawberries
Pineapple Chunks
Banana Slices
½ Grapefruit

AT HOME

1. Use half of grapefruit (cut side down) on a plate or tray to arrange kabobs.
2. Place fruit on skewers and stick into grapefruit with a few mint leaves tucked in here and there.

— Mrs. Dewey Weaver

CURRIED TOASTA

Yield: 100 each

100 Thin Slices of White Bread, Trimmed
1 Cup Butter, Softened
Curry Powder
Melted Butter

1. Preheat oven to 350 degrees.
2. Trim crusts from white bread and roll slices flat with rolling pin.
3. Blend together softened butter and curry powder to taste.
4. Spread bread slices with curry powder mixture and roll tightly.
5. Place rolls on a baking sheet, seam side down, brush them with melted butter, and bake at 350 degrees, turning them several times until lightly browned.

— Mrs. E. E. Paschal, Jr.

PRETTY PARTY CHEESE BALL

Yield: 2 Cheese Balls

1 Cup Walnuts, Chopped
6 to 10 Ounces Roquefort Cheese
2 8-Ounce Packages Cream Cheese
½ teaspoon Garlic Salt
(Optional) 2 Tablespoons Bell Pepper, Chopped
(Optional) 2 Tablespoons Pimiento, Chopped

1. Preheat oven to 350 degrees. Spread chopped walnuts in shallow pan and toast, stirring occasionally, until golden brown (approximately 8 to 10 minutes).
2. Have cheeses at room temperature and blend together well. Stir in garlic salt, Bell pepper and pimiento if desired.
3. Chill until firm and shape into ball. Roll in toasted walnuts.
4. Chill until serving time. Serve with crisp crackers.

— Mrs. Louise Armour Knowlton

AT HOME

HOT N' SPICY DIP

Yield: 2 Cups

1 Large Onion, Diced
1 Large Bell Pepper, Diced
½ Cup Butter
1 Can Ro-tel Tomatoes with Hot Peppers
2 Cans Fried Beans
2 Rolls Nippy Cheese
Salt and Pepper

1. Saute onion and Bell pepper in butter until soft.
2. Add tomatoes and blend well. Add beans and melt cheese into mixture. Season to taste.
3. Serve with a variety of bland foundations, such as bugles, etc.

— Miss Sidney Dickson

EGG AND BACON SPREAD

Yield: 1½ Cups

16 Hard-Cooked Eggs, Minced
12 Slices Crisp Bacon, Crumbled
4 teaspoons Horseradish
4 teaspoons Onion, Minced
4 teaspoons Worcestershire Sauce
1 Cup Mayonnaise
4 teaspoons Salt

1. Combine all ingredients and chill until serving time.
2. Serve with a choice of crackers, etc.

— Miss Rita Burnley

OLD CROW PUNCH

Yield: 110 4-Ounce Servings

2 12-Ounce Cans Frozen Lemonade, Diluted
2 12-Ounce Cans Frozen Orange Juice, Diluted
1⅓ Cups Maraschino Cherry Juice
2 Fifths of Bourbon
2 Quarts Sparkling Water
4 Quarts Ginger Ale

1. Blend first three ingredients together and chill.
2. Before serving, add last three ingredients to chilled mixture.
3. Float iced fruit ring (note introductory pages to Tea Section) in bowl.

— Mrs. David Love

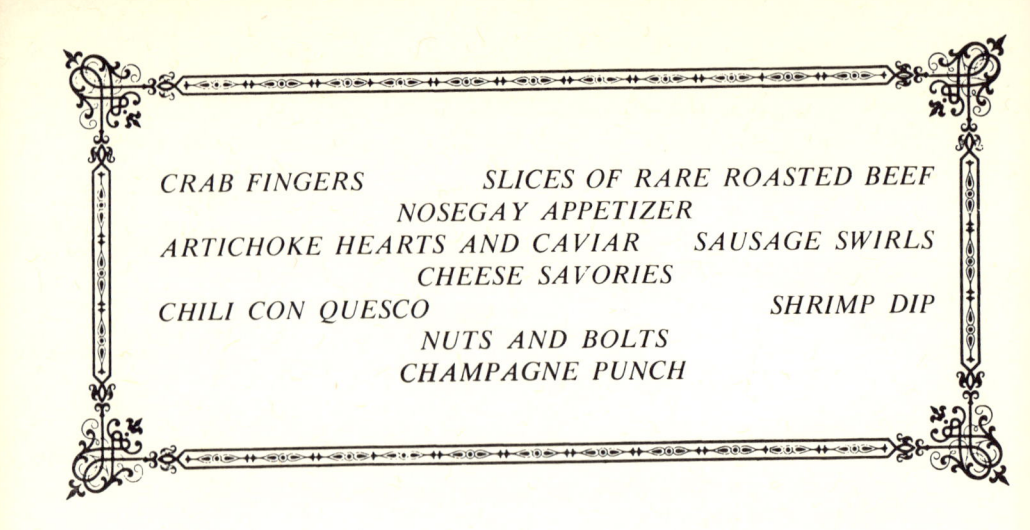

CRAB FINGERS   SLICES OF RARE ROASTED BEEF
                NOSEGAY APPETIZER
     ARTICHOKE HEARTS AND CAVIAR   SAUSAGE SWIRLS
                  CHEESE SAVORIES
CHILI CON QUESCO   SHRIMP DIP
                   NUTS AND BOLTS
                 CHAMPAGNE PUNCH

CRAB FINGER DIP

Yield: 2 Cups

2 Cups Chili Sauce or Catsup
3 Tablespoons Fresh Frozen Horseradish

1. In blender, blend together chili sauce and horseradish.
2. Serve with crab fingers for something extra delicious!

— Mrs. Charles C. Ford

SPICY BEEF SPREAD

(See page 182)

NOSEGAY APPETIZER

Sharp Cheddar Cheese Cubes
Bottled Cooked Salad Dressing
Snipped Parsley
Frankfurters
Sharp Cheese Spread
Ripe Olives
French Dressing
Cornucopias

1. Arrange the following on white styrofoam circle (9 inches in diameter and 1 inch thick).
2. Spear 17 cubes of sharp cheddar cheese and dip half of each cube into salad dressing and then into snipped parsley. Place in center of styrofoam circle.

AT HOME

3. Slice each frankfurter in half lengthwise and spread cut sides with sharp cheese spread. Place sides back together. Cut into half inch pieces and arrange on picks around cheese cubes on circle.

4. Spear ripe olives that have been tossed in French Dressing and arrange around frankfurters on circle.

Cornucopias:

19 Thin Slices of Salami or Cervelat
Cream Cheese, Softened
Melted Butter
Hot Pepper Sauce

1. Slash each slice of salami or cervelat to center and roll each slice into a cone. Fasten with a pick.

2. Blend together cream cheese, melted butter and hot pepper sauce until right consistency and taste is obtained.

3. Fill each salami cone with cream cheese mixture.

4. Insert tip of cone that has been pierced with pick into outer ring of nosegay.

5. Serve on platter with large doily.

— Mrs. Tom Slaughter

ARTICHOKE HEARTS AND CAVIAR

Artichoke Hearts
Black Caviar
Lemon Juice
Hard-Cooked Egg Yolk, Sieved

1. Fill artichoke hearts with black caviar and sprinkle with drops of lemon juice.

2. Garnish with sieved hard-cooked egg.

— Mrs. Byford E. Wagstaff

SAUSAGE SWIRLS

Yield: 6 Dozen

This is another grand do-ahead recipe. Freeze and bake just before serving.

4 Cups Flour, Sifted
¼ Cup Cornmeal
¼ Cup Sugar, Granulated
2 Tablespoons Baking Powder
1 teaspoon Salt
⅔ Cup Vegetable Oil
⅔ Cup Milk
2 Pounds Hot Sausage

1. Preheat oven to 350 degrees.
2. Sift dry ingredients together. Blend in vegetable oil. Add enough milk to make a stiff dough.
3. Roll out thin on lightly floured board. Spread on sausage and roll up lengthwise.
4. Chill well and slice. Bake at 350 degrees for 15-20 minutes.

— Miss Suzanne Burnley

CHEESE SAVORIES

Yield: 8 Dozen

8 Cups Sharp Cheddar Cheese, Grated
1 Pound Butter
½ teaspoon Salt
3 Cups Flour, Sifted
2 teaspoons Celery Seed
Paprika

1. Preheat oven to 400 degrees.
2. -Cream together butter and cheese. Add dry ingredients and blend well.

3. Form into 1 inch balls and place on ungreased cooky sheet 2 inches apart.
4. Press flat with fork and sprinkle with paprika. Chill for several hours.
5. Bake at 400 degrees for 10 minutes and serve hot.

— Mrs. Ruth D. Williams

CHILI CON QUESO

Yield: 2-3 Cups

1 Pound Velveeta Cheese
1 Large Can Tomatoes, Drained
1 Can Hot Green Chili
Onion Juice

1. Melt cheese in double boiler. Add tomatoes and green chili.
2. Add a little onion juice to taste and serve with crisp potato chips or varied shapes of crackers.
   (If an even hotter flavor is desired, use two cans of green chili.)

— Mrs. Bernard L. Shackleford

SHRIMP DIP

Yield: 2 Cups

1 Can Frozen Shrimp Soup
¾ Cup Shrimp, Diced
1 8-Ounce Package Cream Cheese, Softened
¼ teaspoon Curry Powder
2 teaspoons Lemon Juice
½ Cup Stuffed Olives, Chopped
¼ teaspoon Garlic Salt
Salt and Pepper

1. Thaw soup in a bowl with diced shrimp. Add softened cream cheese.
2. Add the remaining ingredients and blend well.
3. Chill at least 2 hours before serving.
4. Serve with spicy corn chips.

— Mrs. J. C. Stephenson

AT HOME

NUTS AND BOLTS

1 1-Pound Can Mixed Nuts
4 teaspoons Garlic Salt
4 teaspoons Celery Salt
4 teaspoons Worcestershire Sauce
2 teaspoons Tabasco Sauce
¾ Cup Butter, Melted
1 Box each of:
    Corn Chex
    Wheat Chex
    Rice Chex
    Cheese Nips
    Pretzels

1. Preheat oven to 200 degrees.

2. Blend together thoroughly melted butter, garlic salt, celery salt, Worcestershire Sauce, and Tabasco sauce.

3. Combine dry ingredients in pan and add butter mixture. Mix well and bake at 200 degrees for 2 hours, stirring every 15 minutes.

— Mrs. C. Y. Bumgarner

CHAMPAGNE PUNCH

Yield: 100 4-Ounce Servings

8 Quarts Champagne, Chilled
2 6-Ounce Cans Frozen Orange Juice, Undiluted
1 6-Ounce Can Frozen Limeade, Undiluted
2 Quarts Soda, Chilled
2 Quarts 7-up, Chilled
1 Pint Apricot Brandy, Chilled

1. Blend all ingredients together.

2. Float iced moulds of fruit or fresh flowers in punch bowl. (See Introductory pages to Tea Section.)

— Miss Marjorie Chisholm

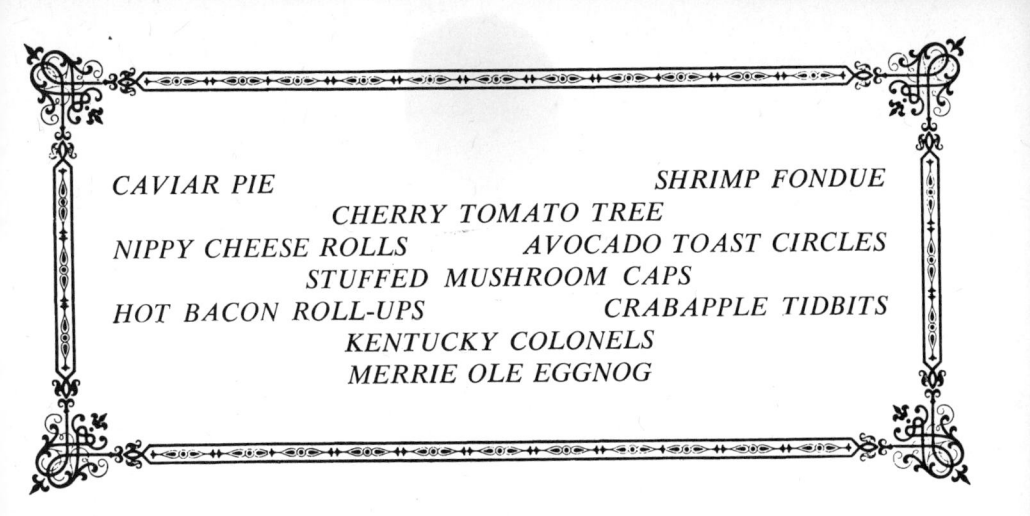

CAVIAR PIE   SHRIMP FONDUE
         CHERRY TOMATO TREE
NIPPY CHEESE ROLLS   AVOCADO TOAST CIRCLES
         STUFFED MUSHROOM CAPS
HOT BACON ROLL-UPS   CRABAPPLE TIDBITS
             KENTUCKY COLONELS
             MERRIE OLE EGGNOG

CAVIAR PIE

Yield: 12 Servings

10 Hard-Cooked Eggs, Chopped
¼ Cup Butter, Softened
½ teaspoon Celery Salt
½ teaspoon Dry Mustard
Salt and Pepper
1 Tablespoon Onion, Minced
1 Cup Sour Cream
Caviar (red or black)
Snipped Parsley

1. Peel and chop hard-cooked eggs while hot. Mash and blend together with butter, celery salt, mustard, salt, and pepper.
2. Press mixture into 8 inch pie pan that has been rinsed in cold water and chill.
3. Combine onion and sour cream and place on top of mixture in pie pan.
4. Garnish with caviar (red or black) and snipped parsley for a colorful treat!

— Mrs. Joseph L. Lombardi

SHRIMP FONDUE

2 Cans Frozen Cream of Shrimp Soup
1 Cup Milk
1 Pound Swiss Cheese, Grated
Paprika

AT HOME

1. In a double boiler heat soup and blend until smooth. Stir in milk and heat. Add grated cheese and cover.
2. Heat until thoroughly blended, stirring occasionally. Pour into a heated chaffing dish and serve with the following foundations: **Toasted French Bread Squares, Artichoke Hearts, Celery Slices, Bell Pepper Slices, Apple Wedges**

— Mrs. Joseph L. Lombardi

CHERRY TOMATO TREE

Styrofoam Cone, 10-12 Inches Tall
Cherry Tomatoes
Sprig of Holly
French Dressing

1. Spear blossom end of cherry tomato with pick.
2. Stick speared cherry tomatoes into styrofoam cone.
3. Tuck sprigs of holly in indiscriminately.
4. Serve with bowl of French Dressing.

— Mrs. McNeill Stokes

NIPPY CHEESE ROLLS

Yield: 5 Dozen

2 Pounds Velveeta Cheese
½ Tablespoon Onion, Minced
1½ Tablespoons Lemon Juice
½ Tablespoon Tabasco Sauce
½ Cup Pecans, Chopped
Paprika
Snipped Parsley

1. Blend all ingredients except paprika together. Chill for at least 12 hours.
2. Sprinkle paprika on waxed paper and roll small balls of the chilled cheese mixture in the paprika. Form into apple shapes and garnish with parsley.
3. You may personally want to vary the amounts of the ingredients depending upon your own taste buds.

— Mrs. Ivan Allen, III

AVOCADO TOAST CIRCLES

Ripe Avocados
Lemon Juice
Onion Juice
Salt
Cayenne Pepper
Crisp Bacon, Minced

Mayonnaise
Toast Rounds
Stuffed or Ripe Olives

1. Mash avocados and sprinkle with lemon juice and a few drops of onion juice.
2. Add seasoning to taste. Blend in small amount of crisp, minced bacon.
3. Spread toast rounds with mayonnaise, add avocado mixture and top with stuffed or ripe olive.

— Mrs. Tom Slaughter

STUFFED MUSHROOM CAPS

Fresh Mushrooms
Butter
Chicken Livers, Chopped
Salt and Pepper

1. Cut stems from fresh mushrooms. Saute mushroom caps in butter.
2. Mince mushroom stems and saute in butter with chicken livers and seasoning. Mash well.
3. Fill mushroom caps and garnish with parsley.

— Mrs. Terrell Burnley

HOT BACON ROLL-UPS

Bacon Slices
Olives
Oysters
Pecan Halves
Roquefort Cheese Spread
Burgundy Wine

1. Preheat broiler unit of range.
2. Cut each bacon slice into 4 pieces. Wrap each piece of bacon around olives, oysters, or pecan halves (placed together with Roquefort cheese spread).
3. Dip each in Burgundy wine, broil and serve hot on individual picks.

— Mrs. Bernard Haight

CRABAPPLE TIDBITS

Spiced Crabapples
Cocktail Sausage

1. Preheat oven to 400 degrees.
2. Core crabapples and insert cocktail sausage into space.
3. Heat at 400 degrees for 5 minutes.

— Mrs. Frank Briggs

AT HOME

KENTUCKY COLONELS

Yield: 6 Dozen

½ Cup Butter
2 Pounds Confectioner's Sugar
Pinch Salt
¾ Cup Bourbon
1 Cup Pecans, Ground
1 1-Ounce Square Unsweetened Chocolate
1 Square of Paraffin (1 x 1 x ¾ inch)

1. Cream butter well.
2. Add Confectioner's sugar and salt gradually and blend well. Add Bourbon and ground pecans.
3. Chill overnight. Next morning form into small balls.
4. In double boiler, melt unsweetened chocolate and paraffin together.
5. Dip balls into melted chocolate mixture and place on waxed paper to dry.
6. When dry, wrap each Kentucky Colonel Ball separately in waxed paper and chill until ready to serve.

— Mrs. Thomas I. Sangster

MERRIE OLE EGGNOG

Yield: 40 Servings

15 Egg Yolks
2½ Cups Sugar, Granulated
½ teaspoon Salt
1 Quart Heavy Cream
1 Quart Milk
1 Quart Bourbon
1 Pint Rye Whiskey
½ Pint Sherry
¾ Pint Dark Jamaica Rum
15 Egg Whites, Stiffly Beaten
Nutmeg

1. Separate eggs and place whites in refrigerator.
2. Blend together sugar, salt and egg yolk until frothy. Let stand. Whip cream and let stand.
3. Add milk to sugar and eggs. Blend well.
4. Combine Bourbon, Rye and whipped cream. Add Sherry and Rum. Blend thoroughly and let stand.
5. Whip egg whites until stiff and fold into mixture.
6. Stir vigorously with long handled wooden spoon. Mixture should develop small "islands."
7. Refrigerate and ripen for about 3 or 4 hours. Serve with grated nutmeg.

— Mr. Byford E. Wagstaff

HOSTESS' NOTES

DINNERS

DINNERS

Roll out the red carpet! Make every dinner party an opening night, whether it is seated or buffet, housed or gardened, formal or informal. A sense of being welcomed, honored, especially emanates when the hostess plans her party with thought, grace and imagination. There is a special warmth about a personal invitation to dinner that reflects the charm and hospitality of Atlanta. In 1879, a bit of real Southern hospitality took place in the city when General Sherman made his second entry. This time, he was guest of honor at a dinner given in McPherson Barracks.

SEATED DINNERS

At a seated dinner it is more important to concentrate on cuisine than on decorations. What could be more decorative than a beautifully set table with fine linen, sparkling glassware and exquisite china with candles casting a soft glow over the table.

INVITATIONS

Invitations may be telephoned at least ten days before the dinner; or written invitations may be sent on attractive notepaper, printed invitation cards or informals indicating a requested reply.

SEATING ARRANGEMENTS

Carefully plan seating arrangements before the dinner party. If there are guests of honor, the woman sits at the right of the host and the man at the hostess' right. Other guests may be seated as the hostess pleases. However, for a more stimulating conversation, you may prefer alternating men and women. In order for men and women to be alternated at a dinner for eight, another man should be seated facing the host. The host always maintains his place at the head of the table while the hostess is seated on the side.

TABLE SETTING

Successful table settings follow the basic rules of etiquette but should freely express the hostess' personality. Unusual color combinations and contrasting textures often complement table settings. An immaculate embroidered cloth or place mats of organdy, linen or damask set a fitting stage for dinner. For added color, adorn the table with a pretty pastel sheet covered with a lace cloth and a coordinating floral arrangement.

Not too long after General Sherman's second visit to Atlanta, the dinner topic arose again. Henry Grady sent a questionnaire to a number of Atlantans. Judge Bleckley's reply was a classic to remember. "Henry, if the men were entire strangers to me, I would have a great variety of viands and many kinds of drinks, all served with elaborate plate and much ceremony. If I knew the company very well, I would have fewer dishes and less plate and ceremonious service. If the men were old-time friends of thirty or more years' standing whom I had not seen for a long time, we would sit down to some well-cooked meat and bread and some coffee and have a good time." He then added, "The more feeling, the less need for gaudy and expensive feed."

DINNERS

CONTINENTAL DESSERT

Many people prefer fruit and cheese rather than a sweet dessert; therefore, a taste of cheese after dinner is a pleasant change and can be a spectacular and adventuresome way to end a meal. Arrange different kinds of cheese on a tray, each with a little flag noting its name and type. As a guide, select at least one soft, one semi-soft and one hard cheese; some mild and some sharp. Surround the cheese with an assortment of crackers, miniature loaves of bread and whipped butter. Tart pears, apples, oranges and choicest grapes have an affinity for cheese. Strawberries or raspberries complement the soft cheese, while walnuts in the shell, fresh figs, dates and prunes add to the flavor of all the cheese. Wine is an especially pleasant accompaniment.

BUFFET DINNERS

Is there a crowd party on your agenda? The Buffet Dinner has become a popular way of extending hospitality because of its adaptability. You can serve six or sixty gracefully with less help, equipment and space.

BUFFET SEATING

At large buffet dinners, guests may find their places in the living room or at card tables placed throughout the entertaining area. Eight to twelve guests can serve themselves from a sideboard or service buffet and may be seated at a graciously appointed table.

BUFFET SERVICE

Improvise your buffet service and utilize the top of a low bookcase or chest of drawers. Library steps and small kitchen ladders make apt servers for side dishes. For a large server, group two or three card tables together and cover with a cloth. Remember to arrange a good traffic pattern when improvising. If the guest list is for more than ten, you might center the server so that guests may serve themselves from either side of the table.

DECOR

When the buffet is placed against the wall, special effects can be achieved with big, bold flower arrangements. If you are using a makeshift table and a plain cloth, dash it with color. Overlay the server with wide ribbons and flowers of contrasting colors.

TABLE SETTING

Spread the buffet serving table with a pretty cloth or leave it uncovered. If card tables are used, cover with party cloths or attractive place mats.

Organize the service so that plates, silver and napkins are arranged at a logical starting place at one end of the table. Place platters of food at intervals along the table with service forks and spoons alongside each platter. The food should be bountiful so that second helpings are available. Place water and coffee on a side table or tea cart where guests may serve themselves. Dessert may also be offered from a side table or tea cart.

PATIO DINNERS

When all outdoors is right for partying with lots of background scenery and roaming-around space, you need not have a second's hesitation about a burgeoning guest list. Sometimes a big party is the easiest kind of all to give. The atmosphere of a summer setting puts every guest in a happy, relaxed mood. Years ago, a favorite outdoor party was the Trolley Party. The hostess requested her guests' presence for a trolley ride and an all-day picnic.

The Patio Dinner can be a magnificent affair with elegantly appointed tables and a luxuriant centerpiece of frosted fruit, graced with silver candelabra.

For casual settings, select carefree accessories from curio shops. Colored straw holders for dishes, glasses and flower pots brighten any setting. A special touch at each lady's place might be a tiny basket of garden flowers. If your party is around a swimming pool, rings of fresh or permanent blossoms and leaves secured to round life preservers and miniature floating candles provide an exotic garden.

Garden torches can outline a party area in the back yard, in lieu of a patio, or the yard may be set aglow with garlands of Japanese lanterns. Green and white striped denim cloths intensify the greenery of a summer garden.

Servers on wheels are a great aid to relaxed outdoor entertaining. If you do not have a suitable cart, divert your imagination. A child's red wagon or a garden wheelbarrow furnish unusual servers for casual entertaining. You might enjoy making a canopy for the wagon and serving your party a la cart!

DINNER PARTY IDEAS

Something out of the ordinary is what makes a party enjoyable. With a little imagination, you can make your party an event, an opening night. When you decide on a novel idea, let your guests know in advance; and they will look forward to a fun-filled evening. Launch new and exciting parties your guests will long remember with these suggestions.

To make a party door festive, wire inexpensive musical toys together and spray paint the toys a dazzling white. Attach a generous bow of white ribbon. To festoon a terrace, use small sized garden tools or plastic fruit.

The Luau is a patio favorite. Guests may sit on the ground around the feast which may be set on a green burlap cloth placed on the ground or on a low table. A low table can easily be made from a damaged door placed over two picnic table benches and provides a perfect table height for a Luau. Decorate profusely with flowers, fruits and greenery. Fill the center of the table with assorted Hawaiian fruits. Pineapple-shaped holders or candles add

DINNERS

to the exotic atmosphere. Use bamboo rings or surround napkins with colorful straw flowers. Greet your guests at the garden gate with a lei and a kiss. Make the leis from the straw flowers or fresh flowers which do not wilt quickly, such as carnations, dahlias, or zinnias. Remove the stems and string the flower heads with a needle onto button twist thread. A refrigerator is too cold for the flowers overnight, but they will thrive in a blanket of wet newspapers inside an ice chest.

For a Paris stop, turn the entertainment area into a bistro with red and white checks splashed over the tables. Center the tables with candles in bottles. Dribble candle wax in several colors down the sides of the bottles to give an antiqued effect. Brighten the serving table with a matching cloth and lots of bottles and candles in various shapes and sizes.

Select a South-of-the-border theme and create a gay atmosphere by featuring the hot colors—red, yellow and orange. Decorate with Mexican motifs, such as gourds, gaucho hats and serapes. A pinata from Mexico or a basket filled with green and red peppers and onions would make a delightful centerpiece. Cored green peppers anchoring red candles add spice to the Mexican fare.

Some special period in history always sparks an exciting party. The Gay Nineties Party creates a nostalgic, light-hearted mood. Present the men with mustaches and derby hats and present the ladies with fans and parasols. Use trunks for tables and dub your drinks with personalities of the era, for example, "Lillian Russell Delight" or "Diamond Jim's Joy". The possibilities for table decor are unlimited.

Have an Original Painting Party where all the guests get into the act. In a convenient corner or one room, set up a studio with a large blank canvas placed on an easel or against the wall. Have paints, brushes, smocks and cloths for your "artists" and allot space on the canvas for them to paint. The focal point might be a still life of fruits, vegetables or flowers.

CENTERPIECES

Candles illuminate every setting. When using candles, please use at least four to lend enough light to the subject. Keep candles high and centerpiece low on the dining table at a seated dinner, but on a buffet, both centerpiece and candles can be high.

Potted candle flowers brighten any party, or you may fancy miniature flower candles that drift in water. Candles of varied heights, shapes, and colors are accented on a mirrored base. Use pastel candles with flowers in the springtime; in autumn, use warm, rich colored candles with leaves around the base. A large scented candle inside a glass chimney surrounded with spring flowers, autumn leaves or winter greens creates a handsome table decoration.

DINNERS

For a summer sea, fill a clear glass bowl with beautiful blue-green water. Drift three white candles in the water's cool-looking depth.

For a graceful centerpiece, select a silver candelabra entwined with ivy or tuck flowers around candles which are fastened to individually inverted wine glasses with melted paraffin.

A color-coordinated bird cage filled with flowers and greens adds a cheerful note.

For a conversational centerpiece, arrange all your objets d'art, such as small figurines and tiny easeled pictures, in the center of the table.

Group together wine bottles in various sizes and shapes and fill with colored straw flowers for a casual touch.

A wreath of pears, bananas, oranges and grapes circling a luscious pineapple or a cornucopia overflowing with delicious fruits offers an edible focal point. Arrange a symphony in orange with peaches, persimmons, apricots, oranges and nectarines nestled in a brass bowl. Bright-red geraniums in a beach hat add color to a patio party.

If seafood is on your menu, cover your table with an aqua cloth overlaid with a fishnet. Cork floats as holders for aqua candles and a boat model provide a fitting center of attraction. Sea shells could make appropriate ashtrays. You may enjoy a simpler arrangement of greenery and candles in a large sea shell. For your next Bon Voyage party, why not float a toy boat in a sea of blossoms.

Hospitality is all the little extras that say welcome—a beautifully set table, a well-planned menu, a cordial attitude that rings through your voice and shines through your smile. At your next dinner party, roll out the red carpet. Place a red rug just outside the door and express a gala welcome!

SEATED DINNERS

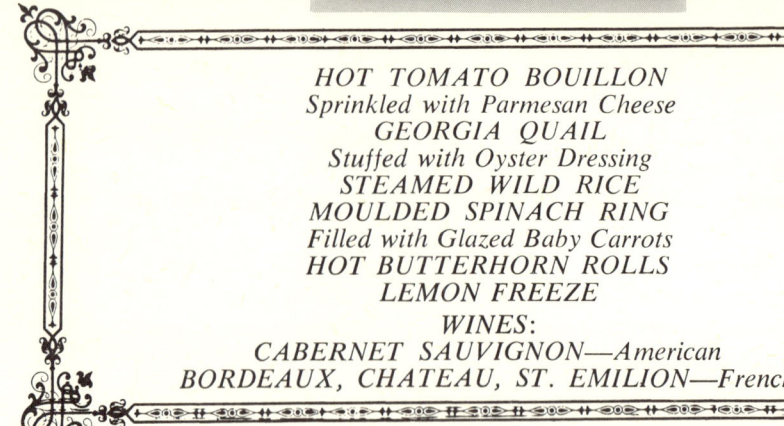

HOT TOMATO BOUILLON
Sprinkled with Parmesan Cheese
GEORGIA QUAIL
Stuffed with Oyster Dressing
STEAMED WILD RICE
MOULDED SPINACH RING
Filled with Glazed Baby Carrots
HOT BUTTERHORN ROLLS
LEMON FREEZE
WINES:
CABERNET SAUVIGNON—*American*
BORDEAUX, CHATEAU, ST. EMILION—*French*

GEORGIA QUAIL STUFFED WITH OYSTER DRESSING

Oysters (4 per each Quail)

Saltines, Crushed (1 per each Quail)

Salt and Pepper

Worcestershire Sauce

Quail

Melted Butter

Sprigs of Parsley

1. Preheat oven to 350 degrees.

2. Roll saltines into fine crumbs and season oysters with salt, pepper and Worcestershire Sauce. Dip oysters in cracker crumbs and place four oysters in each quail.

3. Score quail and brush with melted butter. Bake 15 to 25 minutes at 350 degrees. Garnish with parsley and serve.

— Miss Yolande Gwin

DINNERS

MOULDED SPINACH RING

Yield: 8-10 Servings

3 Pounds Fresh Spinach, Washed and Drained
¼ Cup Onion, Chopped
2 Tablespoons Chives, Chopped
Salt and Pepper
Dash Nutmeg

1. Preheat oven to 300 degrees. Lightly grease ring mould.
2. Wash spinach thoroughly, drain, and place in pan with only the water that clings to the leaves. Cook covered for 5 minutes. Drain.
3. Puree in blender. Add remaining ingredients.
4. Pour into lightly greased ring mould. Place in pan of water and bake at 300 degrees until firm.
5. Fill center with glazed baby carrots and serve.

— Miss Yolande Gwin

CLASSIC YEAST ROLLS

Yield: 5 Dozen

2 Cups Water
1 Cup Shortening
½ Cup Sugar, Granulated
1 Tablespoon Salt
2 Eggs, Slightly Beaten
2 Packages Active Dry Yeast
½ Cup Warm Water
7 Cups Flour, Unsifted
2 teaspoons Vegetable Oil

DINNERS

1. Bring 2 cups water to boil and add shortening, sugar and salt. Cool until lukewarm.
2. Add slightly beaten eggs to shortening-sugar mixture.
3. Dissolve yeast in ½ cup warm water and add to egg mixture.
4. Blend in unsifted flour and mix until smooth.
5. Brush vegetable oil on top of dough and cover with damp cloth.
6. Chill overnight.
7. Turn onto lightly floured board and roll dough to ⅜ inch thick.
8. Cut into pie shapes for butterhorn rolls. Roll up from large end and cover with damp towel. Let rise until double in size (about 2 hours).
9. Bake at 400 degrees until done. (If you would like to freeze part of the rolls for future use, bake at 400 degrees for 8 minutes or until light crust forms. Cool, wrap and freeze.)

— Mrs. Robert S. Grady

LEMON FREEZE

Yield: 8 Servings

4 Egg Yolks, Well-Beaten
2 Cans Eagle Brand Milk
1 Cup Lemon Juice
1 teaspoon Lemon Rind, Grated
4 Egg Whites, Stiffly Beaten
6 Tablespoons Sugar, Granulated

1. Beat egg yolks until thick and lemon colored. Add milk, lemon juice and lemon rind. Stir until thick.
2. Beat whites until stiff and gradually add sugar.
3. Fold egg whites into lemon mixture, and pour into parfait glasses.
4. Freeze until firm and garnish with berries.

— Mrs. Tyrone S. Clifford

LAMB SYMPHONY
BREAST OF CHICKEN AND LOBSTER MARENGO
BUTTERED SPEARS OF BROCCOLI
FRUITED MOULD OF LEMON
PARKERHOUSE ROLLS
CHOCOLATE CALICO PECAN PIE

WINES:
CALIFORNIA RIESLING—American
CHABLIS—French

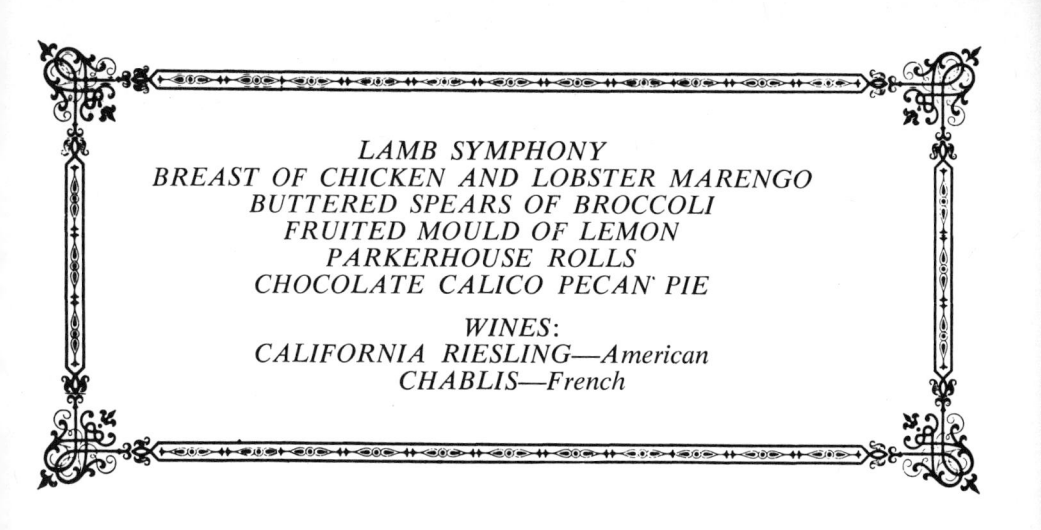

LAMB SYMPHONY

Bone from Roast Leg of Lamb
Carrots
2 Stalks of Celery with Leaves, Sliced
1 Medium Onion, Chopped
1 Can of Tomatoes
Left-over Vegetables
    (i.e., Lima Beans, Corn, String Beans)
1 Cup Wheat, Rice or Barley
Salt and Pepper
Thyme
Oregano
Water

1. In large kettle place bone from a roasted leg of lamb on which there is still plenty of meat. Cover with water and simmer one hour.

2. Add vegetables, wheat, rice or barley.

3. Season to taste with salt, pepper, oregano, and thyme.

4. Add water if necessary, but it should be a thick, hearty soup.

5. Simmer until vegetables are tender. Reheat any leftover soup for future use.

— Mrs. Robert Shaw

BREAST OF CHICKEN AND LOBSTER MARENGO

Yield: 6 Servings

This can be prepared ahead and completed during the last few minutes.

6 Breasts of Chicken (6 Ounces per Half Breast)
2 Boxes Lobster Tails
½ Pound Fresh Mushrooms
¼ Cup Butter
1½ Cups Chicken Stock
2 Tablespoons Flour
1 Tablespoon Tomato Paste
Salt and Pepper
2 Tablespoons Chives, Chopped
3 Ripe Tomatoes (Quartered)
2 Tablespoons Sherry
1½ Cups Rice, Uncooked

1. Preheat oven to 300 degrees.

2. Saute breasts of chicken in butter until browned. Place chicken in shallow casserole, cover, and bake 20 minutes at 300 degrees.

3. In skillet, saute mushrooms in butter.

4. To skillet, add stock and flour. Simmer until thickened. Add tomato paste, salt, pepper, chives, and whole chicken breasts. Simmer 15 minutes.

5. Store in refrigerator, if desired.

6. 15 minutes before serving, add cooked (per package directions) bite-sized lobster, raw tomato wedges, and 2 Tablespoons Sherry.

7. Serve over cooked rice.

— Miss Marjorie Chisholm

PARKERHOUSE ROLLS

(See Page 207)

DINNERS

FRUITED LEMON MOULD

Yield: 6 Servings

1 3-Ounce Package Lemon Gelatin
½ Cup Boiling Water
1 13½-Ounce Can Crushed Pineapple, Undrained
1 Tablespoon Lemon Juice
1 Cup Cheddar Cheese, Grated
1 Cup Heavy Cream

1. Oil 1 quart mould or 6 individual moulds.
2. Dissolve lemon gelatin in boiling water. Stir in undrained crushed pineapple and lemon juice.
3. Chill until slightly thickened and fold in cheese and whipped cream.
4. Pour into oiled mould and chill until firm.
5. Unmould onto lettuce leaves. Fill center with Tokay grapes.
6. Garnish with pineapple slices, sprigs of mint, and small cluster of Tokay grapes.

— Mrs. Wheat Williams, Jr.

CHOCOLATE PECAN PIE

Yield: 8 Servings

2 1-Ounce Squares Unsweetened Chocolate
3 Tablespoons Butter
1 Cup Light Corn Syrup
¾ Cup Sugar, Granulated
½ teaspoon Salt
3 Eggs, Slightly Beaten
1 teaspoon Vanilla Extract
1 Cup Pecans, Chopped
1 Unbaked 9 inch Pastry Shell (See Page 39)
Whipped Cream

1. Preheat oven to 375 degrees.
2. In double boiler melt chocolate and butter together.
3. Combine corn syrup and sugar and simmer together for 2 minutes in separate saucepan.
4. Add chocolate mixture and cool slightly.
5. Add salt to slightly beaten eggs.
6. Slowly dribble syrup mixture into eggs, stirring constantly. Blend in vanilla extract and nuts.
7. Pour into pastry shell and bake for 35 minutes at 375 degrees. Serve with whipped cream.

— Mrs. J. Charles Dukes, Jr.

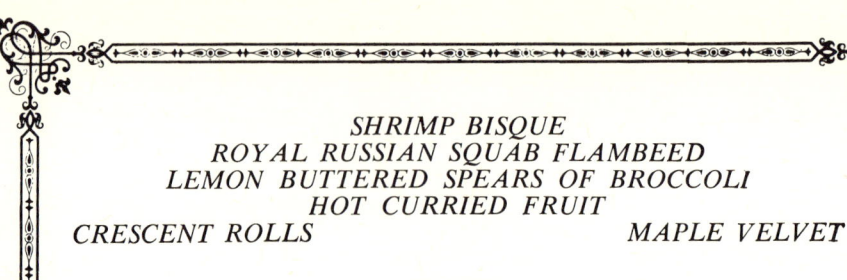

SHRIMP BISQUE
ROYAL RUSSIAN SQUAB FLAMBEED
LEMON BUTTERED SPEARS OF BROCCOLI
HOT CURRIED FRUIT
CRESCENT ROLLS   MAPLE VELVET

WINES:
CABERNET SAUVIGNON—American
BORDEAUX - CHATEAU BOTTLING—French

SHRIMP BISQUE

Yield: 8 Servings

1 Can Frozen Cream of Shrimp Soup
1 Can Cream of Tomato Soup
2 Cups Milk
Dash Curry Powder

1. Add curry powder to milk to dissolve.
2. Blend all ingredients together well.
3. Heat and serve hot in soup turrene or cold in chilled glass soup cups.

— Miss Blanche Thebom

ROYAL RUSSIAN SQUAB FLAMBEED

Yield: 8 Servings

Small, Plump Squab
¼ Cup Butter
½ Cup Dry White Wine
1 Medium Onion, Sliced
5 Green Onions, Chopped
Dash Cayenne Pepper
Dash Salt
⅔ Cup Dry White Wine
1⅓ Cups Sour Cream
Strips of Pimiento

1. Dust squab lightly with flour and poach delicately in plenty of hot butter and ½ cup dry white wine. When light brown, place on hot silver platter and reserve.
2. Saute sliced onion and chopped green onions in butter until clear and tender.
3. Add dry white wine and sour cream.
4. Simmer uncovered gently. Add Cayenne Pepper and salt. Pour mixture over squab. Garnish with strips of scarlet pimiento. Encircle entree with warmed brandy and light for an added gourmet flair.

— Mrs. Robert Sasser

HOT CURRIED FRUIT

Yield: 8 Servings

¾ Cup Brown Sugar
2 Tablespoons Cornstarch
1 Tablespoon Curry Powder
1 Can Pineapple Chunks
2 Cans Fruit Cocktail
¾ Cup Cherries
1 Cup Bing Cherries, Pitted
¼ Cup Butter, Melted

1. Preheat oven to 350 degrees. Grease casserole.
2. Blend together brown sugar, cornstarch and curry powder.
3. Place fruit in greased casserole and add melted butter.
4. Blend in brown sugar mixture.
5. Bake at 350 degrees for 40 minutes.

— Mrs. Ivan Allen, Jr.

MAPLE VELVET

Yield: 8 Servings

2⅔ Cups Light Brown Sugar
2 Cups Sour Cream
2 teaspoons Maple Extract
2 Cups Heavy Cream
8 Cups Blueberries

1. Blend together sugar, sour cream and maple extract until sugar is dissolved.
2. Whip cream and fold into sour cream mixture. Chill until serving time.
3. Mix with berries or fruit and serve in crystal supremes.

— Mrs. Neil Williams

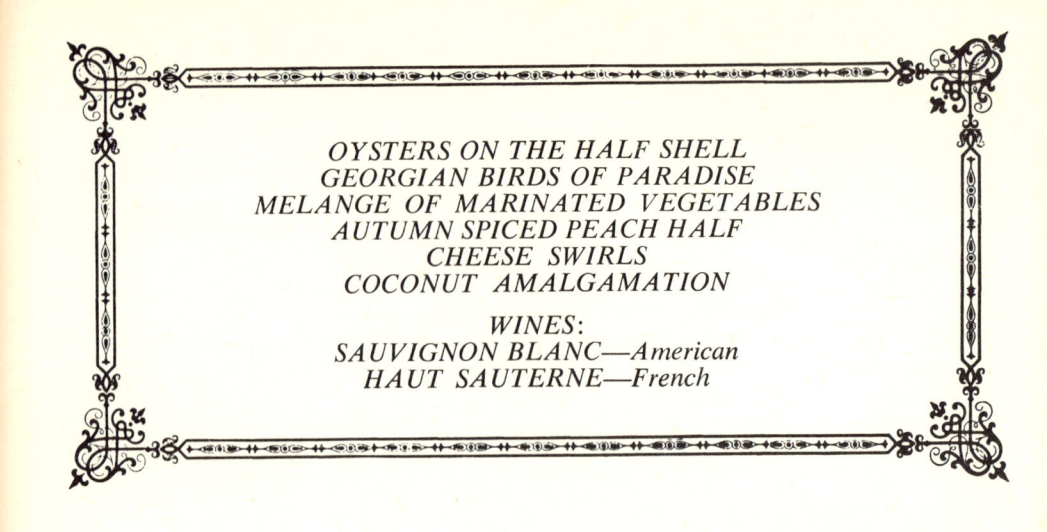

OYSTERS ON THE HALF SHELL
GEORGIAN BIRDS OF PARADISE
MELANGE OF MARINATED VEGETABLES
AUTUMN SPICED PEACH HALF
CHEESE SWIRLS
COCONUT AMALGAMATION

WINES:
SAUVIGNON BLANC—American
HAUT SAUTERNE—French

GEORGIAN BIRDS OF PARADISE

Yield: 8 Servings

½ Cup Vegetable Oil
1 Pound Small White Onions
2 Cloves Garlic, Minced
8 Breasts of Chicken (6 Ounces per Half Breast)
¼ Cup Flour
2 Cups Dry Sauterne
2 teaspoons Salt
¼ teaspoon Pepper
2 teaspoons Thyme
4 teaspoons Parsley, Chopped
2 3-Ounce Cans Sliced Mushrooms
2 Tablespoons Brandy, Warmed

1. In heavy skillet with tight cover, heat oil, slowly.
2. Saute whole onions and garlic in heated oil.
3. Add chicken breasts and brown on both sides. Remove chicken and onions and drain excess oil except ¼ cup.
4. Blend together flour, wine, salt, pepper and thyme. Add to drippings in skillet.
5. Add chicken and onions to gravy. Cover and simmer for 45 minutes.
6. Add parsley and sliced mushrooms. Simmer 10 minutes longer.
7. Place warmed brandy on platter or individual plate and light just before serving chicken.

— Mrs. William Frain

MARINATED VEGETABLES

Yield: 8 Servings

Marinade:

1 Cup Vegetable Oil
2 Cups Vinegar
2 Tablespoons Salt
2 Cups Sugar, Granulated
2 Tablespoons Water
Dash Cayenne Pepper

Vegetables:

3 Cans Whole Blue Lake Green Beans
1 Can Le Seur Peas
1 Cup Bell Pepper, Diced
1 Cup Celery, Minced
1 Cup Onions, Thinly Sliced
¼ Cup Pimiento, Diced

1. Blend marinade ingredients together and let stand one hour.
2. Pour marinade over vegetable mixture.
3. Marinate overnight. To serve, drain marinade and reserve for future use.

— Mrs. James Saxon Childers

AUTUMN SPICED PEACH HALF

Yield: 8 Servings

8 Peach Halves
½ Cup Mincemeat
½ Cup Butter

1. Preheat broiler unit of range.
2. Spoon 1 Tablespoon mincemeat into each peach half. Top with 1 Tablespoon butter.
3. Broil and serve hot.

— Mrs. Wheat Williams, Jr.

DINNERS

CHEESE SWIRLS

(See page 99)

COCONUT AMALGAMATION

Yield: 12 Servings

1 Cup Butter
2 Cups Sugar, Granulated
4 Cups Flour, Sifted
2 teaspoons Baking Powder
1 teaspoon Vanilla Extract
1 Cup Milk
8 Egg Whites, Stiffly Beaten

1. Preheat oven to 350 degrees. Grease and flour 4 layer cake pans.
2. Cream together butter and sugar. Sift baking powder and flour together. Add to creamed butter and sugar mixture.
3. Blend in vanilla extract and milk. Fold in stiffly beaten egg whites.
4. Divide batter among 4 layer cake pans.
5. Bake at 350 degrees for 20-30 minutes or until done.

Filling:

8 Egg Yolks
2 Cups Sugar, Granulated
1 Cup Butter
1½ Cups Pecans and Walnuts, Chopped
1¼ Cups Dark Seedless Raisins
1¼ Cups Coconut, Shredded
1 Tablespoon Wine

1. In a double boiler blend together egg yolks, sugar and butter. Cook until thick.
2. Beat egg mixture in double boiler, cool, and blend in remaining ingredients.
3. Spread filling between layers. Frost top and sides of cake with your choice of white icing. Sprinkle shredded coconut on top of cake.

— Mrs. Samuel N. Gardner

CHILLED V-8 JUICE COCKTAIL
Served with Crisp Carrot Stick Stirrers
ENGLISH ROAST A LA MARINE
SPINACH AND ARTICHOKES EN CASSEROLE
COQUILLE OF MELON BALLS
HOT BUTTERED ROLLS
APPLE CRUMB PIE

WINES:
PINOT NOIR—American
REGIONAL BORDEAUX—French

ENGLISH ROAST A LA MARINE

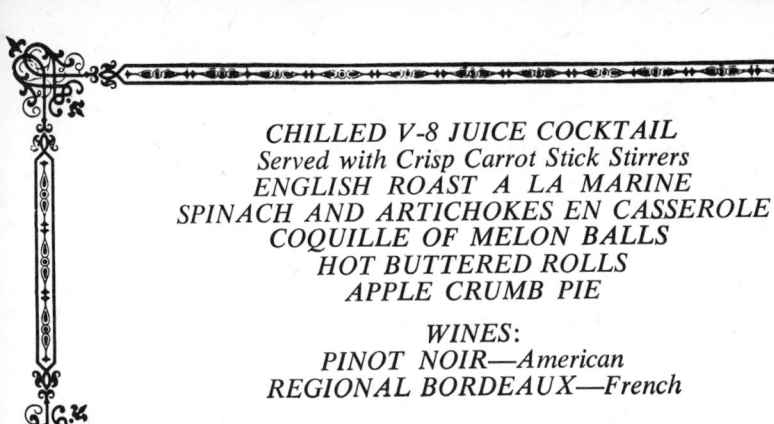

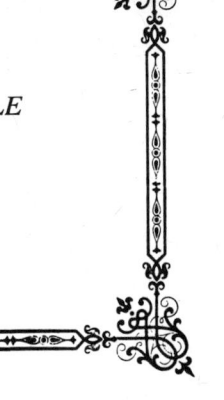

Yield: 6 Servings

Guests enjoy the aroma from this cooking almost enough to forfeit the eating!

1 Clove Garlic, Pressed
1 Cup Soy Sauce
1½ Tablespoons Vinegar
¼ Cup Bourbon
1 Cup Water
1 Tablespoon Meat Tenderizer
1 6-Pound English Cut Roast

1. Combine pressed garlic clove, soy sauce, vinegar, Bourbon, water and meat tenderizer. Pour over roast and marinate for twenty-four hours.

2. Charcoal forty-five minutes on an open grill, or 30-35 minutes on a covered grill.

— Mrs. Harry G. Haisten, Jr.

DINNERS

SPINACH AND ARTICHOKES EN CASSEROLE

Yield: 6 Servings

2 10-Ounce Packages Frozen Spinach, Chopped
1 Package Frozen Artichokes
½ Cup Butter, Melted
1 8-Ounce Package Cream Cheese, Softened
1 teaspoon Lemon Juice
Cracker Crumbs

1. Preheat oven to 350 degrees. Grease casserole.

2. Cook spinach and artichokes according to directions on packages. Drain well.

3. To cooked spinach add butter, cream cheese, and lemon juice. Blend together.

4. Place artichokes in bottom of greased casserole. Add spinach mixture.

5. Top with cracker crumbs, dot with butter and bake at 350 degrees for 25 minutes.

— Mrs. Marvin G. Gregory, Jr.

COQUILLE OF MELON BALLS

(See page 44)

This salad is excellent topped with Celery Seed Dressing.

CELERY SEED DRESSING

Yield 1½ Cups

⅓ Cup Sugar, Granulated
1 teaspoon Dry Mustard
1 teaspoon Salt
1 teaspoon Paprika

1 teaspoon Celery Seed
1 teaspoon Onion, Grated
⅓ Cup Vinegar
1 Cup Salad Oil

1. Blend together dry ingredients. Add onion.
2. Slowly add salad oil alternately with vinegar. Beat vigorously after each addition.
3. Dribble over fresh fruit and serve.

— Mrs. Richard Courts, II

APPLE CRUMB PIE

1 Unbaked Pastry Shell (See page 39)
6 Apples, Sliced
½ Cup Sugar, Granulated
½ teaspoon Salt
¼ teaspoon Nutmeg
¼ teaspoon Cinnamon
¼ Cup Honey or Light Corn Syrup

1. Preheat oven to 350 degrees. Prepare pastry shell.
2. Place apples in pastry shell. Blend together other ingredients and spoon over apples.

Topping:

6 Tablespoons Butter, Melted
½ Cup Light Brown Sugar
¼ Cup Flour, Sifted
½ Cup Pecans, Chopped

1. Blend together ingredients and sprinkle over top of pie. Bake at 350 degrees for 45 minutes.

— Mrs. Richard Courts, II

FROSTED RASPBERRY SHRUB
BEEF FONDUE
BUTTERED BLUE LAKE GREEN BEANS
CURRIED ONIONS
FRESH MUSHROOM AND ROMAINE SALAD
POPPY SEED LOAF BREAD
CHESS PIE
WINES:
CALIFORNIA GAMAY—American
ST. EMILION—French

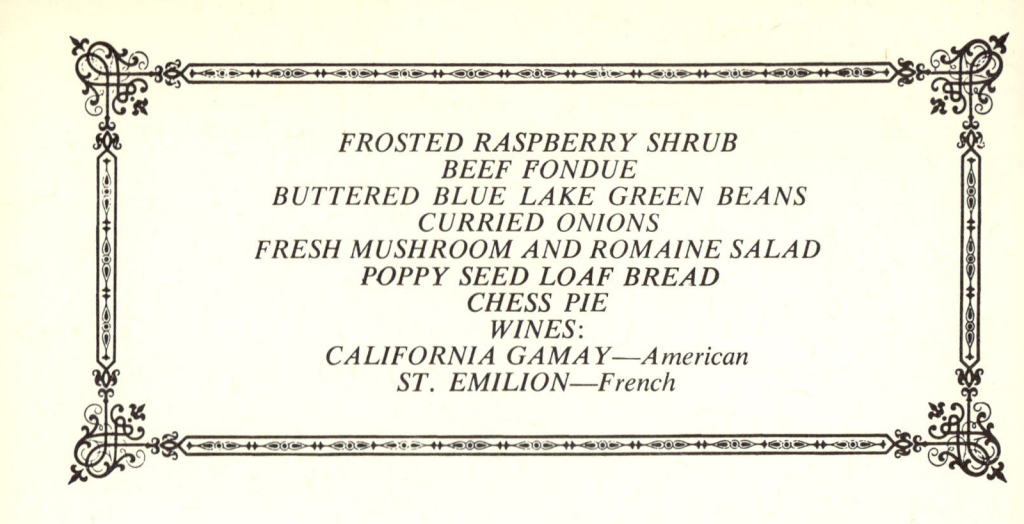

FROSTED RASPBERRY SHRUB

Yield: 6 Servings

6 Tablespoons Frozen or Fresh Raspberries, Crushed
1 Cup Orange Juice*
1 Cup Grapefruit Juice*
 *(Any 2 fruit juices may be used.)

1. Frost fruit glasses by chilling in the freezer. Place 1 Tablespoon crushed raspberries in bottom of glass.
2. Blend 2 chilled fruit juices together and pour into frosted glasses. Add a sprig of mint and serve.

— Mrs. Ogden Stokes

BEEF FONDUE

Yield: 6 Servings

3 Pounds Fillet Mignon, Cut into 1 Inch Cubes
2 8-Ounce Bottles Olive Oil
Crisp Salad Greens

1. Trim beef cubes of all fat. Cover and chill until serving time.
2. Just before serving, mound beef on 2 platters of crisp salad greens.
3. For 6 people, it is ideal to have 2 Fondue pots, one at each end of the table.
4. Heat olive oil in pan on top of range. (It should be hot enough to brown a one inch bread cube in 1 minute).
5. Pour heated olive oil into fondue pots. Ignite burners.
6. Using long handled fondue forks to spear meat, place speared meat in hot olive oil and remove when meat is brown and crusty on the outside and juicy on the inside.
7. Dip in various sauces listed below.

— Mrs. Joseph R. Manning

HORSERADISH SAUCE

1 Cup Sour Cream
2 Tablespoons Horseradish
½ teaspoon Lemon Juice
¼ teaspoon Worcestershire Sauce
⅛ teaspoon Salt
⅛ teaspoon Pepper

1. Combine all ingredients and chill.

CURRIED FRUIT SAUCE

Yield: 1½ Cups

1 Cup Sour Cream
½ Cup Crushed Pineapple, Drained
½ Unpared Medium Apple, Chopped
1 teaspoon Curry Powder
½ teaspoon Garlic Salt

1. Combine all ingredients and chill.

BLEU CHEESE SAUCE

Yield: ¾ Cup

½ Cup Sour Cream
¼ Cup Bleu Cheese, Crumbled
1 teaspoon Worcestershire Sauce
¼ teaspoon Salt

1. Blend all ingredients together and chill.

CURRIED ONIONS

Yield: 6 Servings

2 1-Pound Jars Tiny Whole Onions, Drained
1 Can Cream of Mushroom Soup
2 Tablespoons Mayonnaise
¼ teaspoon Curry Powder

½ Cup Bread Crumbs
2 Tablespoons Butter, Melted
2 Tablespoons Parsley, Chopped

1. Preheat oven to 350 degrees.
2. Place drained onions in casserole. Combine soup, mayonnaise, and curry powder. Spoon over onions.
3. Toss bread crumbs in melted butter and chopped parsley. Sprinkle on top of casserole.
4. Bake for 30 minutes at 350 degrees.

— Mrs. Paul Grigsby

FRESH MUSHROOM AND ROMAINE SALAD

Yield: 6 Servings

½ Pound Fresh Mushrooms, Sliced
Lemon Juice
2-3 Heads Romaine

1. Peel and slice mushrooms (with stems). Sprinkle with lemon juice.
2. Wash and drain romaine lettuce. Tear into bite-size pieces and arrange on salad plate. Add sliced mushrooms and serve with Herb dressing.

— Mrs. Harry I. Talbert

HERB DRESSING

Yield: 1 Cup

1 Cup Vinegar
2 Tablespoons Sugar, Granulated
1 teaspoon Salt
1 teaspoon Paprika
1 Tablespoon Worcestershire Sauce
1 Tablespoon Salad Herbs

1. Blend ingredients together over a low flame for 8 minutes.
2. Let cool and add ½ cup salad oil and 3 cloves of garlic.

— Mrs. Carl E. Sanders

POPPY SEED LOAF BREAD

(See page 261)

CHESS PIE

Yield: 8 Servings

This falls into the "best I've ever eaten" category!

    1 Cup Sugar, Granulated
    ½ Cup Brown Sugar
    1 Tablespoon Flour
    1 Tablespoon Cornmeal
    3 Egg Yolks, Slightly Beaten
    ¼ Cup Milk
    ¼ Cup Butter, Softened
    ½ teaspoon Vinegar
    1 teaspoon Vanilla Extract
    1 Unbaked Pastry Shell (See page 39)
    2 Egg Whites, Stiffly Beaten
    ½ Cup Sugar, Granulated

1. Preheat oven to 425 degrees. Prepare unbaked pastry shell.

2. Blend together well granulated sugar, brown sugar, flour and cornmeal. Add slightly beaten egg yolks, milk, softened butter, vinegar and vanilla extract. Blend well.

3. Pour into unbaked pastry shell. Bake at 425 degrees for 10 minutes. Reduce heat to 350 degrees and bake for 15 to 20 minutes or until set.

4. Cool. Beat egg whites until foamy and gradually add sugar until stiff peaks form.

5. Top pie with meringue and bake at 350 degrees for 15 to 20 minutes.

— Miss Irene Burba

RUSSIAN BORSCHT
BEEF BOURGUINONE
YELLOW SQUASH SOUFFLE
Topped with Tiny Green Peas
PARKERHOUSE ROLLS
FRENCH FANTASIA

WINES:
CALIFORNIA GAMAY—American
COTE DE BEAUNE—French

RUSSIAN BORSCHT

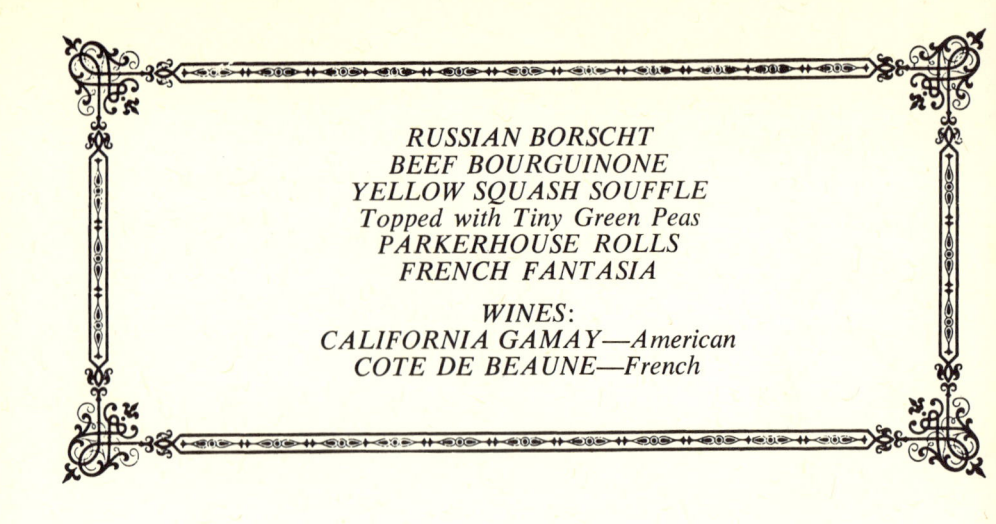

Yield: 10 Servings

Borscht is a mainstay of the Russian diet. It is served as a soup, or a meal in one. The basic ingredients are beets and cabbage, but almost anything can be added.

2 Cans Consomme
2 Cans Beets, Diced
1 Large Can Strained Tomatoes
1 Medium Head Cabbage, Shredded
2 Large Whole Onions
Chunks of Beef with Soup Bone
2 Quarts Water
1 teaspoon Citric Acid, or ¼ Cup Vinegar, or Juice of 2 Lemons
½ Cup Sugar, Granulated
½ teaspoon Salt

1. Combine all ingredients. Cover kettle and cook until meat is tender.
2. Remove whole onions and serve topped with sour cream blended with black caviar.
3. Store remainder of Borscht in refrigerator for future use.

— Mrs. Herbert Taylor

BEEF BOURGUINONE

Yield: 6 Servings

This is a true gourmet's delight!

4-5 Pounds Beef Tenderloin, Sliced
Flour
3 Tablespoons Olive Oil
3 Tablespoons Butter
5 Shallots, Sliced or Minced
1 Large Onion, Diced
¾ Pound Fresh Mushrooms, Sliced
8 Slices Bacon
¼ Cup Cognac, Warmed
1½ Cups Burgundy
1½ Cups Beef Stock

1. Roll beef lightly in flour, shaking off any excess flour.
2. Saute beef slices in skillet with shallots and onions in olive oil and butter. Add peeled fresh mushrooms and bacon. Saute until mushrooms are soft.
3. Add warmed cognac and light. Add burgundy and beef stock and simmer until beef is tender.
4. Serve on a bed of wide noodles.

— Mrs. McNeill Stokes

YELLOW SQUASH SOUFFLE

Yield: 6 Servings

2 Pounds Fresh Yellow Squash, Sliced
½ Pound American Cheese, Cubed
4 Slices White Bread (Broken in Small Bits)
2 Eggs, Slightly Beaten
Salt and Pepper
¼ Cup Butter

1. Preheat oven to 350 degrees. Grease casserole.
2. In small amount of water, cook squash approximately 10 minutes. Mash cooked squash, and blend in cheese.
3. Add remaining ingredients. Place in greased casserole and bake at 350 degrees for 30 minutes. Sprinkle with tiny green peas and serve immediately - hot!

— Mrs. Louise Armour Knowlton

FRENCH FANTASIA

Yield: 6 Servings

3 Quarts Vanilla Ice Cream, Solid but not Frozen
9 Ounces Blackberry Brandy
6 Ounces Scotch Whiskey

1. Blend ice cream, brandy and scotch in mixer to creamy consistency.
2. Serve in stemmed goblets.

— Mrs. Curtis A. Rogers

SALSA ROSATA SHRIMP
CURRIED TOASTA
COLD GLAZED ROAST OF BEEF
BARLEY AMANDINE
THICK SLICES OF TOMATO
Topped with Watercress
MEDLEY OF FRESH FRUIT AND CHEESES

WINES:
CALIFORNIA GAMAY—American
BEAUJOLAIS—French

SALSA ROSATA SHRIMP

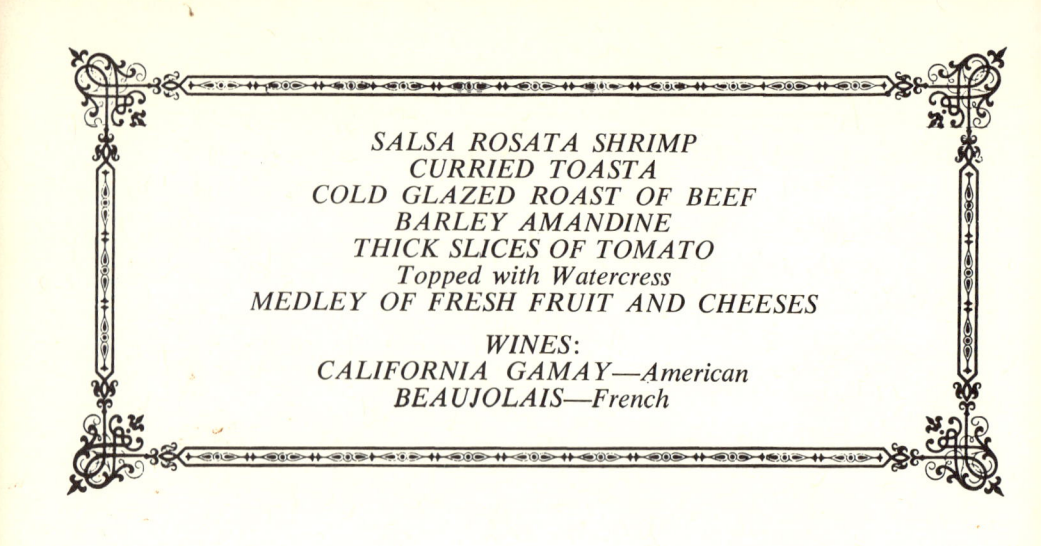

Yield: 6 Servings

2 Quarts White Wine Court Bouillon
36 Large Shrimp, Uncooked
Hearts of Chicory, Shredded
½ Cup Mayonnaise
½ Cup Heavy Cream or Sour Cream
1 Tablespoon Catsup
2 teaspoons Brandy

1. In a kettle bring white wine court bouillon to a boil. Add shrimp and simmer covered for 5 minutes.
2. Remove from heat and let shrimp cool in the court bouillon for 20 minutes.
3. Drain, shell and devein shrimp, chill.
4. Line bottom of 6 individual crystal serving dishes with shredded hearts of chicory. Place 6 shrimp on each bed of chicory.
5. Blend together remaining ingredients. Top shrimp with sauce, chill thoroughly and serve.

— Mrs. Sanford S. Atwood

CURRIED TOASTA

(See page 188)

COLD GLAZED ROAST OF BEEF

Rib Roast of Beef
Pate de Foie Gras
2 Cups Consomme
2 Tablespoons Plain Gelatin
2 Tablespoons Madeira

1. Rub a rib roast of beef with butter or oil and place fat side up on a rack in a roasting pan.
2. Set the beef in a cold oven, turn on the oven to 300 degrees and roast the meat, without basting, until done. (Allow about 20 minutes per pound for rare, 25 minutes for medium and 28 to 30 minutes for well done.)
3. Remove the meat from pan and chill thoroughly. Trim excess fat from roast and spread meat with a thin layer of pate de foie gras.
4. In a saucepan heat consomme, dry gelatin and Madeira until gelatin is dissolved.
5. Remove pan from heat, set it in a bowl of cracked ice and stir sauce with a metal spoon until it is cold and starts to turn syrupy.
6. Spoon the sauce over the meat immediately, before it sets, coating the meat smoothly and completely. Put the roast on a chilled platter and surround it with parsley and chopped set aspic.

— Mrs. Sanford S. Atwood

BARLEY AMANDINE

Yield: 6 Servings

1 Cup Dry Barley
2 Cups Consomme
1 Large Onion, Chopped
½ Pound Fresh Mushrooms, Chopped
4-5 Tablespoons, Butter
Toasted Almonds, Chopped

1. Preheat oven to 350 degrees.
2. In a large shallow pan, toast dry fine pearly barley in oven.
3. Add consomme and simmer until tender. Add more consomme if needed.
4. Saute onions and mushrooms in butter. Combine barley, onions and mushrooms in casserole. Season to taste.
5. Top with toasted almonds. Bake covered at 350 degrees for 30 minutes. Add more consomme periodically to keep mixture moist but not wet.

— Mrs. Sanford S. Atwood

HOT CHICKEN BOUILLON
With Snipped Parsley
BAKED PORK CHOPS
Plumped with Herbed Mushroom Dressing
GREEN RICE   MINCEMEAT GLAZED APPLES
BUTTERMILK BRAN MUFFINS
LEMON ICE

WINES:
ROSE - GRENACHE—American
RHINE WINE—Germany

BAKED PORK CHOPS

Yield: 6 Servings

This is a husband favorite! It may be cooked ahead and browned just before serving.

6 2-Inch Thick Pork Chops with Pocket
   (Cut by Butcher)
Salt and Pepper
Accent
1 8-Ounce Package Pepperidge Farm Stuffing
2 3-Ounce Cans Sliced Mushrooms

1. Preheat oven to 350 degrees.

2. Season inside of pork chop pockets with salt, pepper, and accent. Fill pork chop pockets lightly with stuffing and mushrooms. Close with a pick.

3. Bake in a covered casserole for 1 hour at 350 degrees.

4. Brown without cover for 15 minutes and serve piping hot.

— Mrs. Dan M. Hodges

GREEN RICE

Yield: 6 Servings

This will make you dear to many a guest's heart!

2½ Cups Rice, Cooked
¾ Cup Milk
3 Tablespoons Cheddar Cheese, Grated
¼ Cup Parsley, Minced
¾ teaspoon Worcestershire Sauce
2 Eggs, Well-Beaten
3 Tablespoons Butter
1½ teaspoons Onions, Grated
1 10-Ounce Package Frozen Spinach
1½ teaspoons Salt

1. Preheat oven to 325 degrees. Grease casserole or ring mould.
2. Cook and drain frozen spinach. Blend together all ingredients.
3. Turn into greased casserole or ring mould.
4. Bake at 325 degrees for forty-five minutes.

— Mrs. Harry G. Haisten, Jr.

MINCEMEAT GLAZED APPLES

Yield: 6 Servings

1 3-Ounce Package Cherry Gelatin
1 3-Ounce Package Orange Gelatin
1½ Cups Boiling Water
1 Cup Cold Water
6 Baking Apples
1 Cup Prepared Mincemeat

1. Preheat broiler unit of range.
2. Dissolve gelatins in boiling water. Add cold water.
3. Core apples and starting at the stem end, peel each apple down about one inch.
4. Place apples with peeled end up in large skillet. Fill apples with mincemeat.
5. Pour gelatin mixture over apples and bring to a boil over melium heat.
6. Cover, reduce heat and simmer 15 minutes or until apples are tender.
7. Remove cover and place under broiler, basting frequently, for 15 minutes. When done, apples will be glazed and lightly browned.
8. Serve warm or cold with syrup.

— Miss Blanche Thebom

BUTTERMILK BRAN MUFFINS

(See page 105)

LEMON FROST ICE CREAM

(See page 251)

WATERCRESS AND CORN SOUP
CANTONESE SWEET AND SOUR PORK
FLUFFY WHITE RICE   CHILLED TOMATO QUARTERS
ARTICHOKE AND BEAN SPROUT SALAD
PARSLIED FANTANS
LUSCIOUS LEMON SQUARES

WINES:
RICE WINE (SAKE)—Japanese

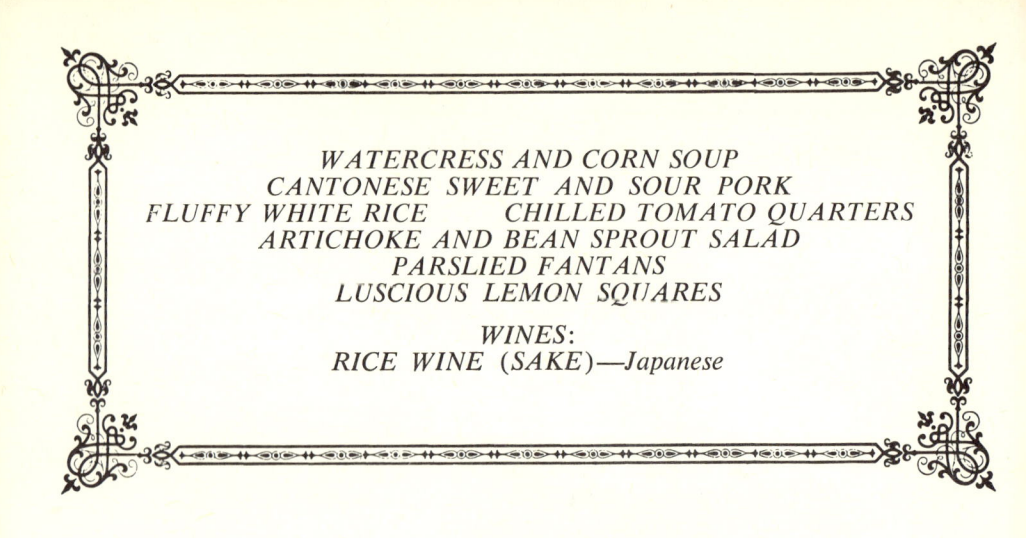

WATERCRESS AND CORN SOUP

Yield: 4 Servings

4 Cups Beef Broth
1 teaspoon Parsley, Chopped
¼ teaspoon Marjoram
2 Cups Corn Kernels, Uncooked
½ Cup Watercress, Chopped Finely
3 Tablespoons Butter
Salt and Pepper
Hard-Cooked Egg Slices
Strips of Pimiento

1. In a saucepan simmer together beef broth, parsley and marjoram for 5 minutes.

2. Add corn, cut from the cob, and simmer for 20 to 25 more minutes.

3. Strain through a coarse sieve and stir in chopped watercress and butter. Season to taste.

4. Garnish with hard-cooked egg slice and strip of pimiento.

— Mrs. Tom Slaughter

CANTONESE SWEET AND SOUR PORK

Yield: 4-6 Servings

2 Pounds Cooked Pork (Cut Into 2 Inch Cubes)
2 Tablespoons Soy Sauce, Kirkkoman
2 Tablespoons Cornstarch
2 Cups Sesame Seed Oil
3 Carrots, Sliced
1 Medium Onion, Sliced
1 Can Fresh Frozen Pineapple Chunks
1 Large Bell Pepper, Cut in 1 Inch Squares

1. Dredge pork cubes with mixture of soy sauce and cornstarch.

2. Heat sesame seed oil until very hot and fry meat until brown. Remove meat and drain.

3. Reheat pan and add 2 Tablespoons of the drained oil. Saute onion, carrots, pineapple and Bell pepper in the re-heated oil.

Sweet and Sour Sauce:

¾ Cup Sugar, Granulated
¼ Cup Soy Sauce, Kirkkoman
3 Tablespoons Cornstarch
⅔ Cup Water
⅓ Cup Vinegar

1. In a saucepan blend all ingredients together and cook until thick.

2. Add sweet and sour sauce to sauteed fruit and vegetables. And pork cubes and heat thoroughly.

3. Serve with fluffy white rice.

— Miss Margaret M. Withington

DINNERS

ARTICHOKE AND BEAN SPROUT SALAD

Yield: 4 Servings

½ Can Bean Sprouts, Drained
½ Can Cut Green Beans, Drained
½ Can Artichoke Hearts, Drained
½ Can Water Chestnuts, Drained and Sliced

1. Marinate in Herb-Garlic Dressing for several hours, drain. Serve on bed of crisp chicory.

— Mrs. M. D. Dunlap

PARSLIED FANTANS

Yield: 6 Each

2 Tablespoons Butter, Melted
1 teaspoon Lemon Juice
6 Brown-and-Serve Butterflake Rolls
2 Tablespoons Parsley, Chopped
2 teaspoons Chives, Chopped

1. Preheat oven to 400 degrees.

2. Blend together butter and lemon juice. Partially separate sections of rolls.

3. Brush lemon butter between roll sections and sprinkle with parsley and chives.

4. Place roll in muffin cups and brush tops with lemon butter. Sprinkle with parsley and chives.

— Mrs. Joseph R. Manning

LUSCIOUS LEMON SQUARES

(See page 68)

> FRUIT FANTASY
> SHRIMP LUDMILA
> HERBED SPINACH BAKE
> WHOLE BABY CARROTS
> *Sprinkled with Capers*
> OATMEAL LOAF BREAD
> BOMBE GRANDEE
> WINES:
> CALIFORNIA RIESLING—*American*
> PUILLY FUISSE—*French*

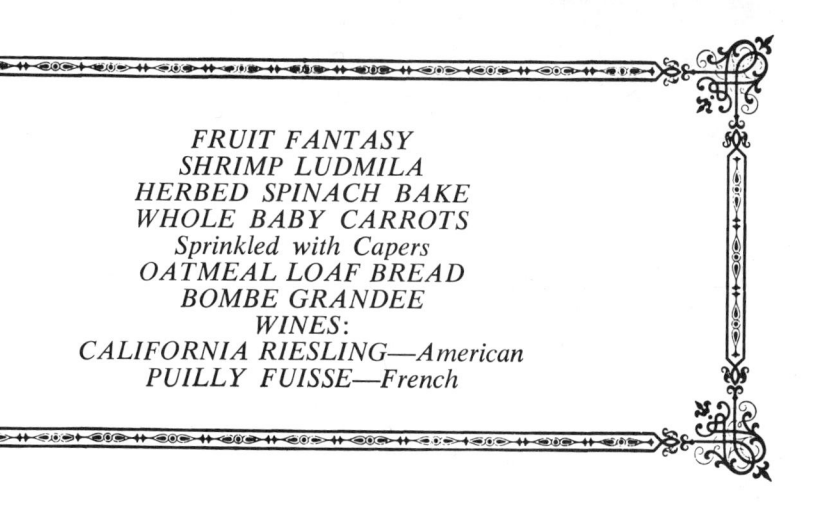

FRUIT FANTASY

Yield: 6 Servings

1 11-Ounce Can Mandarin Orange Segments, Drained
1 13-Ounce Can Pineapple Chunks, Drained
½ Pint Sour Cream
1 Cup Tiny Marshmallows

1. Place drained pineapple and orange segments, marshmallows, and sour cream in large bowl.
2. Blend together and chill overnight.
3. Serve in stemmed crystal compotes, garnished with strawberry flower.

— Miss Pauline Smith

SHRIMP LUDMILA

Yield: 6 Servings

36 Shrimp, Uncooked (Headed but with Shells on)
¾ Cup Olive Oil
¼ teaspoon Oregano
Pinch of Rosemary
5 Cloves Garlic, Sliced
½ Lemon, Sliced
1 Bay Leaf
Salt and Pepper

1. Combine all ingredients in pan. Cover and simmer slowly for 15 minutes.
2. Remove lid and simmer for 5 more minutes, stirring occasionally. Drain and reserve sauce for serving.
3. Serve on large platter of crisp salad greens. Guests peel their own shrimp, using sauce shrimp was simmered in as a dip.

— Mr. J. Lee Friedman

HERBED SPINACH BAKE

Yield: 6 Servings

1 10-Ounce Package Frozen Chopped Spinach
1 Cup Rice, Cooked
1 Cup American Cheese, Grated
2 Eggs, Slightly Beaten
2 Tablespoons Butter, Softened
⅓ Cup Milk
2 Tablespoons Onion, Chopped
½ teaspoon Worcestershire Sauce
1 teaspoon Salt
¼ teaspoon Thyme

1. Preheat oven to 350 degrees. Grease 10 x 16 x 1½ inch casserole.

2. Cook and drain spinach. Combine all ingredients and pour into 10 x 16 x 1½ inch casserole. Bake at 350 degrees for 20-25 minutes. Cut into squares and serve.

3. Top with Hollandaise Sauce (See page 27) for something extra special!

— Mrs. Paul Hanes

OATMEAL LOAF BREAD

Yield: 2 Loaves

2 Packages Active Dry Yeast
½ Cup Warm Water
1½ Cups Boiling Water
1 Cup Quick-Cooking Oatmeal
½ Cup Light Molasses
⅓ Cup Shortening
1 Tablespoon Salt
6½ Cups Flour, Sifted
2 Eggs

1. Soften yeast in ½ cup warm water.

2. In large bowl combine 1½ cups boiling water, oatmeal, molasses, shortening and salt. Cool to lukewarm.

DINNERS

3. Stir in yeast and blend well.
4. Add flour, 2 cups at a time, until dough is moderately stiff and smooth.
5. Grease top lightly. Cover tightly and chill overnight.
6. Turn out on well-floured surface and shape dough into 2 loaves.
7. Place in greased 8½ x 4½ x 2½ inch loaf pans.
8. Cover and let double in warm place (about 2 hours).
9. Bake at 375 degrees for 40 minutes. Serve warm with whipped butter.

— Mrs. Joe MacMillan

BOMBE GRANDEE

Yield: 6-8 Servings

Tall, conical, or fancy melon-shaped moulds create an elegant two-toned dessert, to be moulded in a 2½ quart mould.

1½ Cups Chocolate Wafers, Crushed
3 Tablespoons Butter, Melted
1 Large Package Vanilla Frosting Mix
3 Pints Heavy Cream
1 Tablespoon Instant Coffee
3 Tablespoons Brandy Extract

1. Oil mould. Place two one-inch wide strips of aluminum foil across bottom and sides of mould.
2. Reserve ½ cup chocolate wafer crumbs, combining remaining crumbs with melted butter. Press onto bottom and sides of mould.
3. Blend dry frosting mix into cream in a large mixer bowl, beating until soft peaks begin to form.
4. Reserve about ⅓ of frosting-cream mixture. To the remaining ⅔ frosting-cream mixture, add dry instant coffee, brandy extract, and remaining ½ cup chocolate wafer crumbs. Blend well.
5. Spread coffee mixture over sides and bottom of mould.
6. Spoon frosting-cream mixture into center of mould. Freeze until firm (at least 4 hours).
7. Remove from mould by placing hot, moist cloth on bottom of mould and inverting on serving plate. Keep frozen until serving time. Top with whipped cream and shaved chocolate.

— Mrs. Tom I. Patterson

SENEGALESE SOUP
SMALL ROCK LOBSTER TAILS
ASPARAGUS MIMOSA
GEORGIA PEACH JUBILEE
BUTTERED BRIOCHE
BLUEBERRY ALASKA PIE

WINES:
GEWURTZTRAMINER—American
MEURSAULT—French

SENEGALESE SOUP

Yield: 8 Servings

2 10½-Ounce Cans Cream of Chicken Soup
1 Soup-Can Water
1 Can Evaporated Milk
1 Soup-Can Water
¼ Cup Butter
1 Tablespoon Curry Powder
½ Apple, Unpeeled and Sliced Thinly
½ Avocado, Peeled and Sliced Thinly
Lemon Juice
Chives Chopped

About fifteen minutes before serving:

1. Place in a saucepan, cream of chicken soup, water and milk. Add butter and curry powder and heat until bubbly.

2. Brush thin slices of unpeeled apple and peeled avocado with lemon juice, and chill.

3. Serve each bowl of soup, topped with chives and slices of apple and avocado.

— Miss Martha Haines

DINNERS

SMALL ROCK LOBSTER TAILS

Yield: 8 Servings

8 Frozen Small Rock Lobster Tails
Pink Sauce

1. Place frozen lobster tails in large kettle and cover with boiling salted water. Cover kettle and simmer for 5 minutes.
2. Drain and cool. With scissors cut through thin undershell of each tail.
3. Insert fingers between top shell and pull meat out in one piece. Reserve shells. Chill meat.
4. Cut meat into half inch slices and re-fill shells with red side up.

Pink Sauce:

Yield: 1 Cup

1 Tablespoon Tomato Paste
1 Pimiento, Diced
Pinch Dried Tarragon
Pinch Basil
1 Cup Mayonnaise
Lemon Juice

1. Puree tomato paste, pimiento and spices. Blend together with mayonnaise and lemon juice. Top with chopped chives.

— Mrs. McNeill Stokes

ASPARAGUS MIMOSA

2 Packages Frozen Spears of Asparagus
Hard-Cooked Egg

1. Prepare asparagus according to package directions.
2. As serving, sieve hard-cooked egg yolk over asparagus spears.

— Mrs. I. J. W. Johnston

GEORGIA PEACH JUBILEE

(See page 65)

DINNERS

BRIOCHE

Yield: 2 Dozen

Recipe for yeast rolls (See page 207)
1 Egg White, Slightly Beaten
1 Tablespoon Sugar, Granulated

1. Set aside one-fourth of dough. Cut remaining 3 pieces in half and roll into 24 balls.
2. Place large balls of dough in greased muffin pans. Cut reserved dough into 4 wedges and divide each wedge into 6 pieces. Form 24 small balls.
3. Make indentation in top of each large ball in muffin pans. Brush holes lightly with water and press each small ball into indentation. Let rise.
4. Brush tops with egg white-sugar mixture. Bake at 375 degrees for 15 minutes or until done.

— Mrs. Louie Lathem

BLUEBERRY ALASKA PIE

Yield: 8 Servings

This is one of the most fun and delicious desserts ever!

Coconut Butter Crust:

2 Tablespoons Butter, Softened
1½ Cups Coconut, Shredded

1. Preheat oven to 300 degrees.
2. Spread softened butter evenly on bottom and sides of pie pan. Completely coat inside of pan with the softened butter.
3. Sprinkle with coconut and press evenly into butter.
4. Bake at 300 degrees for 15 to 20 minutes or until brown.

1 Quart Lemon Custard Ice Cream
2 Egg Whites, Stiffly Beaten
¾ Cup Sugar, Granulated
1 Can Blueberries
Cornstarch

1. Fill coconut crust with lemon custard ice cream. Cover with aluminum foil to prevent ice crystals from forming and freeze.
2. Beat egg whites until foamy and gradually add sugar. Beat until stiff peaks form. Top pie with meringue and run under broiler to brown (about 1-2 minutes).
3. Heat blueberries and make paste of 1 Tablespoon Cornstarch and water. Add to heated blueberries and stir until thickened.
4. Dribble hot, thickened blueberry sauce over each piece of pie and serve!

— Mrs. McNeill Stokes

BUFFET DINNERS

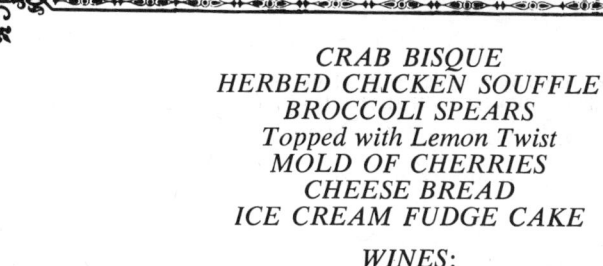

CRAB BISQUE
HERBED CHICKEN SOUFFLE
BROCCOLI SPEARS
Topped with Lemon Twist
MOLD OF CHERRIES
CHEESE BREAD
ICE CREAM FUDGE CAKE

WINES:
EMERALD—*American*
ROSE (ANJOU)—*French*

CRAB BISQUE I

Yield: 10-12 Servings

2 Cups Flaked Crabmeat
1 Cup Sherry
2 Cans Cream of Tomato Soup
2 Cans Green Pea Soup
2 Soup-Cans Light Cream
½ teaspoon Curry Powder
1 teaspoon Paprika

1. Place crabmeat in bowl; add sherry and toss lightly. Let stand 1 hour.
2. Blend other ingredients together and heat slowly. Do NOT boil.
3. Add crabmeat. Reheat and serve immediately. Garnish with added pieces of crabmeat and snipped parsley.

— Mrs. J. Charles Dukes, Jr.

CRAB BISQUE II

Yield: 6 Servings

1 Can Cream of Mushroom Soup
1 Can Cream of Asparagus Soup
1½ Soup-Cans Milk
1 Cup Light Cream
1 6½-Ounce Can Flaked Crabmeat
¼ Cup Sherry

1. Combine soups.
2. Stir in milk and cream. Heat to just boiling.
3. Add crabmeat and heat through.
4. Just before serving, add sherry.
5. Float pat of butter on top.

— Mrs. John E. McGaughey, Jr.

DINNERS

HERBED CHICKEN SOUFFLE

Yield: 10 Servings

1 8-Ounce Package Pepperidge Farm Herb Dressing
3 Cups Cooked Chicken, Diced
½ Cup Butter, Melted or ½ Cup Chicken Fat
½ Cup Flour, Sifted
¼ teaspoon Salt
Dash Pepper
3 Cups Chicken Broth
6 Eggs, Slightly Beaten

1. Preheat oven to 325 degrees. Grease 13 x 9 x 2 inch casserole or souffle dish.
2. Cook chicken (one medium-sized hen) and dice meat.
3. Prepare stuffing according to package directions for dry stuffing.
4. Spread in bottom of 13 x 9 x 2 inch casserole. Add layer of diced chicken.
5. Melt butter (chicken fat adds even more flavor) in saucepan and blend in flour and seasoning.
6. Stir in broth and cook until thick.
7. Stir small amount of hot mixture into slightly beaten eggs.
8. Blend chicken broth sauce and eggs together gradually.
9. Pour over chicken and cook at 325 degrees for 40-45 minutes or until knife inserted in souffle comes out clean.

Pimiento - Mushroom Sauce:

1 Can Cream of Mushroom Soup
1 Cup Sour Cream
¼ Cup Milk
½ Cup Pimiento, Chopped

1. Combine all ingredients of pimiento-mushroom sauce and ladle over souffle when serving.

— Mrs. Joseph R. Manning

MOULD OF CHERRIES

Yield: 10-12 Servings

1 6-Ounce Package Cherry Gelatin
1 Envelope Plain Gelatin
¾ Cup Sugar, Granulated
1 No. 2 Can Pineapple, Diced

1 No. 2 Can Pie Cherries
1 Cup Pecans, Chopped
Rind and Juice of 1 Lemon
Rind and Juice of 1 Orange

1. Oil salad mould(s).
2. Drain fruit and have 3 cups liquid in all (water may need to be added to make 3 cups).
3. Dissolve cherry gelatin in heated syrup made from 2 cups of above liquid and sugar.
4. Dissolve plain gelatin in remaining 1 cup liquid and add to hot mxture. Blend in other ingredients. (Red coloring may be added if desired.)
5. Pour into individual moulds or a large mould and chill. Serve on bed lettuce leaves.

— Mrs. Byron Brooke

CHEESE BREAD

Yield: 2 Loaves

2 Eggs, Slightly Beaten
3 Cups Milk
7½ Cups Bisquick
1½ Cups Sharp Cheese, Grated

1. Preheat oven to 350 degrees. Grease and line with waxed paper 2 loaf pans.
2. Blend together slightly beaten eggs and milk. Stir in Bisquick and cheese. Blend well.
3. Pour into greased, wax-paper lined loaf pans. Bake 1 hour at 350 degrees.
4. Cool 5 minutes, slice ½ inch thick and serve or cool completely and slice thin to serve.

— Mrs. Robert S. Grady

ICE CREAM FUDGE CAKE

1 Slice Pound Cake (See page 17)
1 Scoop Vanilla Ice Cream
Hot Fudge Sauce

1. Top sliced pound cake with scoop of vanilla ice cream and ladle hot fudge sauce over cake and ice cream.

— Mrs. Ogden Stokes

ARROZ CON POLLO
Served on Saffron Rice
GREEN BEANS AND BLACK OLIVES
CHILLED BOWL OF FRESH FRUIT
HOT CRESCENT ROLLS
GINGERED ICE CREAM

WINES:
CABERNET SAUVIGNON—American
BORDEAUX, CHATEAU ST. EMILION—French

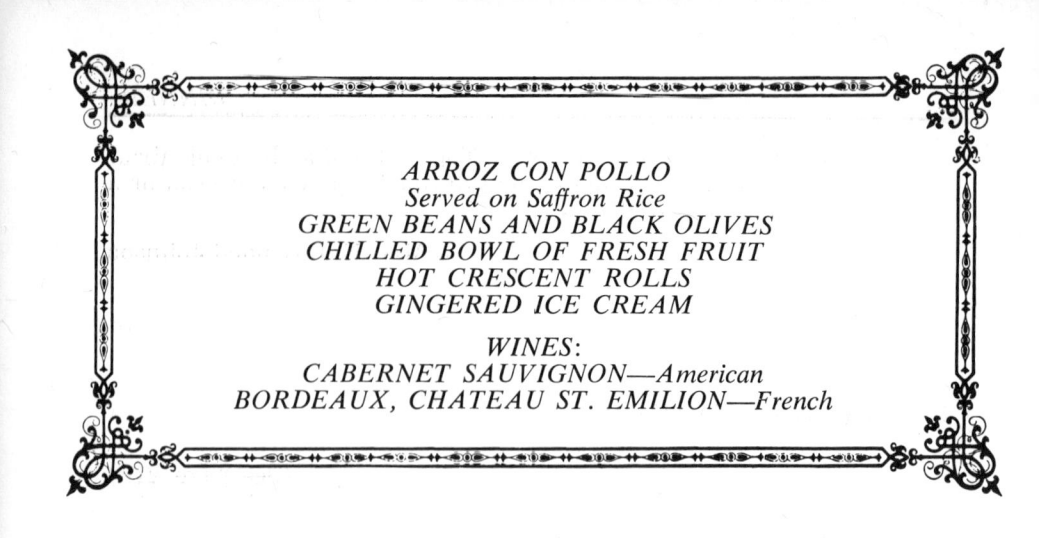

ARROZ CON POLLO

Yield: 4 Servings

1 Large Fryer or Young Hen

2 Large Onions, Chopped

2 or 3 Bell Peppers, Chopped

1 or 2 Cloves Garlic, Minced

2 Tablespoons Olive Oil or Vegetable Oil

1 Large Can Tomatoes

Pinch Saffron

2 Cups Rice, Uncooked

1 No. 2 Can Le Seur Green Peas, Drained

1 Small Can Pimiento

Salt and Pepper

1. Saute chicken lightly in olive oil, merely heat and turn. Do not cook. Remove from frying pan to large pot.

2. Saute onions, Bell pepper, and garlic in olive oil. Add tomatoes and saffron. Saute 5 to 10 minutes and add to chicken in pot.

3. Add rice which has been washed 5 or 6 times and drained. Do NOT stir. Cook very slowly on a low fire; every once in awhile move the pot to relocate the rice, but do NOT stir. Cook about 40 minutes.

4. Add drained peas and reserve liquid. Top with pimiento. Cook about 5 minutes more. To keep moist, add drained liquid from peas or a can of chicken soup if necessary.

— Mrs. E. Raymond Johnson

CELERY SEED DRESSING

(See page 218)

(Served with chilled bowl of fresh fruit)

GINGERED ICE CREAM

Yield: 6-8 Servings

1 Pint Milk
2 Eggs
½ Cup Sugar, Granulated
1 Cup Ginger Preserves, Cut Fine and with Syrup
1 Tablespoon Maraschino Cherries, Chopped
¼ Cup Sherry
1 Quart Heavy Cream
1 Cup Sugar, Granulated
1 teaspoon Vanilla Extract

1. Blend together well milk, eggs and sugar in the top of a double boiler and cook until spoon is coated.

2. Add ginger preserves, cherries, and sherry.

3. Chill overnight. When ready to freeze, add heavy cream, sugar, and vanilla extract, blending well.

— Mrs. Kathryn Grayburn

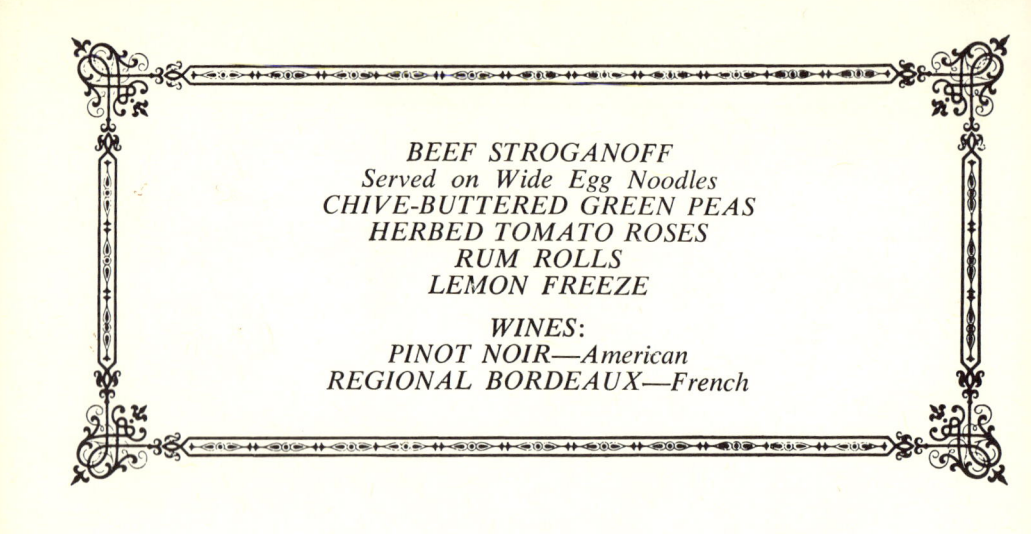

BEEF STROGANOFF
Served on Wide Egg Noodles
CHIVE-BUTTERED GREEN PEAS
HERBED TOMATO ROSES
RUM ROLLS
LEMON FREEZE

WINES:
PINOT NOIR—American
REGIONAL BORDEAUX—French

BEEF STROGANOFF

Yield: 6 Servings

5 Pounds Beef Fillet Tips
Salt and Pepper
Flour
½ Cup Butter, Melted
1 Medium Onion, Chopped
½ Clove Garlic, Minced
½ Pound Fresh Mushrooms, Sliced
1 Can Cream of Mushroom Soup
1 Can Cream of Chicken Soup
½ teaspoon Lea & Perrin's Sauce
¾ teaspoon Soy Sauce
1 Pint Sour Cream
3 Cups Wide Egg Noodles, Cooked

1. Lightly dust fillet tips in seasoned flour. Brown quickly in melted butter in skillet. Remove meat.

2. In same skillet saute onions and garlic. Add mushrooms and saute until tender.

3. Add soups, Lea & Perrin's Sauce and soy sauce. Gently stir in meat.

4. Cover and simmer for 20 to 30 minutes. Add sour cream and heat. Serve over wide egg noodles. (Do NOT simmer after sour cream has been added).

— Mrs. Richard Courts, II

HERBED TOMATO ROSES

Yield: 6 Servings

6 Medium Tomatoes
Herbed Italian Dressing
2-3 Heads Bibb Lettuce
Hard-Cooked Egg Slices

1. Using the tip of a sharp paring knife, make an "X" on the blossom end of the tomato (NOT the stem end). Extend the "X" from the center of the tomato to the base of the tomato only. Cut through the first thick layer of tomato with tip of knife.

2. Divide each of the portions made by the "X" in half.

3. With tip of knife, separate each "petal" from the round of the tomato, allowing "petals" to stand away from the meat of the tomato.

4. Center tomato rose on bed of Bibb lettuce, surround with hard-cooked egg slices and dribble with herbed Italian dressing. Garnish with sprig of parsley.

— Mrs. McNeill Stokes

RUM ROLLS

(See Page 88)

LEMON FREEZE

(See Page 208)

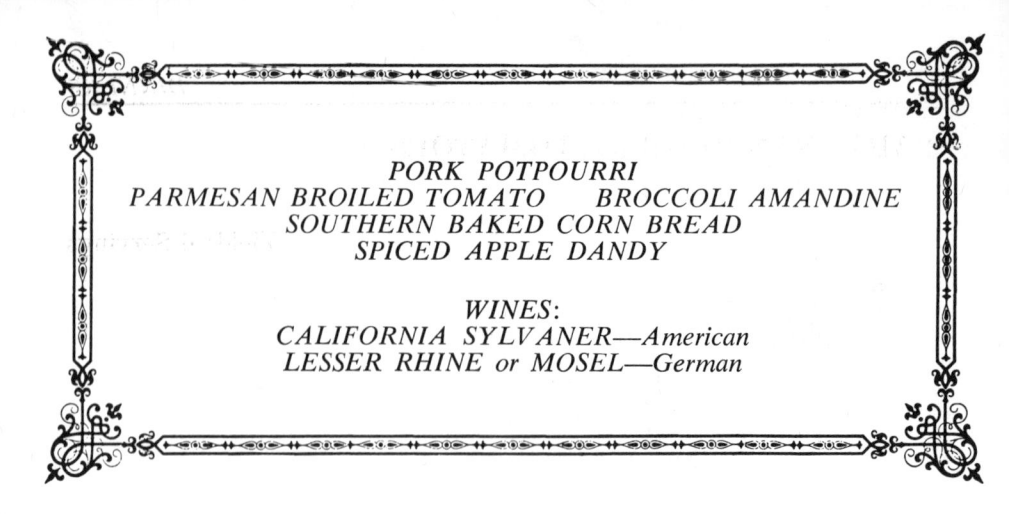

PORK POTPOURRI
PARMESAN BROILED TOMATO   BROCCOLI AMANDINE
SOUTHERN BAKED CORN BREAD
SPICED APPLE DANDY

WINES:
CALIFORNIA SYLVANER—American
LESSER RHINE or MOSEL—German

PORK POTPOURRI

Yield: 6 Servings

6 Loin Pork Chops
Salt and Pepper
Paprika
Vegetable Oil
1 Large Can Sauerkraut, Drained
1 Medum Onion, Chopped
1 Pint Sour Cream

1. Preheat oven to 300 degrees.

2. Brown six loin pork chops that have been sprinkled with salt, pepper and paprika in a small amount of oil. Remove and drain on paper towel.

3. Drain one large can of sauerkraut and blend with chopped onion. Saute until golden. Add one pint of sour cream.

4. Place half of the sauerkraut mixture on bottom of casserole. Arrange pork chops on top and cover with rest of sauerkraut mixture. Cover casserole.

5. Bake at 300 degrees for one hour.

— Mrs. William C. Bartholomay

DINNERS

PARMESAN BROILED TOMATOES

Yield: 6 Servings

6 Whole Tomatoes
Salt and Pepper
Parmesan Cheese
Chives
Garlic Salt
Butter
Saltine Crackers, Crushed

1. Preheat oven to 350 degrees.

2. Wash tomatoes and cut out stems. Do NOT peel. Select tomatoes which are not too ripe.

3. Slice off top fourth and sprinkle generously with salt, pepper, chives, garlic salt, cheese and cracker crumbs.

4. Place a pat of butter on each one.

5. Bake at 350 degrees for 30 minutes. Do not let tomatoes overcook. This can also be done as a casserole dish using canned tomatoes.

— Mrs. Tom I. Patterson

CORN BREAD

Yield: 1 Dozen Pieces

1 Egg
1 Cup Self-rising Corn Meal
¼ Cup Flour

DINNERS

    1 teaspoon Baking Powder
    3 Tablespoons Bacon Drippings
    1 Cup Milk

1. Preheat oven to 450 degrees. Grease cornstick moulds or square pan.

2. Blend all ingredients together and pour into greased pan.

3. Bake at 450 degrees for 40 minutes.

— Mrs. Robert S. Grady

SPICED APPLE DANDY

Yield: 8 Servings

5 Cups Apples, Diced
2 teaspoons Cinnamon
½ Cup Sugar, Granulated
¾ Cup Brown Sugar
¾ Cup Oatmeal
½ Cup Flour, Sifted
½ Cup Shortening
1 teaspoon Baking Powder
¼ teaspoon Soda
Heavy Cream, Whipped

1. Preheat oven to 275 degrees. Grease a shallow pan. Dice apples.

2. Place apples in greased pan, cover with granulated sugar, and sprinkle with cinnamon.

3. In a mixing bowl, blend together until grainy, brown sugar, oatmeal, flour, shortening, baking powder, and soda.

4. Sprinkle this mixture over apples and bake at 275 degrees until apples are tender and top is brown (about 20 minutes).

5. Serve with whipped cream.

— Mrs. Charles P. Netherton

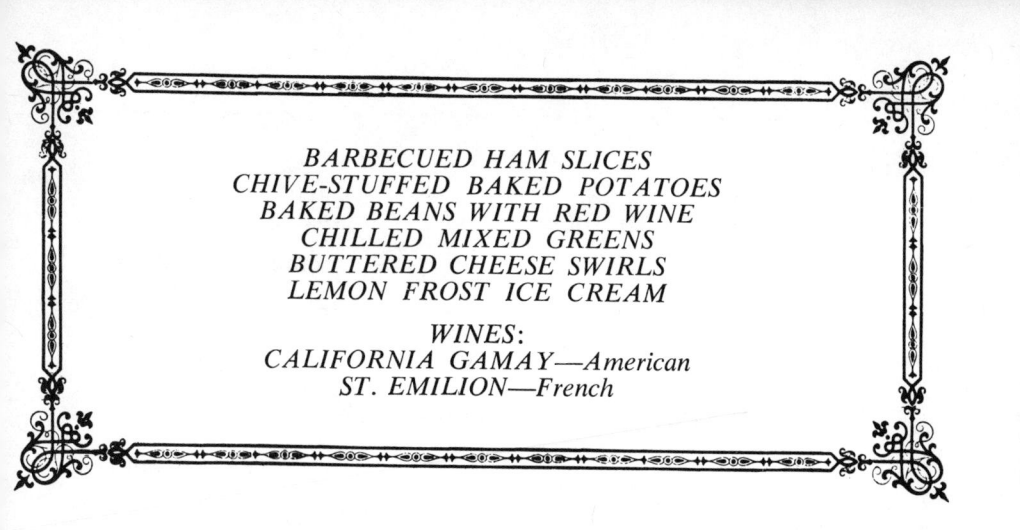

BARBECUED HAM SLICES
CHIVE-STUFFED BAKED POTATOES
BAKED BEANS WITH RED WINE
CHILLED MIXED GREENS
BUTTERED CHEESE SWIRLS
LEMON FROST ICE CREAM

WINES:
CALIFORNIA GAMAY—American
ST. EMILION—French

BARBECUED HAM SLICES

Yield: 6 Servings

Barbecue Sauce:

Yield: 1½ Cups

2 Tablespoons Butter
½ Cup Salad Dressing
½ Cup Vinegar
1 teaspon Paprika
½ Cup Catsup
2 teaspoons Chili Powder
¼ teaspoon Salt
Ham Slices, Thinly Sliced

1. Preheat broiler unit of range.

2. Blend sauce ingredients together and simmer until well thickened.

3. Brush one side of each ham slice with sauce and place on broiler rack 3 inches from moderate flame. Broil for half the cooking time.

4. Turn ham slices over and brush other side with sauce. Continue broiling until done.

DINNERS

Broiling Time:

    ¼ inch slices - broil 3 minutes to a side.

    ½ inch slices - broil 5 to 6 minutes to a side.

— Mrs. Ben Y. Cooper

CHIVE-STUFFED BAKED POTATOES

Yield: 6 Servings

11 Slices Crisp Bacon, Crumbled
6 Large Potatoes, Baked
1½ Cups Sour Cream
2 Tablespoons Chives, Chopped
6 Tablespoons Butter
2 Eggs
Salt and Pepper

1. Fry bacon until crisp. Drain and crumble.
2. Scoop out baked potatoes and mash with sour cream, chives, butter and eggs, salt and pepper to taste.
3. Add bacon to mashed potato mixture and blend.
4. Re-fill potato shells, wrap in foil and freeze.
5. To heat, bake in 400 degree oven 45 to 60 minutes.

— Mrs. William Frain

BAKED BEANS WITH RED WINE

Yield: 6-8 Servings

2 Medium Onions, Diced
2 Tablespoons Butter
1 Thick Slice Ham, Diced
1 Cup Canned Consomme
1 Cup Red Wine
½ teaspoon Salt
¼ teaspoon Cayenne Pepper
2 Cans Kidney Beans
6-8 Slices Bacon, Cut into 1 Inch Squares
½ Cup Cheddar Cheese, Grated

1. Preheat oven to 350 degrees.
2. Saute onions in butter. (Do NOT brown). Add ham, consomme and red wine. Blend well.
3. Simmer until sauce begins to thicken and add salt and Cayenne Pepper. Simmer for 10 minutes and add beans.
4. Blend well and pour into casserole. Top with 1 inch square pieces of bacon and bake at 350 degrees for 30 minutes.
5. Ten minutes before beans are done, sprinkle with grated cheese and finish baking.

— Mrs. Robert B. Ansley, Jr.

CHEESE SWIRLS

(See Page 99)

LEMON FROST ICE CREAM

Yield: 6-8 Servings

2 3-Ounce Packages Lemon Gelatin
2 Cups Boiling Water
1½ Cups Sugar, Granulated
6-8 Ice Cubes
1 No. 2 Can Fruit Cocktail
1 Quart Milk
2 Large Cans Evaporated Milk
1 Tablespoon Vanilla Extract

1. Dissove gelatin in boiling water. Add sugar.
2. When sugar dissolves, add ice cubes.
3. Stir in fruit cocktail including juice. Then add both milks and vanilla extract.
4. Freeze in 1 gallon home ice cream freezer.
5. Top with blackberry, pineapple, or strawberry jam.

— Mrs. Tyrone S. Clifford

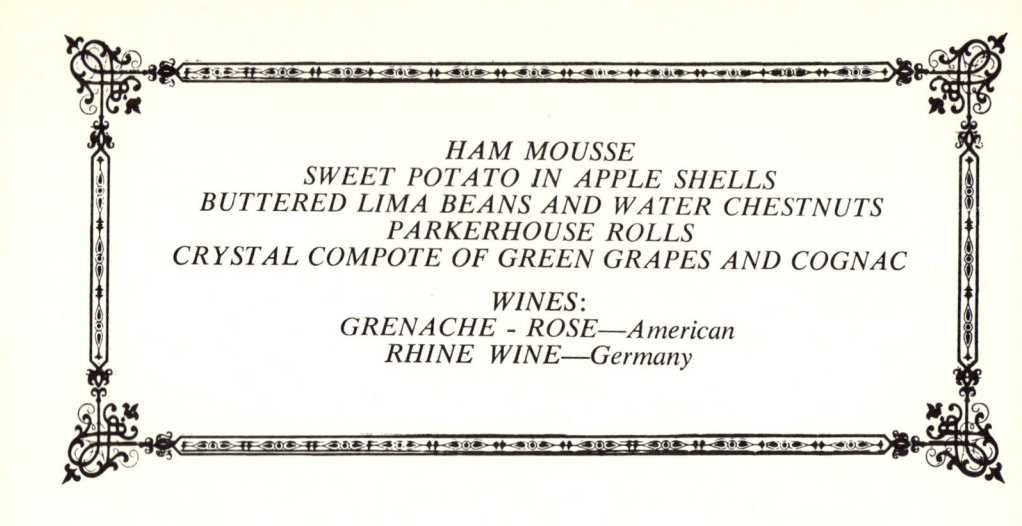

HAM MOUSSE
SWEET POTATO IN APPLE SHELLS
BUTTERED LIMA BEANS AND WATER CHESTNUTS
PARKERHOUSE ROLLS
CRYSTAL COMPOTE OF GREEN GRAPES AND COGNAC

WINES:
GRENACHE - ROSE—*American*
RHINE WINE—*Germany*

HAM MOUSSE

Yield: 6 Servings

1 Tablespoon Plain Gelatin
¼ Cup Cold Water
1 Cup Milk, Heated
1 Tablespoon Vinegar
1 teaspoon Prepared Mustard
1 Tablespoon Horseradish
2 Cups Baked or Boiled Ham, Ground
1 Tablespoon Bell Pepper, Minced
1 teaspoon Onion, Minced

1. Oil mould.
2. Soften gelatin in cold water. Dissolve in hot milk.
3. Add vinegar, mustard, and horseradish. Chill until partially set.
4. Add remaining ingredients. Pour into oiled mould.
5. Unmould onto crisp lettuce and serve with Russian dressing.

— Mrs. Fletcher Wolfe

SWEET POTATO IN APPLE SHELLS

Yield: 6 Servings

3 Large Red Baking Apples
½ Cup Brown Sugar
3 Cups Sweet Potatoes, Cooked and Mashed
3 Tablespoons Butter
3 Tablespoons Heavy Cream

(Optional) Pecans or Walnuts, Chopped
Melted Butter

1. Preheat oven to 400 degrees.
2. Cut apples in half crosswise. Remove core and seeds and sprinkle cavity with half of brown sugar.
3. Place in shallow pan containing small amount of water. Bake in oven at 400 degrees, 10 to 20 minutes or until almost tender.
4. Scoop out pulp of apple leaving a shell about ½ inch thick. Reserve pulp.
5. Add apple pulp, butter and cream to hot mashed sweet potato. Beat until fluffy and season to taste. Add chopped nuts, if desired.
6. Pile sweet potato mixture lightly into apple shells or force through a decorating tube. Place in shallow pan.
7. Sprinkle with remaining brown sugar and pour a little melted butter on top. Run under broiler until lightly browned.

— Mrs. Lester G. Maddox

GREEN GRAPES IN COGNAC

Yield: 6 Servings

3 Pounds Thompson Seedless Grapes, Fresh
¾ Cup Honey
¾ Cup Cognac
1 Tablespoon Lemon Juice
1-2 Cups Sour Cream

1. Drain washed grapes thoroughly.
2. Remove from stems. Combine honey, Cognac and lemon juice. Toss grapes with honey mixture.
3. Chill at least 5 hours, stirring occasionally. Serve in chilled crystal compote and top with sour cream.

— Mrs. Robert Malone

FLAKED CRABMEAT SOUFFLE
BOUQUET OF CHILLED VEGETABLES
CINNAMON SPICED CRESCENTS
ORANGE LADYFINGER DELIGHT

WINES:
GEWURTZTRAMINER—American
MEURSALT—French

FLAKED CRABMEAT SOUFFLE

Yield: 8 Servings

3 Tablespoons Butter, Melted
5 Tablespoons Flour
1½ Cups Heavy Cream, Heated
1⅓ Cups Velveeta Cheese, Grated
1 Pound (3 Cups) Flaked Crabmeat
4 Egg Yolks, Well-Beaten
1 teaspoon Cream of Tartar
4 Egg Whites, Stiffly Beaten

1. Preheat oven to 325 degrees. Grease large souffle dish or individual souffle cups.
2. Add flour to melted butter and cook until bubbly. Stir in cream and cook until thick.
3. Blend in cheese and stir until thoroughly melted.
4. Add crabmeat (pick shells out carefully) and egg yolks.
5. Add cream of tartar to egg whites and beat until stiff but not dry. Fold in stiffly beaten egg whites.
6. Pour into greased souffle baking dish(es), and set in a pan of hot water. Bake at 325 degrees for 1 hour.
7. Serve on thick slices of pineapple or tomato and top with thin cream sauce and chopped parsley.

— Mrs. McNeill Stokes

BOUQUET OF CHILLED VEGETABLES

Baby Okra
Tiny Butterbeans
Whole Green Beans
Small Artichoke Hearts
Tiny Carrots
Small Mushroom Caps

1. In separate bowls marinate in French Dressing each of the above cooked vegetables.
2. Attractively arrange on shallow platter with fresh cherry tomatoes and serve cold with additional French Dressing.

— Mrs. Robert Minnear

CINNAMON SPICED CRESCENTS

(See page 101)

ORANGE LADY FINGER DELIGHT

Yield: 8-10 Servings

1 Tablespoon Plain Gelatin
¼ Cup Cold Water
2 Cups Milk
2 Tablespoons Cornstarch
¾ Cup Sugar, Granulated
¾ Cup Orange Juice (or Lemon Juice)
2 Egg Yolks, Slightly Beaten
2 Egg Whites, Stiffly Beaten
¼ Cup Sugar, Granulated
1 teaspoon Orange Rind (or Lemon Rind), Grated
2 Packages Lady Fingers
Whipped Cream

1. Soak gelatin in cold water.
2. Add a little cold milk to cornstarch. Scald rest of milk in top of double boiler.
3. Add sugar to milk and then add cornstarch-milk mixture.
4. Simmer for 20 minutes, and stir until thickened and add gelatin and orange juice.
5. Add gelatin-orange juice mixture a little at a time to slightly beaten egg yolks. Cook for 5 minutes more.
6. Cool before adding stiffly beaten egg whites to which ¼ cup extra sugar has been added. Blend well and cool completely.
7. Arrange split lady fingers around edge of bottom of mould. Add custard, then more lady fingers on top, if desired. Serve with whipped cream.

— Mrs. John C. Hopkins, Jr.

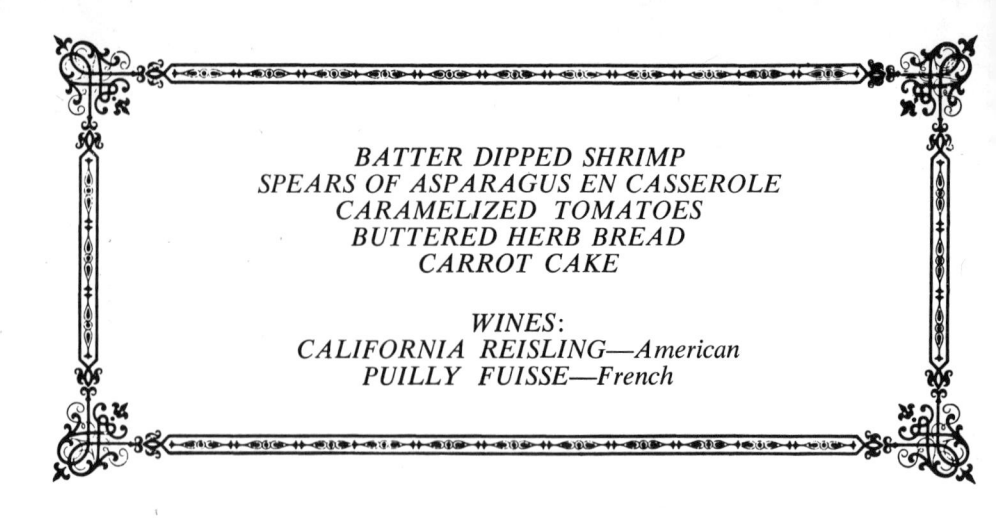

BATTER DIPPED SHRIMP
SPEARS OF ASPARAGUS EN CASSEROLE
CARAMELIZED TOMATOES
BUTTERED HERB BREAD
CARROT CAKE

WINES:
CALIFORNIA REISLING—American
PUILLY FUISSE—French

BATTER DIPPED SHRIMP

Yield: 8 Servings

1 Pound Shrimp, Uncooked
1 Egg, Slightly Beaten
1 Cup Milk
1 Cup Flour, Sifted
1 teaspoon Baking Powder
½ teaspoon Salt
Vegetable Oil

1. Wash, shell and devein shrimp. Drain shrimp on paper towels.

2. Blend egg and milk together. Sift flour with baking powder and salt.

3. Add egg-milk mixture to dry ingredients and blend until smooth. Dip shrimp in batter and fry in just enough heated oil to float shrimp. (Heat oil to 385 degrees before adding shrimp.) Drain golden brown shrimp on paper towels.

— Mrs. Albert W. Boam

SPEARS OF ASPARAGUS EN CASSEROLE

Yield: 8 Servings

2 10-Ounce Packages Frozen Asparagus
1 10-Ounce Package Tiny Green Peas
1 Can Cream of Mushroom Soup
1 Cup Cheddar Cheese, Grated

1. Preheat oven to 350 degrees. Grease casserole.
2. Combine all ingredients, reserving part of cheese.
3. Top with reserved cheese and bake at 350 degrees for 30-40 minutes or until bubbly.

— Mrs. William Frain

CARAMELIZED TOMATOES

Yield: 8 Servings

6 Medium Tomatoes
3 Slices White Bread, Trimmed and Cubed
⅓ Cup Butter, Melted
⅓ Cup Brown Sugar
¾ teaspoon Salt
Dash Pepper
Chopped Parsley

1. Preheat oven to 350 degrees. Grease baking pan.
2. Slice off top fourth of tomatoes (at stem end). Scoop out most of tomato pulp and reserve.
3. Place shells in greased baking pan. Combine bread cubes, 1 cup of tomato pulp, melted butter, brown sugar and seasonings. Blend thoroughly.
4. Re-fill tomato shells with this mixture and bake at 350 degrees for 30 minutes. Garnish with chopped parsley.

— Miss Ann O'Hara Boswell

DINNERS

HERB BREAD

(See page 33)

CARROT CAKE

Yield: 12 Servings

This one will surprise and please your guests and family. A spicy, moist, rich cake with a delicious icing. No! You can't taste the carrots.

2 Cups Flour, Sifted
2 Cups Sugar, Granulated
¼ teaspoon Salt
1 teaspoon Baking Powder
1 teaspoon Baking Soda
1 teaspoon Cinnamon
4 Eggs
1½ Cups Vegetable Oil
2 Cups Carrots, Grated

1. Preheat oven to 375 degrees. Grease and flour 2 layer cake pans.
2. Sift dry ingredients together (not carrots).
3. Blend together eggs and vegetable oil.
4. Add dry ingredients and carrots.
5. Bake 30 to 40 minutes at 375 degrees.

Icing:

1 8-Ounce Package Cream Cheese, Softened
½ Cup Butter
1 teaspoon Vanilla Extract
1 Box Confectioner's Sugar
1 Cup Pecans, Chopped

1. Cream together softened cream cheese and butter.
2. Add vanilla extract and Confectioner's sugar.
3. Frost cake and sprinkle with chopped pecans.

— Mrs. J. Robert Douglas, Jr.

PATIO DINNERS

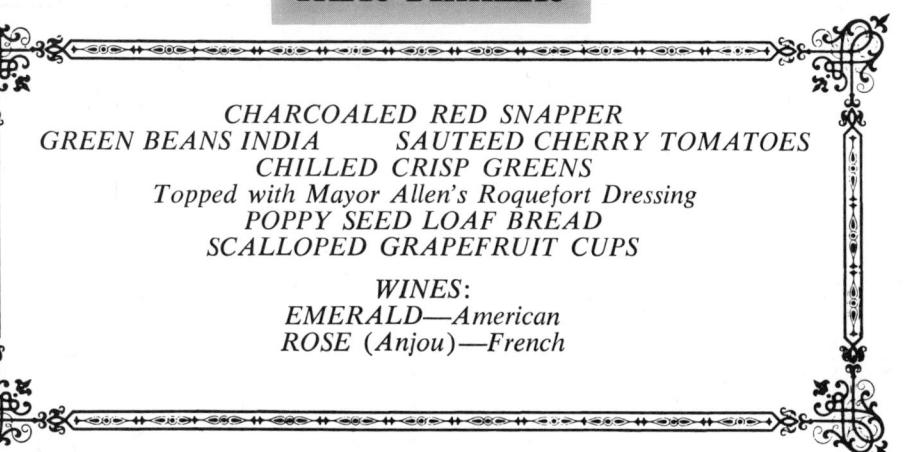

CHARCOALED RED SNAPPER
GREEN BEANS INDIA   SAUTEED CHERRY TOMATOES
CHILLED CRISP GREENS
Topped with Mayor Allen's Roquefort Dressing
POPPY SEED LOAF BREAD
SCALLOPED GRAPEFRUIT CUPS

WINES:
EMERALD—American
ROSE (Anjou)—French

CHARCOALED RED SNAPPER

Yield: 4 Servings

1 Large Red Snapper
¼ Cup Lemon Juice
1 Cup Butter, Melted
Salt
Pepper

1. Prepare charcoal for grilling.

2. Blend together lemon juice, butter and seasonings.

3. Brush fish with lemon-butter sauce and wrap in aluminum foil or place in greased pan or grill.

4. Cover pan and/or grill and cook about 15-20 minutes or until done. Baste frequently.

5. Garnish with twists of lemon and sprigs of parsley.

— Mrs. Charles C. Ford

DINNERS

GREEN BEANS INDIA

Yield: 8 Servings

8 Slices Bacon, Crumbled
½ Cup Sugar, Granulated
½ Cup Vinegar
2 Cans French Style Green Beans
½ Medium Onion, Diced
3 Tablespoons India Relish

1. Preheat oven to 275 degrees.

2. Fry bacon and remove from pan. Saute sugar, onions and vinegar in bacon drippings.

3. Place green beans in casserole and pour sugar mixture over beans. Crumble bacon and mix with relish. Top beans with this mixture and cover.

4. Bake at 275 degrees for 1½ hours.

— Mrs. Tyrone S. Clifford

SAUTEED CHERRY TOMATOES

(See Page 182)

MAYOR ALLEN'S ROQUEFORT DRESSING:

Yield: 1½ Cups

1 Cup Sour Cream
½ Cup Mayonnaise
½ Cup Roquefort Cheese, Crumbled
Salt and Pepper

1. Blend all ingredients together, seasoning to taste.

Mayor Ivan Allen, Jr.

POPPY SEED LOAF BREAD

Yield: 1 Loaf

1 Package Active Dry Yeast
1¼ Cups Warm Water
2 Tablespoons Butter
2 Tablespoons Sugar, Granulated
2 teaspoons Salt
3 Cups Flour, Sifted
1 Egg
2 Tablespoons Poppy Seeds

1. Soften yeast in warm water. Grease loaf pan.
2. Add remaining ingredients except 1 cup flour.
3. Beat two minutes at medium speed and blend in remaining flour with spoon.
4. Let double in bulk in covered bowl.
5. Punch down and pour into greased loaf pan.
6. Bake at 375 degrees for 45 minutes.

This is an extremely light and airy bread and does not store particularly well. This warning is probably unnecessary, as seldom will a loaf last more than one meal. It's delicious!

— Mrs. Joe MacMillan

SCALLOPED GRAPEFRUIT CUPS

Yield: 8 Servings

4 Grapefruit or Oranges
⅓ Cup Flour, Sifted
⅓ Cup Sugar, Granulated
3 Tablespoons Butter
¼ teaspoon Nutmeg
¼ teaspoon Cinnamon

1. Preheat oven to 375 degrees.
2. Cut fruit in half (scalloping as fruit is cut), scoop out sections with spoon, discarding membrane and return sections to shells.
3. Combine remaining ingredients and cut in butter until mixture resembles coarse cornmeal.
4. Sprinkle mixture over top of scalloped fruit cups.
5. Place on baking sheet and bake at 375 degrees for 40 minutes.
6. Serve warm or cold for a real treat!

— Mrs. William Berry Hartsfield

LAMB EN KYATHION
CASSEROLE OF GREEN BEANS AND WATER CHESTNUTS
WHOLE SPICED PICKLED PEACH
SLICED TOMATOES
Topped with Cucumber Cream Dressing
HEAVENLY RUM ANGEL CAKE

WINES:
CABERNET SAUVIGNON—American
PETIT CHATEAU - BORDEAUX—French

LAMB EN KYATHION

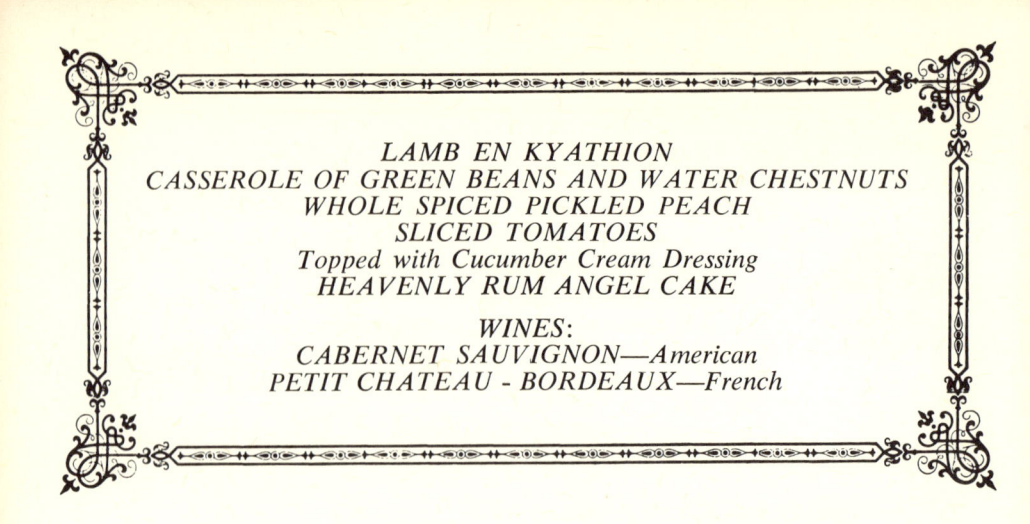

Yield: 6 Servings

3 Pounds Lamb, Cubed
½ Cup Pineapple Juice
Juice of 1 Lemon
¼ Cup Vegetable Oil
1 teaspoon Salt
½ teaspoon Pepper
¼ teaspoon Sage
¼ teaspoon Dry Mustard
Pinch of Oregano
1 Medium Onion, Chopped
1 Bell Pepper, Chopped
1 Clove Garlic, Minced

1. Combine all ingredients and marinate overnight. Stir several times.
2. Drain and charcoal in pan over grill for 20 to 30 minutes. (This also may be cooked under broiler unit of range.)

— Mrs. Robert Malone

HOT GREEN BEAN SALAD

Yield: 6 Servings

This is a quick, do-ahead easy delicious salad!

1½ Cans Frenched Green Beans
1 Medium Onion, Thinly Sliced
4 Slices Crisp Bacon, Crumbled
½ Cup Vegetable Oil

— 262 —

½ Cup Vinegar
½ Cup Sugar, Granulated
½ Cup Water Chestnuts or Almonds

1. Preheat oven to 300 degrees. Grease casserole.
2. Blend together oil, vinegar and sugar. Pour this mixture over beans and chill overnight.
3. Drain crumbled bacon and place in greased casserole. Bake at 300 degrees for 30-45 minutes until thoroughly heated. Top with water chestnuts or almonds.

— Mrs. J. S. Roberts

CUCUMBER CREAM DRESSING

Yield: 1 Cup

1 Large Cucumber, Grated
1 Cup Sour Cream
1 teaspoon Green Onion, Minced
2 teaspoons Lemon Juice
Salt

1. Peel and remove seeds from cucumber. Grate and drain excess moisture from cucumber.
2. Combine all ingredients and chill until ready to serve.
3. Serve over sliced tomatoes.

— Mrs. William Berry Hartsfield

RUM ANGEL FOOD CAKE

Yield: 12 Servings

1½ Cups Milk
2 Eggs
½ Cup Sugar, Granulated
¼ teaspoon Salt
1 Envelope Plain Gelatin
⅓ Cup Cold Water
¼ - ½ teaspoon Rum Extract
1½ Cups Heavy Cream
1 Angel Food Cake

1. Blend first four ingredients together in top of double boiler. (Do not let water boil in bottom). Stir until mixture is of custard consistency and coats spoon. Remove from heat.
2. Add plain gelatin softened in ⅓ cup cold water. Add to custard and heat. Add rum extract. Chill until firm.
3. Whip heavy cream into peaks and fold into chilled custard. Pile onto angel food cake and serve for something extra delectable!

— Mrs. John C. Hopkins, Sr.

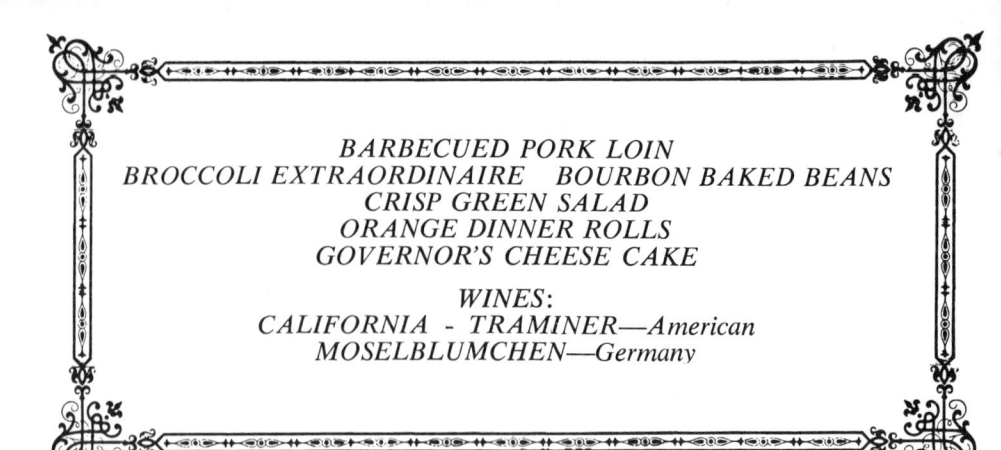

BARBECUED PORK LOIN
BROCCOLI EXTRAORDINAIRE   BOURBON BAKED BEANS
CRISP GREEN SALAD
ORANGE DINNER ROLLS
GOVERNOR'S CHEESE CAKE

WINES:
CALIFORNIA - TRAMINER—American
MOSELBLUMCHEN—Germany

BARBECUED PORK LOIN

Yield: 8 Servings

1 (5-6 Pound) Pork Loin, Boned, Rolled and Tied
Salt and Pepper

1. Preheat oven to 325 degrees. Prepare charcoal for grilling.
2. Rub pork loin with salt and pepper. Place in open roasting pan with fat side up. Insert meat thermometer.
3. For first part of cooking, roast in 325 degree oven for 2-3 hours. Remove from oven for remainder of cooking time which is to be done over charcoal on the grill outside. Roast over charcoal for aproximately 1-2 hours or until meat thermometer registers 185 degrees.
4. Baste periodically with barbecue sauce.

Harvey's Barbecue Sauce

Yield: 3 Cups

½ Cup Mustard, Prepared
6 Tablespoons Catsup
½ Cup Vinegar
¼ Cup Worcestershire Sauce
3 Cups Water
2 teaspoons Onion Salt
2 teaspoons Garlic Salt
½ teaspoon Hot Pepper Sauce

¼ Cup Lemon Juice
5 Tablespoons Brown Sugar
1 teaspoon Cayenne Pepper (Optional)

1. In a saucepan blend all ingredients together well.
2. Bring to a boil and simmer for 15 minutes. Baste and serve with pork loin.

— Mrs. Andrew N. Foster

BROCCOLI EXTRAORDINAIRE
Yield: 8 Servings

10 Ounces Spaghetti, Uncooked
8 Scallions, Chopped
2 Tablespoons Butter
2 10-Ounce Packages Frozen Broccoli
Dash Pepper
¾ teaspoon Salt
10 Ounces American Cheese Slices
¾ Cup Light Cream

1. Preheat oven to 375 degrees. Grease casserole.
2. Cook and drain spaghetti. Cut cooked broccoli into chunks.
3. Saute scallions in butter until limp. Add broccoli and seasoning and cook 5 minutes over low heat.
4. Put spaghetti in greased casserole and cover with half of cheese slices.
5. Pour cream over cheese, add broccoli mixture and cover with remaining cheese.
6. Bake 30 minutes at 375 degrees.

— Mrs. Joseph R. Manning

BOURBON BAKED BEANS
Yield: 8 Servings

4 No. 2 Cans Baked Beans
1 Tablespoon Molasses
¼ teaspoon Dry Mustard
½ Cup Chili Sauce
½ Cup Bourbon
⅓ Cup Strong Coffee
1 Small Can Crushed Pineapple
½ Cup Brown Sugar
Crisp Bacon

1. Blend together all but brown sugar, pineapple and bacon. Let stand 3 hours.

DINNERS

2. Bake 30 minutes at 300 degrees. Add pineapple and brown sugar and bake 30 more minutes at 300 degrees.
3. Add crisp bacon slices before serving.

— Mrs. J. S. Roberts

ORANGE DINNER ROLLS

Yield: 3 Dozen Small Rolls

1 Package Active Dry Yeast
¼ Cup Lukewarm Water
1 Cup Milk, Scalded
½ Cup Shortening
⅓ Cup Sugar, Granulated
1 teaspoon Salt
5-5½ Cups Flour, Sifted
2 Eggs, Slightly Beaten
2 Tablespoons Orange Rind, Grated
¼ Cup Orange Juice
Orange Glaze

1. Soften yeast in luke warm water.
2. Combine milk, shortening, sugar, and salt in a large mixing bowl. Cool to lukewarm.
3. Stir in about 2 cups of the sifted flour. Blend well. Add eggs and blend well.
4. Stir in softened yeast.
5. Add orange rind, orange juice and enough of remaining flour to make a soft dough.
6. Cover and let rest 10 minutes.
7. Knead dough 8-10 minutes on a lightly floured surface until smooth and elastic.
8. Place in lightly greased bowl, turning once to grease the surface.
9. Cover: let rise in warm place until double (about 2 hours).
10. Punch down; cover and let rest 10 minutes.
11. Roll dough out and cut into strips.
12. Take enough dough to roll into the shape and size of a small cigar. Tie the cigar-shaped dough into a knot.
13. Place on greased baking sheets, cover, and let rise until double (about 45 minutes).
14. Bake at 400 degrees for 12 minutes or until golden brown.
15. Glaze with orange glaze while hot. Cool on rack and serve.
16. (These rolls can be prepared in advance and frozen by baking to the brown and serve stage. The glaze is applied when rolls are browned for serving).

Orange Glaze:

    1 teaspoon Orange Rind, Grated
    2 Tablespoons Orange Juice
    1 Cup Confectioner's Sugar, Sifted

1. Blend ingredients together and brush on hot rolls.

— Mrs. Joe MacMillan

GOVERNOR'S CHEESE CAKE

Yield: 12 Servings

This is a favorite of visiting Congressmen!

Graham Cracker Crumb Crust:

    ¼ Cup Butter, Melted
    1½ Cups Graham Cracker Crumbs

1. Preheat oven to 300 degrees.
2. Blend together melted butter and graham cracker crumbs.
3. Line sides and bottom of 10-inch spring mould.
4. Bake at 300 degrees for 10 minutes. Let cool before adding the cheese cake mixture.

Cheese Cake Mixture:

    2 Tablespoons Plain Gelatin
    ½ Cup Cold Water
    1 Cup Hot Water
    4 Egg Yolks, Well-Beaten
    1 Cup Sugar, Granulated
    Juice of 6 Lemons
    4 Egg Whites, Stiffly Beaten
    2 Cups Heavy Cream
    2 12-Ounce Packages Cottage Cheese

1. Soften plain gelatin in cold water for 5 minutes.
2. Dissolve softened gelatin in 1 cup of hot water, then cool.
3. Beat egg yolks until lemon yellow and add sugar and lemon juice.
4. Cook egg-lemon juice mixture in top of double boiler until it coats the spoon. (Do not allow water to boil under top of double boiler). Cool.
5. Beat egg whites until stiff but not dry. Whip heavy cream until stiff.
6. Blend cottage cheese until smooth. Add lemon custard and gelatin. Beat until mixture begins to set. Fold in whipped cream and stiffly beaten egg whites.
7. Pour into 10-inch spring mould and chill for several hours until set. Serve with favorite fruit topping.

— Governor and Mrs. Carl E. Sanders

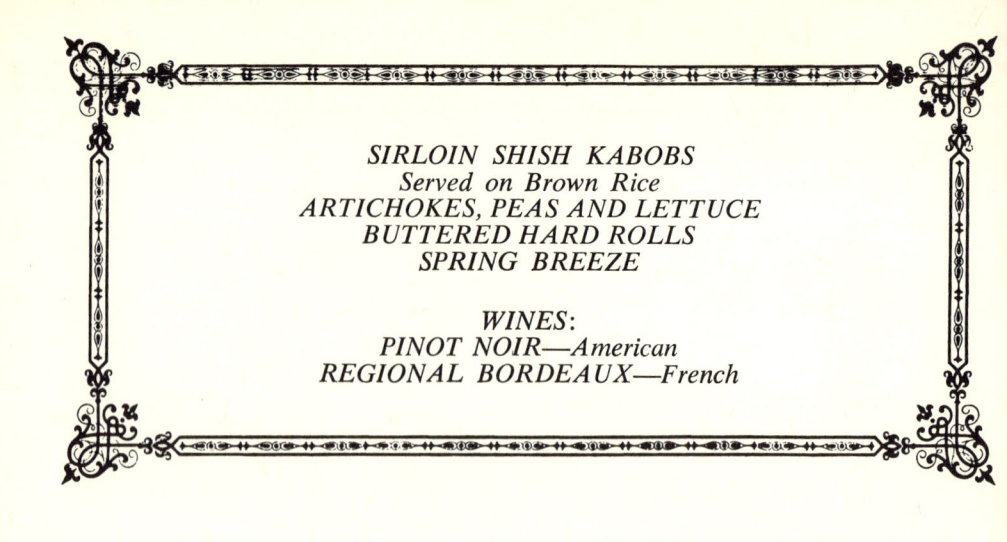

SIRLOIN SHISH KABOBS
Served on Brown Rice
ARTICHOKES, PEAS AND LETTUCE
BUTTERED HARD ROLLS
SPRING BREEZE

WINES:
PINOT NOIR—American
REGIONAL BORDEAUX—French

SIRLOIN SHISH KABOBS

Yield: 6 Servings

3 Pounds Sirloin Beef, Cut into Cubes
Tomatoes
Small Whole Onions
Bell Pepper
Pineapple Chunks

1. Marinate beef cubes in marinade sauce for 12 hours.
2. Put on skewers with quartered tomatoes, small onions, Bell pepper slices and pineapple chunks.
3. Broil about 7 minutes per side and serve on brown rice.

Marinade Sauce

Yield: 1 Cup

1 teaspoon Ginger
1 teaspoon Dry Mustard
½ Cup Soy Sauce
½ Cup Vegetable Oil
3 Cloves Garlic, Pressed

1. Combine all ingredients and let stand 24 hours.
2. Marinate meat for 12 hours.

— Mrs. Tyrone S. Clifford

BROWN RICE

Yield: 6 Servings

1½ Cups Rice, Uncooked (Not Instant)
1½ Tablespoons Butter
1½ teaspoons Salt
3½ Cups Water

1. Preheat oven to 350 degrees.

2. Place dry rice in skillet with butter and stir over moderate heat until rice is an even, pale, golden brown.

3. Reduce heat to low, add salt and water and let come to a boil.

4. Cover and place pan in a moderate oven (350 degrees) for 30 minutes.

ARTICHOKES, PEAS, AND LETTUCE

Yield: 6 Servings

6 Artichokes
⅓ Cup White Wine
⅓ Cup Olive Oil
Salt and Pepper
1 Small Head Lettuce, Shredded
3 Green Onions, Sliced
½ teaspoon Sugar, Granulated
¼ teaspoon Thyme
¼ Cup Butter, Melted
3 Cups Fresh Green Peas, Shelled
¼ Cup Water

1. Discard tough outer leaves of well-rinsed artichokes. Trim base and stem of each artichoke.

2. In a saucepan, cover with boiling, salted water and cook for 5 minutes. Drain.

DINNERS

3. Combine white wine and olive oil in heavy kettle. Place artichokes upright and close together in kettle. Sprinkle with salt and pepper, separating leaves slightly.
4. Pour 1 Tablespoon olive oil and 3 Tablespoons white wine inside each artichoke.
5. Cover kettle and bring liquid to a boil. Reduce heat and simmer for 30 minutes or until leaves will pull out easily. Drain artichokes upside down.
6. In a skillet, saute shredded lettuce, green onions, sugar and Thyme in butter. Add green peas and ¼ cup water.
7. Cover skillet and simmer for 6 to 10 minutes or until peas are tender.
8. Serve artichokes upright surrounded by above vegetables. Garnish with bits of pimiento, if desired.

— Miss Ann O'Hara Boswell

SPRING BREEZE

Yield: 6 Servings

Strawberries
1½-2 Cups Heavy Cream
1-2 Tablespoons Strawberry Juice
Red Food Coloring
Candied Violets

1. Frost 6 crystal compotes in freezer.
2. Place halved strawberries, sweetened to taste, in bottom of frosted compotes.
3. Whip cream and flavor with strawberry juice and small amount of red food coloring.
4. Swirl whipped cream on top of strawberries and top with candied violets. (See Introductory pages to Tea Section).

— Mrs. Robert Minnear

HOSTESS' NOTES

HOLIDAYS

HOLIDAYS

Happy Holidays! Holidays are a magic time, a time for reverie and reverence, fun and frolic, a time to look forward to and a time to look back upon, a time to strengthen bonds between family and friends. Some holidays are associated with religious occasions, such as Christmas and Easter. Thanksgiving is a family day. Historic and patriotic holidays such as the Fourth of July remind us of our heritage. Watch-night services in Atlanta's churches mark the solemnity of the expiring year as the Happy New Year unfolds.

NEW YEAR'S

As the clock strikes twelve midnight, horns toot, clocks chime, bells ring; and everyone joins in the merry madness that accompanies the advent of a new year.

Party Ideas

Your friends would be "Ah-so-pleased to attend honorable Oriental party" when they receive invitations printed in red and black ink. To set the scene the minute guests arrive, have wind chimes tinkling outside the door and several pairs of shoes placed at the entrance so guests will know to remove their shoes.

Take inspiration from the Japanese, who for centuries have been masters of elegant chairless dining, and arrange a low table by placing a damaged door on picnic benches or stacks of bricks.

Oriental dolls, fans and parasols can be arranged attractively in a centerpiece or set them about for decoration. Bonsai gardens add to the serene mood. Prepare a miniature garden by securing a tree branch to the bottom of a shallow pan with floral clay and surrounding it with tiny pebbles. Trim the branch with blossoms and small Japanese umbrellas. For a festive glow throughout the party area, hang Japanese paper lanterns.

EASTER

Atlantans set out before dawn to attend the worship at sunrise sponsored by churches of all faiths on top of historic Stone Mountain on Easter Sunday.

The City commemorates the resurrection of Christ as six hundred and ten magnificent bells ring out from the Carillon, which is the largest of six in the world.

Beautifully appointed tables await worshippers at home for the Easter Sunday dinner on this joyful day.

Centerpieces

Down the middle of the table, parade four small Easter baskets filled with decorated eggs and spring tulips.

A captivating focal point on any table is the Easter Basket Cake frosted pink and overflowing with delicate marshmallow daisies. Use a wire hanger covered with aluminum foil for the basket handle. Wrap the foil-covered

HOLIDAYS

handle in pastel ribbon secured with cellophane tape, and press the handle into the top of the cake basket. Tie a contrasting bow onto the handle. To make the daisies, snip the sides of a large marshmallow to make individual petals. Use tiny yellow marshmallows for the centers of the daisies, and snip large green marshmallows for the leaves.

FOURTH OF JULY

Rippling flags, marching soldiers, pounding drums—Atlanta hails its "Salute To America Parade" on the Fourth of July. After the spectacular display, the day is climaxed in alfresco entertaining with all outdoors as the resplendent dining room.

CENTERPIECES

Spark the table with a blue and white skyrocket, trailing a blaze of red carnations and ribbon streamers. To create your rocket, cover a small oatmeal box with blue paper or felt. Staple a slim stick to the open end for a tail; then fill in the opening with Oasis which has been cut to fit. Snip carnation stems to varied lengths and insert in the Oasis. Glue a nose cone of styrofoam to the opposite end of the box. Bend a wire hanger to form a support for the rocket, and conceal the hanger with short branches of greenery. Attach red ribbon streamers and "blast off!"

Stand toy soldiers in Revolutionary uniforms at attention around a toy drum. Cut bright blue felt with pinking shears in a circle eighteen inches in diameter. Glue white felt stars about an inch in diameter all around the edge. Place in the center of the table and over the blue felt place a circle of red felt, fourteen inches in diameter, so that a blue border of white stars shines from beneath. Center the toy drum from which one side has been removed and line with a dish, filled with white flowers.

THANKSGIVING

Branches of autumn leaves set outside the door wave a special holiday greeting as the family gathers for the first big feast of fall.

The very mention of Thanksgiving brings thoughts of warm country kitchens and good things to eat. To present your Thanksgiving dinner, you might enjoy arranging an autumn centerpiece.

CENTERPIECES

Frosted fruit glisten in a compote mingled with greenery. To frost fruit, dip red apples, pears, lemons, oranges and assorted grapes into egg white beaten until frothy; then dip into granulated sugar. Let fruit set on cake rack over waxed paper until dry.

One Atlanta hostess recommends a versatile ring of pine cones for a centerpiece base. She halves the pine cones with a saw-type knife and then wires the cones, that resemble roses after cut, onto a small florist ring. In the fall, she fills the ring with either brightly-colored gourds, a pumpkin, ears of corn, autumn leaves, or golden apples. She might center the wreath with a frosty snowman or red candles in the wintertime.

CHRISTMAS

Atlantans treasure the old lamppost called, "The Eternal Flame" that was first lit on Christmas Day, 1855. At its base is a hole torn by a shell during the seige of Atlanta in 1864. The gas lamp was again connected for the premiere of the screen version of GONE WITH THE WIND in December, 1939, and now burns as a memorial to the South of that period. The lamppost is located at the corner of Whitehall and Alabama Streets.

At Christmas time, lights from glowing candles illuminate the warmth and brightness of this most revered of all holidays. Candles belong all over the house at Christmas. If you have wall sconces, set them with your finest tapers; decorate them with festoons of greens and Christmas tree decorations. The sideboard will hold Christmas candles and the table in the entrance hall should have lighted candles to give a holiday welcome to all who enter.

CENTERPIECES

Decorate the dining table with a generous Christmas wreath and tall red candles in the center. Add a few pine cones, and tie a big red bow to the wreath.

A boxwood tree can be made from fresh or artificial boxwood tucked into a styrofoam cone that has been covered with wire mesh. Trim with red velvet bows or berries.

The following carefully selected and tested recipes will add joy to holiday eating and drinking. All are old Southern favorites. WASSAIL!

NEW YEAR'S

STEAK TARTARE   SHRIMP ARNAUD
TOP HAT OF CRISP VEGETABLES
SCALLOPED EDAM
EGG ROLLS   BACON-WRAPPED WATER CHESTNUTS
CHEESE STRAWS
CONFETTI DIP
MERRYMAKING CHEER

STEAK TARTARE

2 Pounds Sirloin or Beef Fillet
2 Raw Egg Yolks
2 Tablespoons Onions, Grated
1 Tablespoon Worcestershire Sauce
1 Tablespoon Lemon Juice
2 teaspoons Prepared Mustard
1 Tablespoon Cognac
1 teaspoon Salt
½ teaspoon Black Pepper, Freshly Ground
¼ teaspoon Cayenne Pepper
1 Small Can Anchovy Fillets
1 Small Bottle Capers

1. Remove all fat from beef. Put through meat grinder twice.

2. Mix ground meat, raw egg yolks, grated onions, Worcestershire sauce, lemon juice, mustard, Cognac, salt, black pepper, and Cayenne pepper together.

3. Mold into desired shape and garnish with anchovy fillets and capers.

4. Serve with sliced and buttered French bread.

— Mrs. Harry G. Haisten, Jr.

HOLIDAYS

SHRIMP ARNAUD

(See page 181)

TOP HAT OF CRISP VEGETABLES

1. Line inside of hat with plastic saran or aluminum foil.
2. Fill with crisp vegetable flowers (see page 175).
3. Serve with spicy dip of your choice.

— Mrs. John C. Hopkins, Sr.

SCALLOPED EDAM

1 Round Edam Cheese
Onion Juice
Prepared Mustard
Light Cream

1. With cheese at room temperature, press cooky cutter into top of cheese, cutting a deep circle.
2. Remove circle of cheese and scoop out center leaving a ¼ inch wall.
3. Scallop edge of cheese with sharp knife.
4. Whip cheese with electric mixer and blend with onion juice and mustard to taste. Add enough cream to reach spreading consistency.
5. Mound cheese in shell. Chill.
6. Remove from refrigerator 1 hour before serving.

— Mrs. Colburn Coe

EGG ROLLS

1. Heat packaged frozen egg rolls and serve hot with red mustard sauce.

Red Mustard Sauce:

Yield: 1 Cup

¾ Cup Catsup
¼ Cup Water
1-1½ Tablespoons Dry Mustard
1 teaspoon Salt

1. Blend all ingredients together thoroughly and chill.

— Miss Delma Sangster

HOLIDAYS

BACON WRAPPED TIDBITS

(See page 178)

CHEESE STRAWS

Yield: 6-7 Dozen

These are absolutely marvelous!

4 Cups (1 Pound) New York Sharp Cheddar Cheese
1 Cup Butter, Softened
4 Cups Flour, Sifted
4 teaspoons Baking Powder
½ teaspoon Cayenne Pepper
1½ teaspoons Salt

1. Break cheese into chunks and blend with butter in mixer.
2. Add remaining ingredients. Chill. Put in cooky press and squeeze onto greased baking sheet.
3. Bake at 300 degrees for 15 minutes.

— Mrs. Robert Sasser

CONFETTI SNACK DIP

Yield: 2½ Cups

1 Package Onion Soup Mix
1 Pint Sour Cream
¼ Cup Bell Pepper, Diced
¼ Cup Cucumber, Diced
¼ Cup Pimiento, Diced

1. Combine all ingredients. Chill at least one hour to blend flavors.
2. Serve with assorted crackers or chips.

— Miss Suzanne Burnley

MERRYMAKING CHEER

Yield: 25 Servings

2 Quarts Scotch Whiskey
1 Quart Ginger Wine
3 Tablespoons Honey
Juice of 4 Oranges
Rind of 2 Oranges, Cut into Spirals
    and Studded with Cloves

1. In large saucepan combine all ingredients and heat thoroughly. Do NOT let boil.
2. Garnish each serving with a strip of clove-studded orange peel.

— Mrs. C. M. Moye

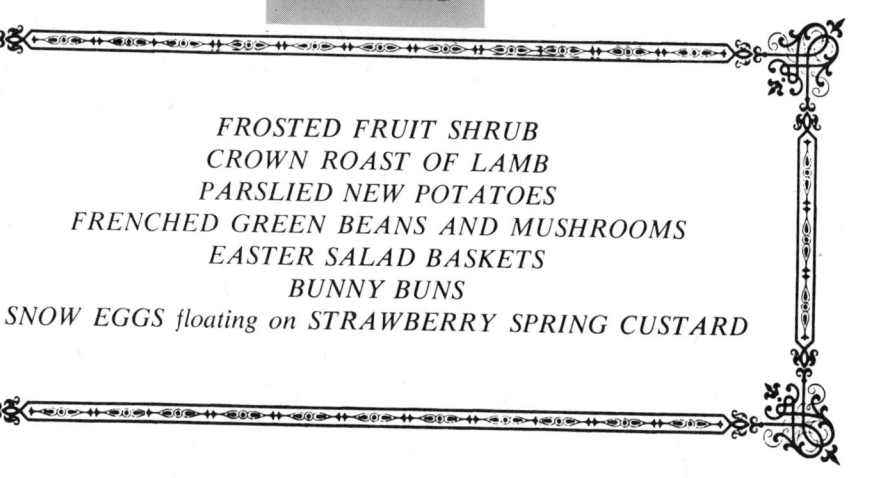

EASTER

FROSTED FRUIT SHRUB
CROWN ROAST OF LAMB
PARSLIED NEW POTATOES
FRENCHED GREEN BEANS AND MUSHROOMS
EASTER SALAD BASKETS
BUNNY BUNS
SNOW EGGS floating on STRAWBERRY SPRING CUSTARD

FROSTED FRUIT SHRUB

(See Page 220)

Although raspberry has been designated, any fruit and combination of two fruit juices may be used. Let your imagination be your guide!

CROWN ROAST OF LAMB

10-16 Rib Crown Roast of Lamb
10-16 Pieces of Bacon
Salt and Pepper
Accent

1. Preheat oven to 325 degrees. Wrap rib ends with bacon pieces to prevent charring.
2. Place roast upside down in roasting pan so fat from roast bastes rib ends.
3. Fill center with sauteed Cherry tomatoes (see page 182).
4. Serve with paper frills (gold or pastel colors for Easter).

— Mrs. Solon P. Patterson

HOLIDAYS

EASTER SALAD BASKETS

Lettuce Cups
Mixed Salad Greens
Radish Roses
Carrot "Chrysanthemums"
Bell Pepper Strips
Bleu Cheese, Crumbled
Creamy Bleu Cheese Dressing

1. Chill all salad ingredients until well crisped. Fit two lettuce cups together to make the shell of a basket.
2. Fill "basket" with tossed salad. Garnish with radish roses (using sharp paring knife, slice thin "Petals" from side of radish, leaving "petals" attached). Add carrot Chrysanthemums (using sharp paring knife, deeply notch 4 petals in large horizontal slice of carrot. Top with carrot chunks spearing both on toothpick). . .

— Miss Ann O'Hara Boswell

MAYOR ALLEN'S ROQUEFORT DRESSING
(See Page 260)

BUNNY BUNS
Yield: 1½ Dozen

1 Recipe Yeast Rolls (See Page 207)

Curlicue Bunnies:

30 10-Inch Strips of Dough
30 5-Inch Strips of Dough
30 Small Balls of Dough

1. Grease baking sheet.
2. Make a loose swirl of 10 inch strip for body of bunny on greased baking sheet. (Dough will "grow" together as it rises).
3. Pinch off ½ inch strips and roll into cigar shapes for ears. (Make point at one end for tip of ear. Snip off other end and place next to bunny's head.)
4. Make small ball of dough for bunny's tail. Let rise until almost double for baking in 375 degree oven for 12-15 minutes.

Twist Bunnies:
Yield: 1½ Dozen

30 14-Inch Strips of Dough
30 Small Balls of Dough

1. Grease baking sheet.
2. On baking sheet, lap one end of 14 inch strip of dough over the other end to form a loop.
3. Bring underneath end over top end, letting each end extend on the sides to form ears. Make points at end of ears.

HOLIDAYS

4. Form small ball of dough for bunny tail and place at bottom of loop of dough.
5. Let "bunnies" rise until almost double. Bake at 375 degrees for 12 to 15 minutes.
6. The curlicue and twist bunnies can also be frosted with a simple sugar-water glaze if desired.

— Mrs. Thomas I. Sangster

SNOW EGGS
floating on STRAWBERRY SPRING CUSTARD

Yield: 4-6 Servings

Milk
4 Egg Whites
½ teaspoon Cream of Tartar
¾ Cup Sugar, Granulated

1. Heat milk to simmering.
2. Combine egg whites and cream of tartar. Beat until stiff and gradually add sugar.
3. Form meringue into egg shapes and place in simmering milk. Poach meringue eggs for 2 minutes, turn them, and poach for 2 more minutes.
4. Remove meringue eggs and drain.

STRAWBERRY SPRING CUSTARD

1 Cup Milk, Scalded
1 Cup Heavy Cream, Scalded
1½ teaspoons Vanilla Extract
5 Egg Yolks
½ Cup Sugar, Granulated
Fresh Strawberries, Sliced
Slivered Almonds

1. In top of double boiler scald milk and cream. Add vanilla extract.
2. Blend together egg yolks and sugar until light and slowly add to cream mixture, stirring constantly.
3. Cook until custard is thick and coats the spoon. (Stir continuously while custard is cooking).
4. Strain sauce through a fine sieve for an added taste of velvet. Chill.
5. Pile fresh, sliced strawberries in bottom of deep, large crystal dish.
6. Arrange meringue eggs on top. Pour chilled custard around eggs and sprinkle with slivered almonds.

— Mrs. McNeill Stokes

FOURTH OF JULY

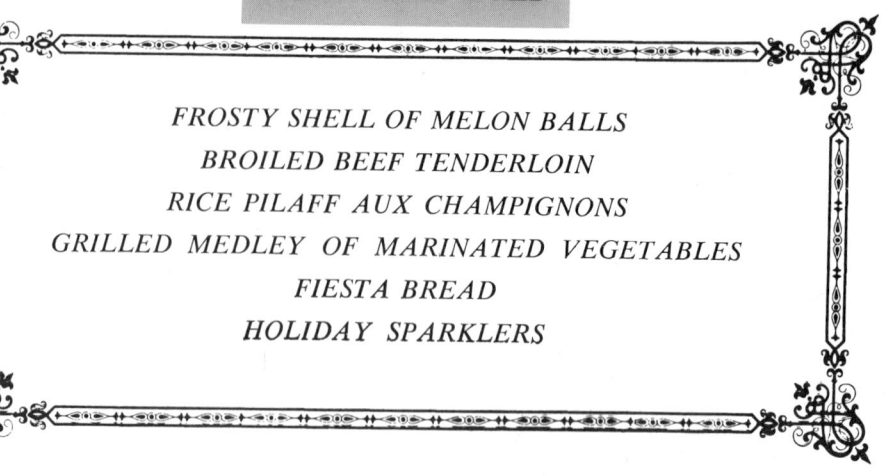

FROSTY SHELL OF MELON BALLS
BROILED BEEF TENDERLOIN
RICE PILAFF AUX CHAMPIGNONS
GRILLED MEDLEY OF MARINATED VEGETABLES
FIESTA BREAD
HOLIDAY SPARKLERS

FROSTY SHELL OF MELON BALLS

Yield: 8-10 Servings

1 Medium Watermelon, Chilled
2 Honeydew Melons, Chilled
2 Cantaloupes, Chilled
½ Pint Blueberries
½ Pint Strawberries
1 Medium Bunch Thompson Seedless Grapes
Sprigs of Mint

1. Cut watermelon lengthwise, slicing off top third of melon.
2. Scallop edges of watermelon with sharp knife, using rim of cup as a guide.
3. Using French melon baller or measuring teaspoon, scoop balls of chilled melon from each of the three melons.
4. Fill scalloped shell of watermelon with melon balls and garnish with remaining fresh fruit and sprigs of mint.

— Mrs. Thomas I. Sangster

BROILED BEEF TENDERLOIN

Beef Tenderloin, 1½ Inches Thick
Kirkkoman's Soy Sauce

1. Prepare charcoal for fire. (Charcoal is ready when white ash covers top of coals.)
2. Forty-five minutes prior to cooking, trim excess fat from steak and brush tenderloin with Kirkkoman's Soy Sauce.
3. Use a wire basket to hold steak 1 inch above coals.
4. To control flame during cooking, hold basket vertically to stop dripping.
5. Turn steak only once while cooking. Length of cooking time will depend upon the number of pounds to be cooked and the desired doneness.

— Mrs. Sam N. Gardner

RICE PILAFF AUX CHAMPIGNONS

Yield: 8 Servings

2 Cups Rice, Uncooked
1 3-Ounce Can Sliced Mushrooms
¾ Cup Butter
6-8 Green Onions, Chopped
3 Cans Beef Consomme
2 Cans Water
Salt

1. Preheat oven to 350 degrees.
2. Saute rice and mushrooms in butter.
3. Add chopped onion and liquid.
4. Add salt to taste and bake at 350 degrees for one hour. Top wth sprigs of parsley and serve.

— Mrs. Robert B. Ansley, Jr.

CHILLED MEDLEY OF MARINATED VEGETABLES

Yield: 8-10 Servings

2 Cans Clear Chicken Broth
1 Cup Dry White Wine
½ Cup Olive Oil
3 Cloves Garlic, Pressed
16 Drops Tabasco Sauce
10 Peppercorns
½ Cup Parsley, Chopped
½ Pound Mushroom Crowns
½ Pound Whole Small Yellow Onions, Peeled
6-8 Green Onions
1 Pound Summer Squash, Sliced
½ Pound Zucchini, Sliced
6-8 Hearts of Celery, Sliced 4 Inches Long
1 Package Frozen Green Beans

1. In a saucepan simmer together for 15 minutes chicken broth, wine, olive oil, garlic, Tabasco, peppercorns, and parsley. Remove parsley after simmering.
2. In a covered saucepan, simmer vegetables one group at a time in above broth.
3. Simmer yellow onions 12 minutes; Zucchini, 10 minutes; Summer Squash, 7 minutes; Green Beans, 5 minutes; Green Onions, 5 minutes.

HOLIDAYS

4. Arrange simmered vegetables in a shallow dish and add with strained broth.
5. Chill in refrigerator for 24 hours before serving.

— Mrs. Harry G. Haisten, Jr.

HOLIDAY SPARKLERS

Yield: 8 Servings

8 Pottery Flowerpots
8 Slices Pound Cake
1 Quart Lemon Custard Ice Cream
½ Pint Fresh Strawberries, Sliced
½ Pint Fresh Blueberries
8 Egg Whites, Stiffly Beaten
2 Cups Sugar, Granulated
1½ teaspoons Cream of Tartar
16 "Sparklers"
16 Tiny American Flags

1. Sterilize flowerpots through dishwasher or by pouring boiling water over them.
2. Cut each slice of pound cake into pieces that will fit into the flowerpots.
3. Place piece of pound cake in the bottom to cover the hole. Add layer of blueberries topped with lemon custard ice cream to fill flowerpot three fourths full.
4. Add top layer of strawberries and pound cake.
5. In large bowl, beat egg whites until frothy and add cream of tartar.
6. Gradually add sugar and continue beating until stiff peaks form.
7. Force soda straw into middle of flowerpot and cut off even with the rim of the flowerpot, if fresh or permanent flowers are to be inserted in lieu of the sparklers and flags.
8. Pile flowerpots high with meringue (leaving space over straw open).
9. Place flowerpots under broiler flame for about 1 minute until golden brown.
10. Place two sparklers at an angle (secure in the dessert) and two American flags at opposite sides from the sparklers. Turn all lights out, ignite sparklers and serve an extra sparkling Fourth of July!
11. These may also be used for patio functions, bridge luncheons, showers, etc. (Insert fresh or permanent flowers into the soda straw and serve a touch of spring!)

— Mrs. McNeill Stokes

THANKSGIVING

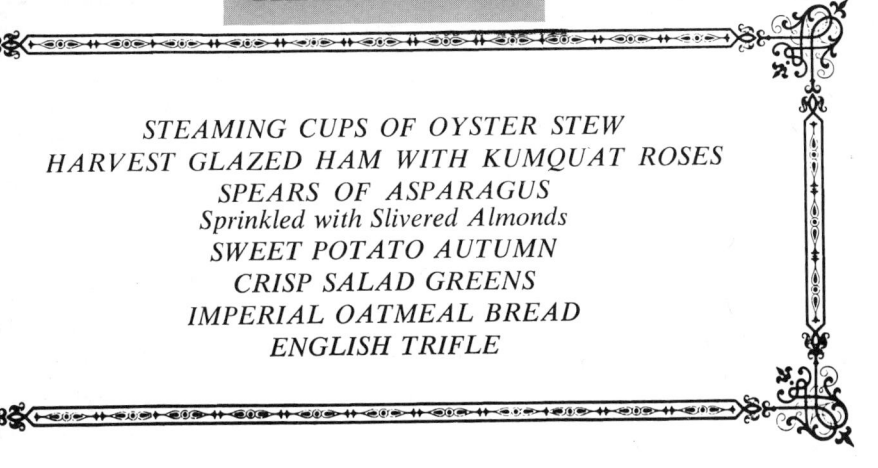

STEAMING CUPS OF OYSTER STEW
HARVEST GLAZED HAM WITH KUMQUAT ROSES
SPEARS OF ASPARAGUS
Sprinkled with Slivered Almonds
SWEET POTATO AUTUMN
CRISP SALAD GREENS
IMPERIAL OATMEAL BREAD
ENGLISH TRIFLE

OYSTER STEW

Yield: 6 Servings

3 Tablespoons Butter, Melted
1 Tablespoon Flour
Salt and Pepper
1 Quart Milk, Heated
1½ Pints Soup Oysters
Chopped Chives

1. Melt butter, add flour and cook until bubbly. Add seasoning to taste.
2. Blend in milk and heat entire mixture thoroughly.
3. Add oysters and let cook about 5 minutes until edges curl. Serve immediately. Top with chopped chives.

— Mrs. John Hitchens

HAM GLAZE

Prepared Mustard
Brown Sugar
Ground Cloves
Madeira
4-5 Pound Ham

HOLIDAYS

1. Make thick paste of the mustard, brown sugar, ground cloves, and madeira.
2. Score ham with knife or cooky cutter. Brush fatty surface of ham with thick sugar paste.
3. If desired, garnish scored places with chunk pineapple and Maraschino cherries.
4. Bake uncooked ham until an internal temperature of 160 degrees is reached (approximately 25 minutes per pound).
5. Bake cooked (ready-to-eat) ham until an internal temperature of 130 degrees is reached (approximately 15 minutes per pound).

— Mrs. Troy Gaunt

KUMQUAT ROSES

6-8 Kumquats

1. Leave kumquat whole. Make 4 petals by cutting peel in fourths from blossom end almost to stem end.
2. Peel petals about ¾ back. Chill kumquats in ice water and garnish platter of ham.

— Mrs. Frank Briggs

SWEET POTATO AUTUMN

Yield: 6 Servings

4 Cups Sweet Potato, Finely Grated
2 Cups Milk
2 Cups Dark Brown Sugar
1 Cup Raisins
¼ Cup Butter, Melted
1 teaspoon Salt
½ teaspoon Cinnamon
½ teaspoon Allspice
½ teaspoon Ginger
½ teaspoon Cloves, Ground
4 Eggs, Slightly Beaten

HOLIDAYS

1. Preheat oven to 350 degrees. Grease 1½ quart casserole.
2. Combine grated sweet potatoes with ingredients and stir in eggs. Put in greased 1½ quart casserole. Bake uncovered at 350 degrees for 30 minutes, stir, bake 1 hour more. Serve warm with milk or cream.

— Mrs. Clifford Baum

IMPERIAL OATMEAL BREAD

(See page 96)

ENGLISH TRIFLE

Yield: 8 Servings

We are indebted to the Mother Country for this!

Stale Pound Cake
½ Cup Sherry
1 3-Ounce Package Orange Gelatin
1 Can Mandarin Oranges, Drained
2 Bananas, Sliced
1 Package Bird's Dessert Powder
1 Cup Heavy Cream
Maraschino Cherries
Pecans or Walnuts, Chopped

1. Line the bottom of a 2 quart glass bowl with bite-size pieces of fairly stale pound cake.
2. Add sherry, making sure that the cake absorbs all the sherry.
3. Drain can of orange segments, reserving juice and place fruit on top of cake. Place sliced bananas on top of oranges.
4. Prepare orange gelatin according to package directions, incorporating the reserved juice as part of liquid. Pour over the contents in the bowl and chill until set.
5. When set, make the custard according to package directions of Bird's Dessert Powder, and when slightly cooled pour over congealed gelatin.
6. Chill well, and just before serving, top with whipped cream and decorate with Maraschino cherries and nuts.

— Mrs. William J. Suttles

CHRISTMAS

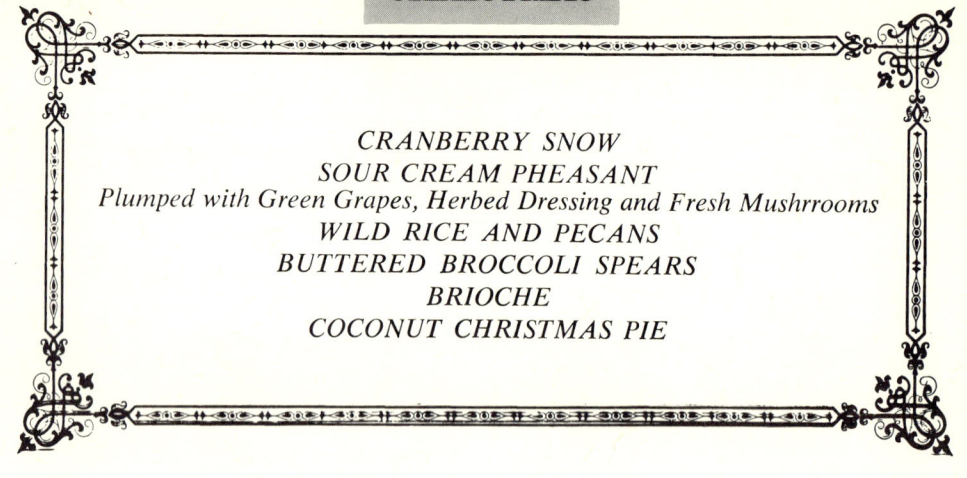

CRANBERRY SNOW
SOUR CREAM PHEASANT
Plumped with Green Grapes, Herbed Dressing and Fresh Mushrrooms
WILD RICE AND PECANS
BUTTERED BROCCOLI SPEARS
BRIOCHE
COCONUT CHRISTMAS PIE

CRANBERRY SNOW

Yield: 12 Servings

4 Cups Cranberries
2½ Cups Water
2 Cups Sugar, Granulated
2 teaspoons Plain Gelatin
½ Cup Cold Water
Juice of 1 Lemon

1. Cook cranberries in 2½ cups water until skins pop.
2. Force cranberries through sieve. Add sugar to sieved cranberries and cook until sugar dissolves.
3. Soften gelatin in cold water. Add to cranberry mixture. Cool.
4. Add lemon juice and freeze in refrigerator trays.
5. Break into chunks and beat until smooth with blender or electric mixer.
6. Return quickly to cold trays.

— Mrs. Charles C. Ford

SOUR CREAM PHEASANT

Yield: 6 Servings

Herbed Dressing:

½ Pound Fresh Mushrooms, Chopped
¼ Cup Butter, Melted
½ Cup Butter, Melted
1 Cup Water
1 8-Ounce Package Pepperidge Farm Dressing
1 Small Can Thompson Seedless Grapes
¼ Cup Parsley, Chopped
1 Pheasant or Hen (approximately 6-8 pounds)
1½ Cups Sour Cream
½ Cup Heavy Cream

1. Saute chopped, fresh mushrooms in ¼ cup butter until tender.
2. Combine ½ cup melted butter, 1 cup water and 1 package dressing.
3. Stir in sauteed mushrooms, Thompson Seedless grapes and parsley.
4. Stuff wishbone cavity of bird lightly and skewer neck skin to back. Tuck wing tips behind shoulder joints.
5. Rub cavity with butter and salt and spoon in stuffing. Do NOT pack.
6. Close opening by placing skewers across it and lacing shut with cord.
7. Tie drumsticks to tail and grease skin thoroughly.
8. Dust pheasant lightly with seasoned flour and brown slowly in melted fat.
9. Wrap bird in foil with breast side up on rack in roasting pan.
10. Blend together sour cream and heavy cream. Pour over pheasant in aluminum foil and cover tightly.
11. Bake at 325 degrees until tender (one to two hours) depending on size of bird.

HOLIDAYS

12. Baste pheasant occasionally with the sour cream sauce. (Sauce will appear curdled after cooking).
13. If desired, heat (Do NOT boil) extra sour cream sauce for ladling over individual servings of pheasant and dressing. (This sauce should be smooth and velvety).

— Mrs. McNeill Stokes

BRIOCHE

(See Page 238)

COCONUT CHRISTMAS PIE

Yield: 12-16 Servings (2 Pies)

½ Cup Sugar, Granulated
¼ Cup Self-rising flour
1 Envelope Plain Gelatin
½ teaspoon Salt
1¾ Cups Milk
¾ teaspoon Vanilla Extract
3 Egg Whites
¼ teaspoon Cream of Tartar
½ Cup Sugar, Granulated
½ Cup Heavy Cream, Whipped
1 Cup Coconut, Shredded
2 Baked Pastry Shells (See page 39)
Holly

1. Blend together ½ cup sugar, flour, plain gelatin and salt.
2. Gradually stir in milk. Cook over medium heat until mixture simmers. Stir constantly. Simmer 1 minute.
3. Place pan in cold water and cool until mixture mounds slightly when dropped from a spoon. Add vanilla extract.
4. In separate bowl, beat egg whites until frothy and add cream of tartar.
5. Gradually add ½ cup sugar to egg whites and beat until stiff peaks form.
6. Fold cooked mixture into meringue.
7. Fold in whipped cream and shredded coconut.
8. Pile into cooled baked pastry shells. Sprinkle with coconut and garnish with holly. Chill thoroughly.

— Mrs. Terrell M. Burnley

HOSTESS' NOTES

Carte des Vins

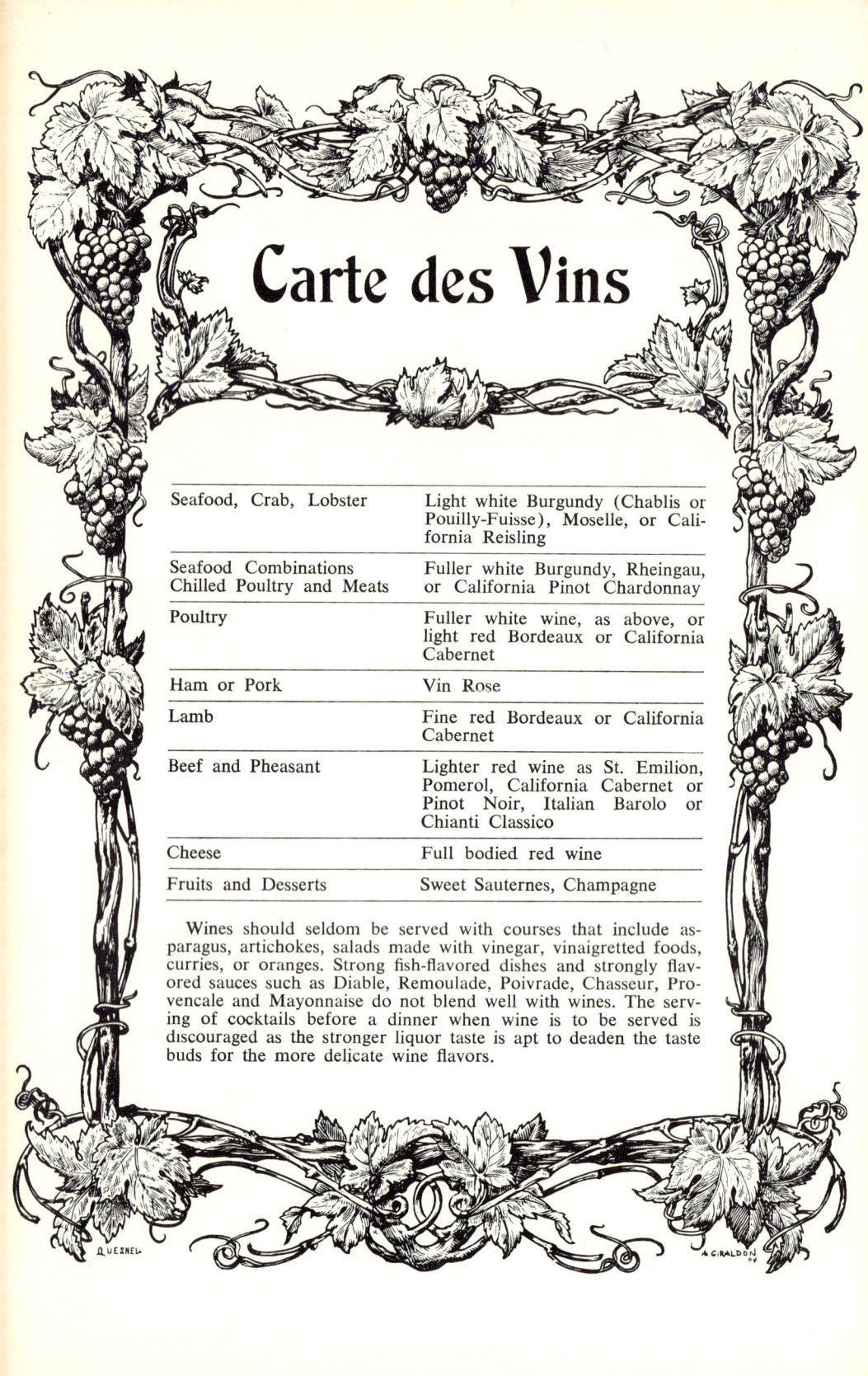

Seafood, Crab, Lobster	Light white Burgundy (Chablis or Pouilly-Fuisse), Moselle, or California Reisling
Seafood Combinations Chilled Poultry and Meats	Fuller white Burgundy, Rheingau, or California Pinot Chardonnay
Poultry	Fuller white wine, as above, or light red Bordeaux or California Cabernet
Ham or Pork	Vin Rose
Lamb	Fine red Bordeaux or California Cabernet
Beef and Pheasant	Lighter red wine as St. Emilion, Pomerol, California Cabernet or Pinot Noir, Italian Barolo or Chianti Classico
Cheese	Full bodied red wine
Fruits and Desserts	Sweet Sauternes, Champagne

Wines should seldom be served with courses that include asparagus, artichokes, salads made with vinegar, vinaigretted foods, curries, or oranges. Strong fish-flavored dishes and strongly flavored sauces such as Diable, Remoulade, Poivrade, Chasseur, Provencale and Mayonnaise do not blend well with wines. The serving of cocktails before a dinner when wine is to be served is discouraged as the stronger liquor taste is apt to deaden the taste buds for the more delicate wine flavors.

WINES

The pleasure and romance of serving wines are being discovered in ever-growing numbers by Atlantans, many of whom have become highly knowledgeable of fine wines. The hostess who wants her dinners to be as delectable as possible will acquaint herself with some of the hundreds of table wines available, for the main objective of a good wine—according to a well-known connoisseur of wines in Atlanta—is to cleanse the palate between bites of food to make each taste of food as exhilarating as the first. Without devoting a lifetime to research, the hostess can acquaint herself through this brief guide to wines with a few of the basic rules for selecting and serving wines.

Wines are divided into several classifications: still wines, which include the reds, whites and roses; champagne and sparkling wines, which require a second fermentation in the bottle; and fortified wines, including port, sherry and madeira, which have brandy, a certain amount of alcohol or sugar added.

There is a wide variety of wine glasses available to the hostess for the many different types of wine, but she need not feel that she must have all types—nor the most expensive—in order to enjoy serving wines. The trend is toward an all-purpose glass suitable for red, white, rose, sparkling wines and champagnes. Preferably, it should be a stemmed clear tulip-shaped glass about two inches wide and with a capacity of six to ten ounces. The glass should never be more than half-filled, so the delightful aroma can concentrate in the upper half of the glass. For variety, a small two and a half to three ounce, tulip-shaped wine glass is appropriate for appetizers and dessert wines. With these two basic types of glasses, the hostess is equipped for any wine serving occasion.

If wines bought for future use are in corked bottles, they should be laid on their sides in a relatively dry storage area at a temperature of sixty-five to seventy degrees. This keeps the cork moist and therefore airtight. A bottle with a screw cap may remain upright. Check with a reliable dealer to determine how long your wines may be properly stored to maintain their quality. Although some red and white wines improve with age, other wines should be enjoyed while still young. Roses are ready to be enjoyed when bottled.

Before serving, white and rose wines should be cooled. Red wines should be at a cool room temperature (70 degrees) and champagnes, of course, are most delightful when thoroughly chilled.

At a seated dinner the wine glass should be placed to the right of the water goblet. The wine bottle, sometimes wrapped in a napkin, should be placed on a small tray at the host's end of the table. If a red wine is served,

WINES

it should already be uncorked to allow it to "breathe". As the main dish is served, the host may pour a few drops into his own glass; not only to taste it for quality, but to assure that none of his guests receive any tiny bits of cork. This practice is not obligatory, however, and it is just as correct to fill the glasses around the table without ceremony. For maximum enjoyment, remember, the glasses should be only half-filled to heighten the bouquet.

Now that the hostess knows how to store and serve wines, she should acquaint herself with the names of the most famous wine-growing regions; and the logical place to begin is France! What is the magic secret that causes French wines to be so talked about and desired? The answer is that France has actually been endowed by nature with the climate, moisture and—most of all—the soil that best enhances the wine grape. The following are several labels from various famous wine-growing regions of the world.

FRENCH WINES

A TYPICAL CHATEAU-BOTTLED BORDEAUX LABEL

1. France is the country of origin.
2. B & G is the company that shipped the wine.
3. Browne-Vintners Company imported the wine.
4. Bordeaux is the region in which the wine was produced.
5. Medoc is the district (a smaller portion of Bordeaux).
6. St. Julien is the township (a smaller area of the Medoc).
7. "Chateau Beychevelle" is the name of the vineyard.
8. "Mis en Bouteuille au Chateau" means placed in the bottle at the chateau. Estate bottled is the English term and tells that the vintner bottled it in his cellars. This is usually a good wine and one of which the vintner is proud.
9. Grand Vin is the wine's official classification or rating, based on the 1855 classification of Bordeaux wines.
10. Achille-Fould is the name of the owner of the vineyard.
11. Appellation St. Julien Controlee means the wine was grown in the delineated area of St. Julien and met certain basic qualifications set down by French law for this area. All true French wines will use an Appellation Controlee.
12. 1961 is the year the grapes were harvested and ventification began. Also shown on the label are the contents of the bottle and the percentage of alcohol.

WINES

Burgundy

From Burgundy come not only the famous red wines (for which the color was named), but also the classic Chablis which is especially enjoyable with seafood.

This Corton Bressandes label is from the region of Burgundy, and Corton Bressandes is the name of the vineyard. It is also an estate bottled wine, but the official nomenclature for estate bottled in Burgundy is "Mise au Domaine." "Tete de Cuvee" is the wine's rating and means that it is at the "head," or top, of the class.

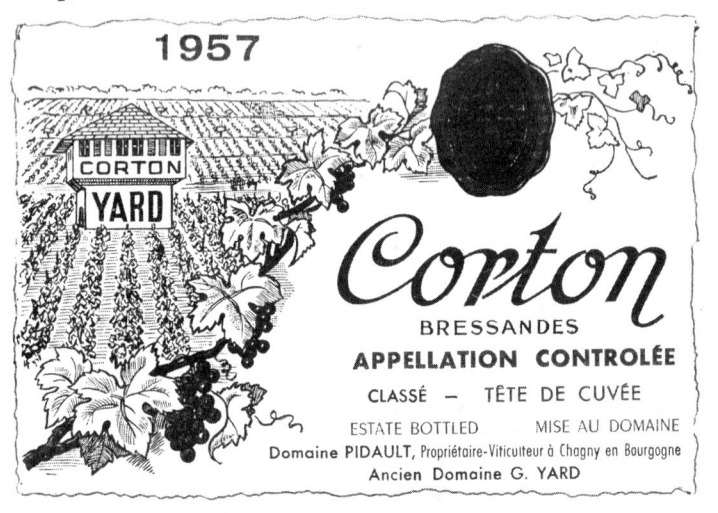

French Chablis, a fine, white Burgundy, is among the most imitated wines in the world. Its dry, flinty taste can hardly be reproduced outside France, and it is rare and expensive. The Appellation Controlee assures that it is a true Chablis, and the classification ler Cru (first pressing) assures that it is a reliably good Chablis. Note the simplicity of this label. Many of the finest French wines have the plainest labels. It is wise to be cautious of a label with too much unnecessary elaboration, for it may be a ruse to mislead the novice wine drinker.

WINES

GERMAN WINES

The best German wines are white. The finest come from the regions of the Rheingau (as the label shown here) and the Moselle. A good indication of quality is the insignia on the label of a black eagle surrounded by the letters "V.D.N.V." and the term "Staatsweinguter" (state-controlled). However, not all good German wines use this seal.

The label pictured says "Original-Abfullung" which means that it is estate bottled. "Reisling" designates the name of the grape used. "Spatlese" means late-picked grapes and puts the wine in a rather sweet class. "1966er" is the year in which the grapes were picked. "Hattenheimer" is the name of the town in which the grapes were grown and "Nussbrunnen" is the name of the vineyard. "Freiherrlich Langwerth von Simmern" is the name of the producer.

Sweeter German wines are classified and priced according to their degree of sweetness. "Spatlese" is less sweet, "Auslese" a little sweeter, "Beerenauslese" is definitely a sweet wine, and "Trockenbeerenauslese" is the sweetest.

ITALIAN WINES

The Italians are noted for their hearty red wines, the most famous of which is Chianti. However, the counterfeit wine industry in Italy is very active and calls for carefully selecting Chianti Classico (authentic Chianti from the Chianti region) for assurance of a good and true Chianti. The best Chianti has a black cockerel on the label, which is a symbol of the Society for Preservation of True Chianti. It is bottled in ordinary Bordeaux bottles rather than the familiar straw jacketed flasks. Other good Italian wines are the Barolo and Barbaresca.

WINES

NEW YORK AND OHIO WINES

New York State and Ohio wines are different from California wines as they use native American grapes rather than European varieties for most of their production. Since the American grape has a raw, foxy flavor, these wines are often more enjoyable when they are the sparkling variety or champagne. Reputable producers are Widmer Wine Cellars, Great Western producers, Gold Seal Vineyards, Taylor Wine Company and Meier Wine Cellars of Ohio. Like the California wines, the best Eastern wines are the varietals which are named for the grape, most successful of which are the Niagara, Delaware, Isabella, Catawba and Diana.

CALIFORNIA WINES

The State of California produces seven times more table wine than is imported into the United States from other parts of the world. Regardless of research and experiments, the wine industry cannot duplicate the taste and fragrance of European wines. California wines have a taste all their own and many are considered quite good.

For this reason, wines with "generic" labels—blends using European regional names such as Chablis, Burgundy, etc.—are generally not reasonable facsimiles of their namesakes. The best California wines are named after the grape from which they are predominently made such as the Riesling, Pinot Noir, Pinot Blanc, Cabernet Sauvignon, etc.

California wines are usually blends of several years; therefore, they are more consistent from year to year. However, a year for which a vineyard may be particularly proud may be bottled with the vintage year included. The most outstanding vineyards include Almaden, Beaulieu, Paul Masson, Louis Martini, Wente Brothers, and Christian Brothers.

Vineyards Established 1852

ALMADÉN
California Mountain
PINOT NOIR
A distinguished, authentic Pinot Noir, velvety and fine, made entirely from grapes of this illustrious Burgundian variety, grown in Mountain Vineyards at Paicines, California

PRODUCED AND BOTTLED BY
Almadén Vineyards, Los Gatos, California
Alcohol 12½% by volume   A-67

WINES

CHAMPAGNES

The festivity and gaiety that champagnes lend to an occasion are an added attraction to a wine and will enhance the flavor of any meal. The only true Champagne is French Champagne although the term is borrowed and used all over the world.

The French Champagne district operates under strict regulations of "Appellations Controlees" laws, but those words which are so important on French wine labels do not appear on Champagne labels. The word "brut" on the pictured label indicates that it is the driest or highest grade. Lesser grades are labelled "Extra Sec" or "Sec" (moderately sweet). The term "blanc de blanc" means that only the white Chardonnay grape has been used, and for a vintage year (1959, 1961, 1962) it will be ultra dry and extraordinarily fine. Unless a vintage year is indicated, the Champagne is a blend of several years but may still be good. There are many reputable Champagne producers whose names may be found in books on wine.

Champagnes and wines are better when they come from a large bottle rather than from a smaller one, but the problems of cooling and serving Champagne make anything larger than the Magnum (double bottle) impractical.

The guidelines in this section have been brief; however, there is a whole new world of wines waiting to be discovered. It is wise to remember that love of wines is a personal thing and that there are exceptions to every rule. The best way to familiarize yourself with wines is to taste them at every opportunity and discover your own favorites. Many authoritative books can acquaint you with the famous regions and the best vineyards. The true connoisseur gains his knowledge from continually tasting, experimenting and making his own judgments—perhaps with the assistance of a knowledgeable retailer.

Characterize your parties as momentous occasions guests will long remember. And in the true tradition of Atlanta, further enhance the evening by serving wine.

BON APPETIT!

INDEX

BEVERAGES

	Page
Champagne Punch	194
Cool Mint Crush	139
Cranberry-Orange Crush	134
Frosty Banana Mist	150
Frosty Mocha Punch	127
Ginger-Ale Fruit Blizzard	131
Hot Russian Tea	166
Hot Spiced Apple Cider	162
Icy Lime Cooler	158
Merrie Ole Eggnog	198
Merrymaking Cheer	278
Mint Juleps	185
Old Crow Punch	189
Orange Frost	143
Party Peach Punch	154
Shangri-La	180
Sparkling Catawba	147
Twenty-four Hour Cocktails	175

CANAPES

Artichoke Hearts and Caviar	191
Avocado Appeteasers	173
Bacon Roll-ups	197
Bacon Wrapped Tidbits	178
Caraway Mound of Cheese	178
Caviar Coated Cheese Ball	184
Caviar Pie	195
Charcoaled Beef Tenderloin	181
Cheese-Bacon Puffs	125
Cheese Puffs	141
Cheese Savories	192
Cheese Smoothies	156
Cheese Straws	278
Cheese Tidbits	149
Cheese Wheels	133
Cherry Tomato Tree	196
Chrissie's Cheezits	162
Corned Beef Roll-ups	163
Cornucopias	191
Crabapple Tidbits	197
Crisp Coconut Chips	183
Crisp Vegetable Flowers	175
Cucumber Bites	178
Curried Toasta	188
Egg Rolls	277
Fruit Kabobs	187
Golden Cheese Straws	131
Hot Ham Puffs	152
Marinated Artichoke Hearts	173
Marinated Mushrooms	187
Meatballs Extraordinaire	176
Nippy Cheese Rolls	196
Nosegay Appetizers	190
Nuts and Bolts	194
Parslied Pecan Cheese Ball	174
Peppery Spiced Nuts	180
Pickled Shrimp	186
Pretty Party Cheese Ball	188
Sausage Swirls	192
Sauteed Cherry Tomatoes	182
Scalloped Edam	277

	Page
Sherried Clams	176
Shrimp Arnaud	181
Shrimp Fondue	195
Smoked Turkey Fingers	172
Steak Tartare	276
Stuffed Mushroom Caps	197
Sweet Potato Crispies	173
Tiny Fried Chicken Drums	186
Toasted Mushroom Rolls	183
Top Hat of Crisp Vegetables	277

DIPS

Anchovy Dip	175
Chili Con Queso	193
Confetti Snack Dip	278
Crab Dip Divine	174
Crab Finger Dip	190
Double Dipper Cheese	179
Egg and Bacon Spread	189
Green Goddess Dip	179
Guacomole	184
Hot n' Spicy Dip	189
Pretty Party Dip	185
Shrimp Dip	193
Spicy Beef Spread	182

SOUPS

Chilled Vichyssoise	113
Crab Bisque I	239
Crab Bisque II	239
Jellied Beet Bouillon	110
Lamb Symphony	209
Oyster Stew	285
Russian Borscht	224
Senegalese Soup	236
Shrimp Bisque	212
Watercress and Corn Soup	230

SAUCES

Barbecue Sauce	249
Bearnaise Sauce	21
Blender Hollandaise Sauce	23
Bleu Cheese Sauce	221
Brandied Cream Sauce	24
Cecile de Vin Sauce	22
Curried Fruit Sauce	221
Golden Ham Sauce	173
Ham Glaze	285
Harvey's Barbecue Sauce	264
Horseradish Sauce	221
Light Cream Sauce	53
Marinade Sauce	268
Mornay Sauce	74
Mushroom Sauce	47, 62
Never Fail Hollandaise Sauce	27
Pimiento-Mushroom Sauce	240
Pink Sauce	237
Red Mustard Sauce	277
Sweet and Sour Sauce	231

— 300 —

INDEX

ENTREES

BEEF

	Page
Beef Bourguinone	225
Beef Fondue	220
Beef Stroganoff	244
Broiled Beef Tenderloin	282
Cold Glazed Roast of Beef	227
English Roast a la Marine	217
Johnnie Maezetti Casserole	40
Melange of Chipped Beef and Mushrooms	84
Rhine Caraway Meat Balls	82
Sirloin Shish Kabobs	268

EGGS AND CHEESE

Charming Cheese Souffle	36
Golden Cheese Souffle	38
Parslied Cheese Souffle	37
Eggs a la Atlanta	24
Eggs Cecile	22
Eggs Royale	31
Eggs Sardou	28
Hearty Egg Delight	26
Mock Eggs Benedict	27
Mousseline Omelette au Fromage	34
Oeufs en Croustade a la Bearnaise	20
Omelettes aux Champignons	32
Poached Eggs Emile	30

LAMB

Crown Roast of Lamb	282
Lamb en Kyathion	262

PORK

Baked Pork Chops	228
Barbecued Ham Slices	249
Barbecued Pork Loin	264
Cantonese Sweet and Sour Pork	231
Coca-Cola Grilled Canadian Bacon	25
Ham and Noodle en Kyathion	80
Ham-Asparagus Bake	78
Ham Mousse	252
Harvest Glazed Ham	285
Pork Potpourri	246

POULTRY

Arroz Con Pollo	242
Breast of Chicken Santo	43
Chicken and Artichokes Chantilly	60
Chicken and Lobster Marengo	210
Crunchy Chicken	64
Georgia Quail Stuffed with Oyster Dressing	206
Georgia Birds of Paradise	214
Golden Orange Chicken	69
Herbed Chicken Souffle	240
Potpourri de Poulet	72
Poulet aux Fromages	62
Roulade of Turkey	76
Royal Russian Squab Flambeed	212

	Page
Sour Cream Pheasant	289
Herbed Dressing	289
South American Chicken	66
Turkey and Broccoli Mornay	74

SEAFOOD

Batter Dipped Shrimp	256
Cajun Shrimp Creole	50
Charcoaled Red Snapper	259
Coquille of Crabmeat Mornay	100
Crab Imperiale	103
Curried Seafood Salad	98
Flaked Crab Deviled Eggs	46
Flaked Crabmeat Souffle	254
Golden Shrimp Chanterelle	92
Hot Crab Salad	106
Melange of Salmon and Mushrooms	48
Shad Roe and Oyster Casserole a la Henry Grady	111
Shrimp and Crabmeat Medley	95
Shrimp and Deviled Egg Casserole	52
Shrimp aux Champignons	86
Shrimp Ludmila	233
Shrimp Rockefeller	90
Small Rock Lobster Tails	237
Tuna Mousse	108

MISCELLANEOUS

Brandied Liver Pate	31
Quiche Lorraine	113
Spinach Casserole Supreme	116

VEGETABLES

Artichokes, Peas and Lettuce	269
Asparagus Mimosa	237
Barley Amandine	227
Beans Baked in Red Wine	250
Bourbon Baked Beans	265
Broccoli Extraordinaire	265
Brown Rice	269
Bouquet of Chilled Vegetables	255
Caramelized Tomatoes	257
Chilled Medley of Marinated Vegetables	283
Chive-Stuffed Baked Potato	250
Crisp Vegetables Flowers	175
Curried Onions	221
Golden Cheese Grits	28
Green Beans India	260
Green Rice	229
Grilled Tomato Florentine	44
Grilled Tomato Parmesan	23
Herbed Spinach Bake	234
Herbed Tomato Roses	245
Marinated Vegetables	215
Moulded Spinach Ring	207
Parmesan Broiled Tomatoes	247
Parslied Rice with Mushrooms	64
Rice Pilaff aux Champignons	283
Sauteed Cherry Tomatoes	182

INDEX

	Page
Spears of Asparagus en Casserole	257
Spinach and Artichokes en Casserole	218
Spinach Casserole Supreme	116
Spinach Sesame	31
Sweet Potato Autumn	286
Sweet Potatoes in Apple Shells	253
Top Hat of Crisp Vegetables	277
Yellow Squash Souffle	225

FRUITS

Apples Stuffed with Sausage	35
Autumn Spiced Peach Half	215
Cinnamon Frosted Pineapple Delight	48
Cinnamon Fruit Cocktail	27
Cranberry Snow	288
Curried Fruit Cascade	107
Frosted Fruit Shrub	279
Frosted Raspberry Shrub	220
Frosty Shell of Melon Balls	282
Fruit Fantasy	233
Green Grapes in Cognac	253
Hot Curried Fruit	213
Hot Raspberry Pear	30
Kumquat Roses	286
Mincemeat Glazed Apples	229
Scalloped Grapefruit Cups	261
Spiced Apple Dandy	248

SALADS

Artichoke and Bean Sprout Salad	232
Canteloupe Ring with Melon Balls	87
Chilled Asparagus	84
Chilled Cinnamon Apple Salad	37
Chilled Melon a la Galax	29
Citrus Greens	109
Coach House Green Salad	111
Congealed Lime-Vegetable Medley	41
Congealed Strawberry-Pineapple Delight	75
Coquille of Chilled Melon Balls	44
Easter Salad Baskets	280
Fresh Mushroom and Romaine Salad	222
Frosty Mould of Cranberries	70
Georgia Peach Jubilee	65
Grapefruit Jubilee	101
Herbed Tomato Roses	245
Hot Green Bean Salad	262
Lemon Fruited Mould	211
Lime Congealed Fruit Fantasy	79
Mould of Avocado	96
Mould of Broccoli and Egg Supreme	114
Mould of Cherries	240
Mould of Party Pretty Fruit	80
Party Pear Salad	72
Pineapple-Apricot Dandy	77
Raspberry Congealed Fruit Medley	53
Raspberry Congealed Medley of Fruit	47

	Page
Sclafani Salad	104
Sweet and Sour Aspic	93
Tangy Spinach Salad	83
White Fruit Salad	117

SALAD DRESSINGS

Celery Seed Dressing	218
Cucumber Cream Dressing	263
Herb Dressing	222
Lime-Honey Fruit Salad Dressing	87
Mayor Allen's Roquefort Dressing	260
Sclafani Salad Dressing	104

BREADS

Apricot Nut Bread	21
Banana Nut Bread	73
Beaten Biscuits	172
Brioche	238
Bunny Buns	280
Buttermilk Bran Muffins	105
Cheese Bread	241
Cheese Drop Biscuits	51
Chocolate Date Bread	129
Cinnamon Crescent Rolls	101
Cinnamon Muffins	29
Classic Yeast Rolls	207
Corn Bread	247
Corn Bread Shortcake	26
Corn Sticks	112
Fiesta Bread	49
Fresh Blueberry Muffins	91
Herb Bread	33
Imperial Oatmeal Bread	96
Miniature Biscuits Supreme	35
Miniature Cheese Swirls	99
Oatmeal Loaf Bread	234
Onion-Dilly Batter Bread	41
Orange Blossoms	146
Orange Dinner Rolls	266
Parslied Fantans	232
Pecan Muffins	25
Peppy Popovers	77
Popovers	61
Poppy Seed Loaf Bread	261
Prune Bread	67
Quick Yeast Rolls	38
Rum Rolls	88
Sally Lunn Bread	93
Scotch Shortbread	54
Southern Spoonbread	44, 65

PARTY SANDWICHES

Amandine Chicken Sandwiches	124
Avocado Toast Circles	196
Bacon-Cheese Sandwiches	159
Carrot-Olive Strips	133
Caviar Bites	148
Caviar Capers	128
Caviar-Cheese Sandwiches	164
Chanterelle Sandwiches	151
Checkerboard Dandies	136
Chicken Salad Baskets	145

— 302 —

INDEX

	Page		Page
Cornucopias Aloha	144	Coconut Kisses	133
Crab Canapes	160	Date-Nut Coronets	139
Cucumber-Cheese Sandwiches	128	Date-Nut Delights	161
Danish Open-Face Appetizers	177	Date-Nut Krispies	126
Deviled Ham Cornucopias	135	Fruit Cake Cookies	141
Deviled Diamonds	141	Gingerbread Gems	134
Flaked Crabmeat Diamonds	132	Ginger Spice Drops	166
Ham Pinwheels	182	Jim Jam Surprises	153
Ham-Walnut Sandwiches	129	Luscious Lemon Squares	68
Hawaiian Nut Sandwiches	151	Oatmeal Coconut Coronets	160
Herbed Egg Sandwiches	163	Oatmeal Crispies	158
Herbed Flowerpots	152	Pecan Delights	142
Herbed Party Triangles	136	Pecan Sandies	147
Herbed Shrimp Sandwiches	156	Pecan Spice Squares	150
Hot Ham Puffs	152	Pershing Point Cookies	149
Maple Nut Sandwiches	149	Praline Strips	75
Olive and Egg Sandwiches	159	Spicy Orange Bites	137
Orange-Nut Sandwiches	155	Strawberry Fakes	130
Parsley Pinwheels	144	Swedish Rose Cookies	126
Pineapple Ribbon Sandwiches	132	Swedish Swirls	157
Poppy Seed Squares	140	Wedding Fiestas	129
Shrimp-Cucumber Rounds	140		
Spring Strawberry Sandwiches	155	**PIES**	
Sunny Lemon Triangles	125	Apple Crumb Pie	219
Tomato-Egg Sandwiches	124	Apple Nut Pie	45
Tomato Wheels	148	Blueberry Alaska Pie	238
		Calico Pecan Pie	79
		Cherry Crunch Pie	97

DESSERTS

CAKES

		Cherry Icebox Pie	83
Applesauce Cake	81	Chess Pie	223
Buttermilk Pound Cake	71	Chocolate Pie	39
Carrot Cake	258	Chocolate Chiffon Pie	88
Coconut Amalgamation	216	Chocolate Meringue Pie	107
Coffee Cake Squares	127	Chocolate Pecan Pie	211
Coffee Crumb Cake	145	Coconut Butter Crust	238
English Trifle	287	Coconut Christmas Pie	290
Governor's Cheese Cake	267	Fudge Fantasy Pie	91
Honey Spice Cake	109	French Silk Pie	102
Ice Cream Fudge Cake	241	Lemon Fluff Pie	51
Imperial Sunshine Cake	73	Pastry Shell	39
Luscious Lemon Cheese Cake	105	Savory Sherbet Pie	61
Old Fashioned Dark Chocolate Cake	99	Slivered Almond Crust	89
Prestige Prune Cake	63	Tiny Jam Tarts	164
Rum Angel Food Cake	263	**MISCELLANEOUS**	
Spring Apple Cake	85	Bombe Grandee	235
Whipped Cream Cake	118	Chocolate Butter Cream Cups	143
		Chocolate Confetti	153

CANDY

		Creme Brulee	94
Divinity Dreams	165	French Fantasia	225
Kentucky Colonels	198	Gingered Ice Cream	243
Pastel Mints	125	Holiday Sparklers	284
		Lemon Freeze	208

COOKIES

		Lemon Frost Ice Cream	251
Accordion Treats	138	Maple Mousse	112
Caramel Capers	157	Maple Velvet	213
Cherry Surprises	115	Meringue Pavlova	49
Cherry Winks	153	Mocha Bourbon Balls	145
Chinese Chews	160	Mocha Delight	42
Chocolate Charmers	137	Orange Lady Finger Delight	255
Chocolate Delights	54	Snow Eggs	281
		Spring Breeze	270
		Strawberry Spring Custard	281

ATLANTA COOKS FOR COMPANY
415 Peachtree Street, N.E.
Atlanta, Georgia 30308

Please send me _____ copies of ATLANTA COOKS FOR COMPANY at $4.00 per copy, plus 35¢ per copy for handling. Enclosed is my check or money order for $_____.

Name_____

Street_____

City_____ State_____ Zip_____

All proceeds from the sale of this cookbook are to benefit Atlanta Music Club Scholarship Funds. Make check payable to Cookbook - Atlanta Music Club.

ATLANTA COOKS FOR COMPANY
415 Peachtree Street, N.E.
Atlanta, Georgia 30308

Please send me _____ copies of ATLANTA COOKS FOR COMPANY at $4.00 per copy, plus 35¢ per copy for handling. Enclosed is my check or money order for $_____.

Name_____

Street_____

City_____ State_____ Zip_____

All proceeds from the sale of this cookbook are to benefit Atlanta Music Club Scholarship Funds. Make check payable to Cookbook - Atlanta Music Club.

ATLANTA COOKS FOR COMPANY
415 Peachtree Street, N.E.
Atlanta, Georgia 30308

Please send me _____ copies of ATLANTA COOKS FOR COMPANY at $4.00 per copy, plus 35¢ per copy for handling. Enclosed is my check or money order for $_____.

Name_____

Street_____

City_____ State_____ Zip_____

All proceeds from the sale of this cookbook are to benefit Atlanta Music Club Scholarship Funds. Make check payable to Cookbook - Atlanta Music Club.